When Communities Design Aid

Praise for this book

'Richard Atkinson has written the rare book that succinctly articulates highly complex challenges and, more importantly, provides practical tools to solve them. Atkinson balances academic research with empirical evidence from the field so the two complement, rather than contradict, each other, all the while doing so without compromising the perspective of the end-user. The lack of true integration of end-users in designing interventions is at the root of so many failed development initiatives. This book provides an actionable blueprint for bringing the end-user into the design of interventions to ensure that well-intentioned projects don't stumble on a lack of understanding of everyday practicalities at the point of intervention. As such, it effectively challenges the supply-side approach that dominates the field, and is a must-read for anyone hoping to design interventions that positively impact the lives of real people.'

Per Braginski, international development consultant

'A valuable and timely book that stimulates both debate and action to redesign aid. Richard's insights and proposals are essential and critical to understand the challenges and possibilities of aid design. This is a book for all of us who want to build and live in better, fairer, and more sustainable communities.'

Dr Shehnaz Suterwalla, Senior Tutor (Research),
Royal College of Art, Kensington Gore, London

'When outsiders design aid interventions, they are planning ways in which we can do good to or for "the poor". Rarely do we really listen to and understand the intricacies and diversity of community life; too often we think we know what is best for others; seldom do we exhibit the necessary humility to learn from our mistakes and do better. This welcome book offers a breath of fresh air as it exposes some of the common mistakes outsiders make; provides insights which can deepen our understanding; and proposes ways by which communities can more truly participate in their own development. If you are involved in any way in designing or planning community development programmes, I urge you to read this necessary, well-written, and important book.'

Richard Carter, water sector specialist and consultant

When Communities Design Aid

Creating solutions to poverty that people
own, use, and need

Richard Atkinson

Practical
ACTION
PUBLISHING

Practical Action Publishing Ltd
27a Albert Street, Rugby, CV21 2SG, UK
www.practicalactionpublishing.com

A catalogue record for this book is available from the British Library.

A catalogue record for this book has been requested from the Library of
Congress.

ISBN 978-1-78853-192-4 Paperback
ISBN 978-1-78853-193-1 Hardback
ISBN 978-1-78853-194-8 eBook

Citation: Atkinson, R. (2022) *When Communities Design Aid: Creating
solutions to poverty that people own, use, and need,* Rugby, UK: Practical Action
Publishing <http://dx.doi.org/10.3362/9781788531948>.

Since 1974, Practical Action Publishing has published and disseminated
books and information in support of international development work
throughout the world. Practical Action Publishing is a trading name of
Practical Action Publishing Ltd (Company Reg. No. 1159018), the wholly
owned publishing company of Practical Action. Practical Action Publishing
trades only in support of its parent charity objectives and any profits are
covenanted back to Practical Action (Charity Reg. No. 247257, Group VAT
Registration No. 880 9924 76).

Typeset by JMR Digital Solutions, India

Contents

About the author   vii

Acknowledgements   ix

Introduction   xi

Part I   When Aid Isn't Wanted

1   Why do the poor reject aid? Common mistakes and
    misunderstandings that lead to failure   3

Part II   Aid through the Eyes of the Poor

2   Who are 'the poor'? Understanding the audience/s for
    development aid   33

3   My village's name will be up in lights: designing for
    communal cultures   47

4   Knots and cages: the myriad problems of reaching the excluded   67

5   Selling the new: making change more attainable and attractive   89

Part III   When Communities Design Aid

6   Building on what exists: hidden infrastructure and scaled-up
    solutions   113

7   Who decides? Who acts? Shifting the power in participative
    development   137

8   Setting participative development goals   173

Appendix: A note on methodology   177

Index   179

About the author

Richard Atkinson is a development researcher with over a decade's experience of conducting ethnographic field studies in low-income communities in the global south. He teaches as Senior Tutor in the Service Design programme at the Royal College of Art in London, where he works on the intersection between development and design, especially participatory design methods.

Acknowledgements

I'd like to thank Kelly Somers, Rosanna Denning, Jenny Peebles, Clare Tawney and everyone else at Practical Action Publishing for making the publication of the book such a smooth and enjoyable process. Their suggestions for further research, recommendations on the text, work on the design, and amendments to the title have made this a much better book than the manuscript I rather tentatively submitted. Having made use of their books for many years, I feel like a fan permitted to put out a record on a favourite label and am thrilled to be a small part of the Practical Action project. I am also very grateful to the anonymous reviewers, whose feedback highlighted important new dimensions that I hadn't considered and gave me encouragement for the final push.

Much of my early interest in this area came when working for 2cv Research, where the encouragement and freedom given by Vincent Nolan and support and camaraderie of my colleagues laid the foundations of this book. Darren, Selena, Alison, Nancy, Alex, Doug, Dan, Claire, Laura, and many others all helped me become a better researcher and a sillier person. Tom, Kat, Josh, Havi, Mamata, and Rajjat all get further thanks in the main text for their huge support and contributions, but I hope they will tolerate a little repetition.

Several universities and countless teachers have shaped my thinking in ways I'll never unpick but will always appreciate. These include Sue Cryne and Adrian Long, Ralph Yarrow, Daniel Limon, Robert Short, and Robert Clark at UEA and Malcolm Bowie at Oxford. In those moments when I'm researching or teaching at my best I often sense Malcolm's warm and patient influence.

At the RCA, Juliette Kristensen, Matt Wraith, Shehnaz Suterwalla, and Jo Pickering created a course that has continually made me think differently about the world. My fellow tutors have influenced the book in ways they may not realize and special thanks go to Ajay Hothi, Kevin Biderman, and Thomas Kelsey. More recently Clive Grinyer, Carolyn Runcie, Nicolas Rebolledo, Qian Sung, Judah Armani, and John Makepeace have helped provide a new, inspiring home in which I can learn and continue my research. I am excited every week by working with students at the RCA, who remind me that no problem is ever totally intractable if you can approach it with enough courage, commitment, and curiosity.

I am also extremely grateful for the support of the many organizations for which I have carried out fieldwork over the years. Particular thanks go to Ruth Hoyal, Laura Baines, Adam Glasner, Matthew Strickland, Lucy Barnett, James Robinson, and Robin Smith.

Jamal Khadar and Per Braginski both read earlier drafts of the book and made many helpful recommendations. They have also discussed the ideas within it with me so often that the text that follows is infused with their thinking. (The customary acknowledgement that all errors are my own most definitely applies here.)

Writing a book is a strange business with no obvious benefits I can see for friends and family. I have been variously absent, fretful, and preoccupied; I am currently writing these acknowledgements when I should be cooking dinner for my family. I have been kept going along the way by so many good friends, including Robin, Leemus, Kane, Jamie, Charlotte, Rose, Hamit, Mary, Amanda, Clem, Parag, Mena, Craig, Ryoko, Catherine, and Ben. I can repay you only with thanks and a bit more of my company now.

The greatest debt is to my family: from my grandmother Janet, who was a brilliant teacher of pupils as capricious as me, to my many aunts, uncles, and cousins, to my nieces and nephews who are now teaching me, to my wonderful extended family of Nora, Joe, Yu-Hsuan, Rod, Lorna, Ken. I grew up myself in a family where it was almost impossible not to keep learning or to feel loved unconditionally – although I'm sure I tested the limits of both propositions and both parents. Sarah, Charles, my mother Judith and father Tony; thank you in so many ways.

There are three other people who have changed my life profoundly and beautifully: my wife Meriel and my twins Frank and Kezia. I love you all and this book is dedicated to you.

Introduction

You can't give away inventions that could potentially save millions of lives? It is an outcome that seems absurd. Yet it happens often in international development. In over a decade in the field I have seen discarded mosquito nets, abandoned medical centres, countless well-intentioned but unused digital apps. Cheap or free clean water products have failed to be adopted on numerous occasions, despite their life-saving potential. When the Monitor Group surveyed a sample of Indian households about their interest in buying purified water, 60 per cent of respondents said they wouldn't switch even if it was free (Karamchandani et al., 2009).

There is much debate about why development aid programmes work – or don't work. Fingers are pointed at poor planning, lack of scale, too much scale, corruption. These problems of the 'supply side' of aid are discussed extensively elsewhere (for instance, Banerjee and Duflo, 2011; Collier, 2007; Easterly, 2006; de Haan, 2009; Moyo, 2009; Sachs, 2005). Sometimes, though, they go wrong for a different reason: people don't want, or cannot use, the aid they are offered. You cannot give them away. This is a book about why this happens and about how to avoid it. It asks a simple question: what kind of aid do people actually want and need?

The book starts by highlighting the common mistakes that outsiders make when designing for the poor. I am one of these outsiders and I write as one who has made all these mistakes. We fail to identify already existing home-grown solutions. We impose individualistic ways of thinking on more communal cultures. We brush over the extent and complexities of inequalities within communities that we term 'poor'. We discount the importance of non-financial resources in the lives of poor people. And as outsiders we over-estimate the appetite for change. (Surely the poorest want change?) I trace how these mistakes are not occasional outliers; they are endemic to much development work. This first part of the book uses a number of case studies from my own and others' work to illustrate why they may happen and why they can be so damaging.

The second part of the book looks at how we can design in ways that are more sensitive to the needs of people on the ground. We will unpick the patterns of daily life in poor communities. We will see how we can create interventions that are easy to share, to organize collectively, and to spread through word of mouth. We will examine the tactics we can use to reach excluded groups and to tackle overlapping webs of discrimination in ways that are sensitive to realities on the ground. We'll explore how we can draw from the fields of design, marketing, and behavioural economics to make interventions more intuitive and appealing, and make change feel more possible. Again, I will illustrate the potential here with case studies from both other development researchers and projects in which I have been personally involved.

As the book evolves we'll see continually the huge capacity for poor people to create and implement their own solutions to poverty. Thus the book's emphasis will shift over time, away from the question of how outsiders can design better and towards the more radical question of how poor people themselves take control. In the third part of the book I examine the power of the poor's own solutions and how outsiders can support and facilitate these. I ask how power, knowledge, responsibility, and money can be transferred away from outside 'experts' and into the hands of the communities who will use them. This is a challenging journey that is barely under way. Although 'participatory development' and 'user-centred design' are becoming fashionable terms in development, too often the poor still remain at the margins of development. I will argue that even when people are consulted in detail and with good faith it is still typically the outside professional who has the last word, whilst implementation is left to 'technical experts'.[1] In addition, we will see that there are major challenges that come with transferring power to those on the ground. What happens when local desires and expert advice clash, or when different members of a community want different things from development, or when certain groups take over the development process? These are significant issues and the book explores how to navigate them pragmatically, with a clear eye on what aspects of development practice are easier and harder to transfer to communities themselves. I firmly believe, though, that the outside-expert model of development I have been working within is not in any sense sustainable. Even if COVID-19 is successfully managed, we cannot continue to fly thousands of miles to ask poor people what they need – when their answer is more often than not, an end to climate change. We cannot continue to guard expert knowledge in the global north, which is then rationed out during two-week visits. We have to shift development's centre of gravity into the communities in which development occurs. In the final chapter I will condense this argument into some practical proposals for how we might do this, set out in a provisional list of 'participatory development goals'.

The book is written to serve as a practical guide for anyone working, or interested, in the field of aid and poverty reduction. This is a fast-expanding audience. Today, interventions to help the poorest come from a huge array of actors: from multinational corporations to tech start-ups, small-scale private NGOs, design studios, and individual entrepreneurs. In the week that I wrote this introduction I have encountered a fundraiser for an education project in India set up by a group of European friends in their retirement, discussed research to help a small private charity working on early years development in East Africa, and talked to a master's student about her ideas for how service design can make an impact on poverty in South East Asia. I am pleased that the problems of development are attracting interest far outside the traditional development 'industry'. I hope that this book will help bring these new actors closer to their audience – encouraging people to find more creative and committed ways to talk to, engage with, and empower their audience and to learn from past participatory projects.

I myself came to this field along an unusual path. I have not worked full-time for a development organization; my master's and doctoral fieldwork were largely conducted in the UK with relatively wealthy young people. I don't teach a course in development, or know my way around Washington institutions. My experience instead comes from research in the field: many dozens of fieldwork visits to poor communities in East, South, and West Africa, South America, the Caribbean, South, and East Asia; many months in total spent listening to, observing, and learning from people, talking about their everyday lives and exploring ideas for improving their standards of living. I am also lucky to be able to make use of the experience of countless colleagues over the years, especially Tom Marriage, Jamal Khadar, Kat Jennings, Josh Sparrow, Mamata Chaudhuri Kathuria, Rajjat Kathuria, Havi Murungi, Carla Rollo, and Per Braginski. It is through listening to their stories of fieldwork visits, comparing notes, and building hypotheses together that so many of the ideas in this book have been formed. Jamal Khadar's name in particular appears frequently in the pages that follow and the book owes a huge debt to his experiences and ideas.

The book also draws on a wide reading of development literature, especially work based on first-hand field interviews, field trials, and ethnography. (For the sake of a clear story, much of this is covered in endnotes.) However wide I have tried to cast the net, the efforts to reduce poverty are vast and global, and my own experiences within them are inevitably limited and partial. As such, this isn't a book with final answers, but I hope it is a book that will help its readers to ask better questions, starting with the most important one: how do the people whom I am seeking to help see the world differently from me?

One of the themes of the book is the importance of diverse voices and plural forms of knowledge within any development project. All authors, though, ultimately write from their own positions. We are informed by our specific knowledge and experience, the power we have or lack, the places we grow up and live in. I don't have lived experience of poverty, and the majority of my time and so many of my ideas and assumptions have been framed by working in the global north. When I write about 'outsiders' and the mistakes that 'they' make when working in development, I am one of these outsiders. Hence when discussing the problems and errors made in development I will often turn to the collective 'we'. Of course, a binary division of this kind between 'outsiders' and 'insiders' obscures more complex gradients. Someone like me who has grown up on a different continent and who is based thousands of miles from the audience is a more obvious outsider than a development worker working in their country of birth, or who has lived there for many years. Conversely, community members who become heavily involved in externally funded projects may take on some of the assumptions and habits of the funding body.

In the pages that follow I often use the idea of 'insiders' and 'outsiders' to highlight the problems of ethnocentrism, but it's useful to remember that in practice this line is often blurred.

Making use of this book

Whilst the book can, and I hope will, be read as a single story, individual chapters provide practical advice on specific elements of development, and readers wishing to use these as a reference might find the following summary helpful:

- Chapter 1 sets out the problem at the heart of the book, asking why many attempts to tackle poverty end up as unattractive or impractical to the people they are meant to help. In this chapter we will highlight a number of mistakes that are commonly made when designing aid interventions and how they reflect often simple but crucial misunderstandings about the daily realities of life in poor communities.
- Chapter 2 is designed to help us understand more clearly the audience for development. How are 'the poor' defined? What are the important differences within this very broad group? What is daily life like in communities that are defined as poor?
- Chapter 3 investigates in detail what we mean by the communal nature of daily life in poor communities. It shows the significant potential for innovation that comes from recognizing close reciprocal ties, shared resources, and the power of word of mouth, whilst questioning a simple divide between 'communal' and 'individual'.
- Chapter 4 looks at the hidden and overt inequalities that exist in poor communities. It explores ways both to navigate around them and to address them head-on, and offers practitioners a range of tactics for making their initiatives more inclusive. The chapter emphasizes the importance of thinking about discrimination in intersectional terms.
- Chapter 5 unpicks the reasons why change can be both unappealing and impractical for people living in poverty and discusses what strategies we can use to make change more natural and inviting. These range from agency-building initiatives, to behaviour-change interventions, to the surprising role of aesthetics in development design. The chapter illustrates a number of areas where development practice can learn from other disciplines.
- Chapter 6 examines how to identify, support, and build upon the poor's own solutions to poverty. It discusses the challenges of finding 'hidden infrastructure', the kinds of support that community solutions do and don't need, the questions to ask before 'scaling up' an intervention, and the pitfalls involved in exporting a local solution to new regions.
- Chapter 7 looks at power and control in development practice. It examines how to balance the expertise of development professionals with the

skills of those on the ground and what kinds of steps are needed to shift the power and knowledge in development to poor people themselves.

- Chapter 8 summarizes lessons from the book. This includes a short summary of design principles for designing development programmes and a list of provisional 'participative development goals' to accelerate the transfer of power to communities.

Note

1. As Cornwall writes (2008: 273), 'delegated power over choosing the colour of paint for a clinic's waiting room in the name of "patient involvement" – in the absence of any involvement in decisions on what the clinic actually does – may count for little in transforming power relations'.

References

Banerjee, Abhijit V. and Duflo, Esther (2011) *Poor Economics: A Radical Rethinking of the Way to Fight Global Poverty*, Public Affairs, New York.

Collier, Paul (2007) *The Bottom Billion: Why the Poorest Countries are Failing and What Can Be Done About It*, Oxford University Press, Oxford.

Cornwall, Andrea (2008) 'Unpacking participation: models, meanings and practices', *Oxford University Press and Community Development Journal*, 43: 269–83 <https://doi.org/10.1093/cdj/bsn010>.

de Haan, Arjan (2009) *How the Aid Industry Works: An Introduction to International Development*, Kumarian Press, Sterling.

Easterly, William (2006) *The White Man's Burden*, Oxford University Press, Oxford.

Karamchandani, Ashish, Kubzansky, Michael, Frandano, Paul (2009) *Emerging Markets, Emerging Models: Market-based Solutions to the Challenges of Global Poverty* [online], Monitor Group, <http://community-wealth.org/sites/clone.community-wealth.org/files/downloads/report-karamchandani-et-al.pdf> [accessed 24 June 2020].

Moyo, Dambisa (2009) *Dead Aid*, Penguin, London.

Sachs, Jeffrey (2005) *The End of Poverty: Economic Possibilities for Our Time*, Penguin, London.

PART I

When Aid Isn't Wanted

CHAPTER 1

Why do the poor reject aid? Common mistakes and misunderstandings that lead to failure

Abstract

Why do so many attempts to tackle poverty end up as unattractive or impractical to the people they are meant to help? In this chapter we will highlight a number of mistakes that outsiders make when designing aid interventions. These often reflect simple but crucial misunderstandings about the daily realities of life in poor communities. Using a number of case studies from my own and others' work I will show how outsiders can under-estimate the communal nature of life in poor communities, ignore the poor's own solutions, underplay local differences, fail to spot inequalities within communities, and under-estimate the risks and time burdens that are placed on users. Ethnocentrism and a tendency to value outside expertise over local knowledge is often at the heart of these problems.

Keywords: ethnocentrism; participation; human-centred design; Orientalism

Introduction

A decade ago I was invited to help a large charity who were working with smallholder farmers. This is a large group of people – bigger than the whole population of North America or Europe, with an estimated 500 million people in the developing world making their living from small plots of land.[1] The charity had therefore commissioned a substantial audience survey. Among the varied, complex data tables it produced was one very simple finding: many of the respondents really didn't want to be farmers. This stopped me in my tracks; the farmers we wanted to help *didn't want to be farmers*?

This shouldn't have surprised me so much. I have worked on farms, and as Paul Polak, the founder of International Development Enterprise and a man who has helped thousands of smallholder farmers, reminds us, 'the everyday work of farming is excruciatingly boring' (2008: 4). But without this insight – that many farmers didn't want to be farmers – we could have spent huge resources trying to improve the efficiency of an activity that people simply didn't want to do. We could have trained these farmers to learn new techniques and use new inputs, helped them adapt to changes to soil and climate, identified new cash crops for them to grow, and all the time we would be fighting their deeper aspirations, making them better at something they would like to stop doing. This crystallized for me a simple, uncomfortable idea: that as 'professional' designers of development programmes we are very often bad at anticipating what the users will find practical or attractive.

Investors make a distinction between high technical uncertainty and high market uncertainty. A zero-emissions aircraft, for instance, is assumed to have little market uncertainty: in other words, people will be willing to pay to travel on one if it can be produced. But creating such a plane has huge technical uncertainty in that the steps and time required to make it a reality are uncertain and challenging. It's easy to assume that development work plays out in this space; that the challenges lie in producing the low-cost irrigation, clean water, or sanitation solution, not in finding an audience who will use it. In reality, we will see that 'market uncertainty' can be just as big a problem as solving technical challenges.

This is clear if we return to humans' most basic need: clean water. There are already sound, sometimes technically brilliant solutions that should help the millions of people at risk from infected drinking water. As Karlan and Appel (2011) highlight, Oral Rehydration Therapy, or ORT, is a product that is cheap, widely distributed, and should, in theory, help save millions of people from dying and yet which hasn't been adopted anything like as widely as logic and theory would suggest.[2] The PuR water purification powder was, on paper, perhaps an even more compelling idea. It was cheap – a 10 cent sachet would purify 10 litres of water – simple to use, and it provided visibly clean water. And yet in most markets sales of PuR never got far beyond 10 per cent of the target audience. As further growth failed to materialize, its manufacturer, Procter & Gamble (P&G), stopped selling PuR as a commercial solution and instead provided the sachets at cost to development charities.[3]

The role here of a large, profit-driven company like P&G reflects how the 'supply side' of development has expanded in recent years to include many thousands of charitable, commercial, and 'third sector' initiatives. Digital technology and rapid prototyping is accelerating this, allowing many more possible solutions to be produced and marketed. But whilst more is being supplied, not enough is meeting actual demand.[4] As corporations from Danone to Nokia have discovered, cheap, innovative solutions to major social problems regularly fail to find large, sustainable audiences. I worked as a consultant for the latter in the global south for several years and saw both the initial excitement around services such as Nokia Life Tools and the challenges of actually getting people to use them.[5] Kilian Kleinschmidt (Fairs, 2017) describes how the UN has analysed more than 6,000 apps designed for refugees, none of which has found real application.[6]

We are not talking about isolated instances of failure. Nor are they limited to either the charitable or commercial sphere.[7] In this book we will see many examples of carefully planned interventions that solve technical problems and make good sense to development professionals, but which are unattractive or impractical for the people they are meant to help. We will encounter farmers whose local knowledge trumps expert agronomic advice, families who have a good rationale to keep their children away from newly built schools, community leaders who subvert a programme to help young fishermen use more effective fishing equipment, users of a new mobile money service who are willing to queue at a bank all day to withdraw and check the physical notes, rather than trust in the digital currency.

One of the starkest examples of this disconnect between the designers and users of aid was identified by field researcher Simon Harragin during the 1998 famine in Sudan. International relief agencies were worried that their efforts were being undermined by food-hoarding by dominant social groups, who they believed were diverting food from the most malnourished people in the region. Harragin observed that the most malnourished members of the community seemed to be complicit in the process, taking the food they were given and handing it back to community leaders to redistribute among everyone – whether malnourished or not. Many outsiders understandably saw corruption and oppression at work. Harragin's research, though, discovered something more complicated: that in this part of Sudan food was traditionally distributed through kinship networks, and so when people were handing their rations back, they were trying to maintain these networks that had served them and fed them for years. As Rao and Walton argue (2004: 6) in their later analysis of Harragin's work, 'survival of the kinship system was seen to be almost as inherently important as physical survival'.

This example is extreme in the sense that thousands of lives were immediately in the balance. It is also quotidian in the sense it captures some of the persistent mistakes that outsiders like myself make when we think about our audience. It is these mistakes that are at the heart of this chapter. In the following pages we will look at eight specific things that people often get wrong when designing development solutions:

1. They think of the poor as individuals not communities.
2. They ignore the poor's own solutions.
3. They disregard vital local differences.
4. They over-estimate the appetite for change.
5. They downplay the major risks they are asking people to take.
6. They miss the huge inequalities within poor communities.
7. They still assume they are the experts.
8. They forget that the poor are busier than them.

I have made each of these mistakes in my own (typically much lower stakes) development work.[8] Worse, I still find myself unconsciously making these mistakes when I work on new projects. However well I know the pitfalls in principle, it is hard to always avoid them in practice. I have found that being aware has made the slips less frequent and the job of getting back on track somewhat easier.[9] The following passages may be particularly helpful for those who are newer to development (and experienced practitioners may want only to skim them en route to later, more solution-focused chapters). But

I hope they offer a reminder and a useful checklist that many can use, as I do, when designing for development.

Mistake #1: To think of the poor as individuals not communities

When I grow up I want to be a cricketer, a famous cricketer. Everyone in India will know my village. My village's name will be up in lights.

Respondent, fieldwork in rural India 2011

You wouldn't often hear a comment like this in the global north. Partly because cricket is an arcane and rather under-appreciated sport, but mostly because Europeans and North Americans tend to think of themselves and their ambitions in more individualistic terms. In the global south identity can be a much more communal affair.[10] Who you are, how you think of your future, how you make decisions: all of these things are defined rather less by the individual and more so by groups. The line between self and family, neighbourhood and community tends to be less sharp. Writing about communities in the Eastern Cape, South Africa, Wilkinson-Maposa (2005: 254) cites the maxim of *ubuntu*, or 'I am because we are', as capturing the strength of reciprocity and collective identity.[11]

When, like me, you have grown up in a very individualized culture, it can be hard to appreciate, *really* appreciate what it means to live in a more communal environment: how much decisions are made collectively; how important peer influence can be; how much more open people can be to sharing products and services. Failing to do so is often a fundamental reason why our projects don't reach their full potential. Decades ago Kottack (1985: 435) identified the significance of this problem. In his review of World Bank projects he laments the number which 'wrongly assumed that the participating units would be small European-type nuclear family farms rather than extended families and descent groups'. Today whilst the influence of human-centred design (HCD) is encouraging more consideration of users' needs, too often HCD treats 'users' of development as individuals, rather than communities.[12]

Communal and individual, though, are broad terms and to appreciate how outsiders need to design differently for more 'communal' cultures, we need to take apart what communal means and explore its different dimensions. The first element is that resources are more likely to be *shared resources* – goods, services, and other assets are owned by groups, who, with little to go round, can set up complex ways of collectively using what does exist. The aid agencies Harragin studied in Sudan, for instance, made the understandable decision that food should be targeted to the most vulnerable individuals in the area. But from the recipients' perspective food had to go through the community as a whole, and then to families to distribute; it couldn't go direct to the hungriest individuals.[13] This again can be hard for the outsider to apprehend. We need to ensure our concepts of personal ownership don't get in the way – many is the time I've run aground in my attempts to pin down 'who owns' a particular tractor, or mobile phones – and we need to think about how we create programmes and services that maximize people's aptitude for sharing. The benefits of designing this way are explored in detail in Chapter 3.

A second way in which life is more 'communal' is a far greater degree of *public scrutiny*. Life can seem startlingly public for visitors used to the relative anonymity of a European or North American town or city. Neighbours may know not just you, but your family – often back through generations. News spreads rapidly through villages – and through the recreated villages hidden in every city. And behaviour is modified knowing that others are watching. Doors are literally and metaphorically open: 'if a neighbour has no salt and comes to me asking, I should give her some if I have it… [if] she comes to find me when my food is ready, I will invite her to sit and eat' a Namibian respondent tells the research team in Wilkinson-Maposa et al. (2005: 69). Writing about life in tribal and rural communities in sub-Saharan Africa, Abraham and Platteau (2004: 212) describe how 'the spheres of private and social life are not neatly separated as they are in modern societies based on wider and more anonymous interactions'.

Such scrutiny may be relatively less acute in urban environments, to which many poor people have migrated in recent years. But *relative* is the operative word. In one of my first ethnographic studies in India I visited a dense urban area of Mumbai, selected partly because it was known to house recent migrants to the city. It would be a microcosm of India went the thinking. After several days of interviews, I discovered that most of my respondents were in fact from a similar, small area of Uttar Pradesh. Whilst none had met previously they could all trace connections; they were far less alone in the city than I would have been. This, I gradually learned is far from uncommon. Wilkinson-Maposa et al. (2005: 59) describe in southern Africa what they call a 're-villagisation process', where, 'as migrants look for urban work, they draw on communal links and create a web of interdependence between their rural home of origin and their urban domicile'. Banerjee and Duflo (2011: 232) cite a study by Munshi which found that 'Mexican villagers migrate to cities where people from their village have already migrated, even if the original round of migration was purely accidental'. Furthermore, as Myers et al. (2018) remind us, the urban/rural binary is not straightforward and some smaller cities and areas on the periphery of cities can be closer in geography and culture to rural areas.

This can have a profound effect on the adoption or rejection of new development ideas. With careful planning, public scrutiny can be a fuel for rapid behavioural change, as we will see in Chapter 3 with the example of Total Community Led Sanitation. But it may also inhibit adoption of new solutions, as people fear criticism, or even ostracism, if they are seen to break tradition, or try to elevate themselves above their peers. Worries can be especially acute for women and girls, who may face particular scrutiny of their 'reputation'. 'She's aware that other people will talk about her if she veers from the norm. People in her community know her and her family; and they will talk', write the authors of a report on girls' lives in India.[14] The pressure to uphold your reputation may sound slightly quaint to someone living in an impersonal modern western society, but with limited state support, reputation is a serious matter.[15] It can be your access to credit when you need it, your saviour when you need someone to look after your children, your emergency service when you or your home is in danger.[16]

This brings us to the third way that life can be more communal. Poor communities tend to have a degree of *mutual self-reliance*, because formal support does not exist. If banks won't lend, neighbours lend among themselves.[17] If there is no formal pre-school, neighbours set up nurseries in their own homes. If there is no qualified doctor, someone will set up as an informal practitioner, maybe with a sign saying doctor above their door. In a fieldwork study across Mozambique, South Africa, Namibia, and Zimbabwe, Wilkinson-Maposa et al. (2005) uncover countless examples of these 'horizontal links', which they contrast with the 'vertical' way that most outsiders see development working. These horizontal support networks range from loans to childcare to repair work. Similarly, Banerjee and Duflo (2011: 144) describe how people 'have access to an extensive network of people who know them well: extended families, communities based on religions or ethnicity ... if those who are doing well now help out those who are having a bad time, in return for similar help when the roles are reversed, everyone can be made better off: Helping each other out does not have to be charity'. Many of the daily social and financial transactions that would be happening impersonally in the global north will be happening face to face with neighbours you know. When we design for a community we have to consider how our solutions fit with these pre-existing ties, a point that I'll expand on shortly when I come to the next of our misconceptions.

These three different dimensions of communal societies play out in a number of the chapters that follow. I look at how they can be a barrier to risk-taking, particularly among more vulnerable members of a community, and at how outsiders are often forced to weigh the value of new opportunities against the value of preserving social ties. But these more communal social structures can also be the basis for successful innovations. The huge development of microfinance, for instance, was in part born out of neighbours' intimate knowledge of one another and their ability to police one another's debts. The notion of a 'sharing economy' may have gathered hype in North America and Europe, but its potential may be greater when designing to help people in poorer countries and communities. We will see numerous ways that word of mouth – a powerful tool in many contexts – can have particular potency in more collectivist poor communities.

Mistake #2: To ignore the poor's own solutions

The second common mistake that outsiders make is to ignore the local solutions to poverty that already exist on the ground. Too often when outsiders design an intervention they don't notice or consider the ways that insiders are already at work on the problem themselves and the often hidden infrastructure that already exists. The outsider then creates new solutions that ignore, replicate, or clash with the solutions that are already in play. Robert Chambers (2014) gives the example of outsiders hoping to bring vital irrigation solutions to smallholder farmers in India.[18] Chambers describes how outsiders assumed there was little in the way of a market for water selling and sharing, because nothing of this kind was officially recorded. But through informal research Chambers and his colleagues stumbled on a number of farmers regularly selling to their neighbours excess water that they had pumped. The farmers had created a marketplace for water already, just without records or official knowledge. The well-meaning outsiders were 'duplicating, displacing and undermining existing water markets and livelihoods' (2014: 54).[19]

This mistake is common, and to an extent understandable, since informal solutions are often invisible solutions, at least to the outsider. The local nursery, savings club, or farming agreement may have no office, registration documents, or website. They may only be known to the people living within a few square miles who sustain and use them. Occasionally, organic solutions may bubble up into wider view – as when recently a Brazilian writer discovered, and started tweeting about, the informal groups on WhatsApp that help citizens negotiate the gaps in transport and security coverage in their cities (Lafloufa and Puff, 2020). But it is below the surface that many exist; widespread, engrained, and vital. Narayan et al. (2009) found that across their sample countries there were an average 2.8 finance groups, 2.3 farming groups, and two health or education groups per community. They note 'innumerable cases, particularly in the African contexts, in which community residents have come together to guard themselves' (2008: 302). Cunningham (2008: 263) describes the wide range of self-help groups found in Ethiopia, including '*idirs* or burial societies ... *iqubs*, or rotating savings and credit associations, *senbetes*, whose members celebrate after church services, and *mahabers*, or rotating feast groups. For hundreds – perhaps thousands – of years these traditional institutions have helped rural communities in Ethiopia survive and thrive'. Research by Udry (1994) in rural Nigeria looking at gifts and informal loans found that the average family owed money to, or was owed money by, 2.5 other families. A diary study of 250 households by Collins et al. (2009: 49) found that 'most transactions are carried out with "informal" partners rather than with formal institutions like banks and insurance companies. The partners are often neighbours, who seldom keep documentation of agreements and certainly nothing that would hold up in court'. The degree of reciprocity is reflected in Collins et al.'s (2009) discovery that the majority of loans between neighbours were interest-free.

These self-created solutions can be more effective than those that outsiders design. A review of projects across Indonesian villages (World Bank, 2004) found that over 80 per cent of those instigated by the community were still in use, compared to only around half for government and NGO initiated projects (privately funded projects were also around 80 per cent in use). The same study found that services provided by outsiders with little community involvement can be seen as distant and hard to identify with. The authors write that 'when communities are not involved in establishing, supporting, or overseeing a school, the school is often seen as something alien. Villagers refer to "the government's" school, not "our" school' (2004: 112).

If, then, local solutions are widespread, often effective, but also invisible to outsiders, what do outsiders do? The first step is to dedicate more time to primary research and exploration. The examples from both Chambers (2014) and Harragin (2004) show the particular value of being there in person, conducting research on the ground. In addition, they reflect the value of an ethnographic approach, which seeks to understand the full complexity of the world as it's experienced by someone different to you (Alasuutari,1995; Denzin and Lincoln,1994; Geertz, 2000, 1973). We also need to take more seriously the opportunities for both sides to learn from the other. Rather than approaching projects looking for the *problems* in the community to solve, we should be looking for the solutions that are already being built and for the untapped resources that might lead to other, organic solutions. The Asset-Based Community Development approach (Mathie and Cunningham, 2008; Neumann and Mathie, 2008; Wilkinson-Maposa, 2008) provides a very productive template, with its aim to 'shift the focus away from deficits and problems and on to people's assets and strengths' (Mathie and Cunningham, 2008: 2).[20] In so doing, it engages with people not as recipients of aid so much as active participants. In the later chapters I focus heavily on the ways in which organic, local solutions can be encouraged and developed and on how insiders can take a leading role in this development. We also need to be clear-eyed about the limitations that informal solutions often face. It's one mistake for outsiders to ignore local solutions; it's another mistake to romanticize them. A society where you rely on your community can sound inviting to many in the global north, but it can be a dangerous one in which to live, especially if you are a woman or a girl, or from a marginal group. When a community loses cohesion, this can have profound effects for people who have come to rely on social networks, rather than on formal provision from the state (Narayan et al., 2000: 147). In addition, anyone who falls out of favour with the community finds themselves very vulnerable indeed, a problem we will return to shortly.

Mistake #3: To disregard vital local differences

Since 2008 I have been involved in numerous initiatives to bring online services to poor communities. There was often, especially in the beginning, great fanfare around such projects, talk of 'bringing a whole world of historical and global knowledge'. Typically, though, the information that people were seeking was extremely local. Countless times I sat in internet cafes or around a low-cost smartphone and watched someone frustratedly search for local buses, a local market, their own home, fields, and nearby rainfall predictions, all on software systems designed to show them the whole world. Here lay one of the biggest tensions between the producers and users of development initiatives: the former are looking at the world, the latter at the world in front of them.

This often leads to development services that simply aren't tailored enough to local needs. It can also lead outsiders to assume that development solutions are more exportable than they really are, that an intervention that works in one location can be transposed relatively easily to another. A striking example comes from work by Robert Jensen (2007) in the Indian state of Kerala, who found that fishers who had bought mobile phones were now able to get better prices for their catch by calling to get the market price at different ports. I'll describe the study in a little detail, as the results were quite dramatic. Jensen found that in 1997, before mobile phone networks arrived, beach market prices ranged from 9.9 rupees a kilo to effectively no money at all for the fishers who arrived to find the buyers now closed for business. He calculated that boats arriving late were losing 3,400 rupees in profit. He also found that there was very little arbitrage – with almost all fishers selling their catch at the closest beach market. Looking then four years later when mobile phones were widespread (used by between 60 and 75 per cent of the fishers depending on location), several changes had materialized. First, fishers were selling to a wider variety of buyers, with the proportion selling *outside* their nearest markets up from near zero to 30–40 per cent on a typical day. Second, price difference had declined from above 60 per cent to 15 per cent. Waste had fallen from 5–8 per cent of daily catch to almost zero and fishers' profits were up by 8 per cent, all on a price that was 4 per cent cheaper to their customers.

This study generated a lot of academic and press attention (Economist, 2007; Wall Street Journal, 2009). Much was made of the potential for mobile phones to disrupt exploitative markets and transform the lives of poor people around the world. I was working a great deal with mobile phone companies at this time and I can remember numerous meetings where we speculated about how phone access might empower millions of fishers and farmers in this way. This did not materialize. One factor was that later research showed that the value of mobile phones to fishers was if not specific to this part of Kerala then significantly heightened by particular local factors, both social and oceanographic. So when Jensen's work was replicated in other areas of the same coastline, the effects were less dramatic (Sreekumar, 2011; Srinivasan and Burrell, 2013; Steyn and Van Greunen, 2014). Jensen himself was careful to note the specific conditions that made mobile phones such an important intervention in the communities he studied. His fishers could typically only get to one market per day because of the costs of transportation and short market hours; their goods were highly perishable; they had no form of storage; and poor quality local roads made it hard to sell inland. These conditions made up-to-date market prices so valuable, but they don't exist to the same extent for many other poor producers, including, it was discovered, fishers further along the same coastline. In much of the reporting and reception of the results, however, these local specificities were glossed over in the rush for a story of digital potential.

There are, of course, examples of development interventions that spread fast across regions and countries, whose benefits connect to, or transcend, vastly different social, geographic, and economic environments. M-Pesa mobile money is one of the most famous examples of a local innovation that has spread. But even here when my colleagues conducted fieldwork in East Africa a few years after the M-Pesa launch, they found, as did Camner et al. (2012), that its utility and uses varied a lot by the country and area in which it operated. And we will see throughout the book that successful interventions tend to pay a lot of attention to local specifics. I will illustrate it here with two brief examples.

The first is from a J-PAL paper (J-PAL, 2017) that reviewed 60 different randomized control trials (RCTs) performed on education interventions across countries and regions. These interventions took almost wildly different approaches to getting children into schools. There were subsidies, conditional cash transfers, free uniforms and meals; there were health interventions, free technology, and information campaigns. The report's clear conclusion is that what works is what works in *that area*. Context matters. For instance, in the Dominican Republic an RCT found that an information campaign listing local earnings by educational level led to boys spending an average of more than two months longer in school. Yet a similar information programme in rural China had no significant effect. The authors conclude that:

> Which strategy is best to pursue will depend on local conditions and challenges. In areas where there are few schools, requiring children to travel outside their local community to attend school, finding ways to provide low-cost local school options is likely a priority. Similarly, in places with high parasitic worm load or very high rates of anaemia, programs that cheaply address these issues should be investigated for feasibility. These are specific strategies that make sense where these specific needs are present (2017: 27).

The second example is from International Development Enterprises (IDE), who have worked for decades to help smallholder farmers in the global south. In order to advise farmers on which crops to grow to meet market demand, IDE have an exhaustive methodology which they apply to each new geographical area they enter. This involves interviewing 50 farmers, a number of expert market traders, and regional and governmental agricultural experts. As their founder Paul Polak writes (2008: 17), 'you can't make practical plans unless you gather a lot of details about each specific village context. What kind of high-value crops you can grow in each depends on the type of soil and the climate... If there is a factory nearby with jobs that pay well, the labor required for intensive horticulture may be hard to come by'.

This painstakingly local approach contrasts with the way many large, international organizations work, but it has helped IDE to expand methodically but dramatically across multiple markets. Chambers (2014) argues along similar lines, giving the example of a project he conducted with rice growers in India in the 1970s. When he and his colleague compared the 12 villages they were studying they found 'each of them had a different system of acquiring, distributing and allocating minor irrigation water, and each differed in its groundwater conditions. We came to realize that had I, or we, studied only one village, we would have supposed its system was the norm, when in fact it was unique. The norm was the uniqueness of diversity' (2014: 53). The message that will unfold in the following chapters is that we have to be extremely alert to local differences of this kind and that to be effective we have to find ways to work at a local scale, even on larger national or regional projects. We will explore how digital resources offer new opportunities and challenges here.

Mistake #4: To over-estimate the appetite for change

A desire for change might seem to be a given in poor communities. If you live in poverty you are surely eager for new solutions, new options, and opportunities. Yet a simple, common reason that development initiatives fail is by over-estimating people's appetite for change. This again reflects ethnocentrism on the part of 'experts' like myself who are based in the global north and who live with an expectation and mantra of constant changes. We absorb the basic tenets: one must learn new skills to adapt to the changing workplace, adopt new technologies, move fast to seize business opportunities, stay in touch with rapidly mutating news stories. The sociologist John B. Thompson (1995: 189) describes how change has permeated our culture and consciousness. He notes how 'the rigidity of traditional ways of life begins to break down as individuals are confronted with alternatives that were previously unimaginable. Social life begins to seem more uncertain as individuals start to wonder what will happen next rather than assuming that the future will resemble the past as it always has'.[21] This ideology of constant and accelerating change feeds into development ideology and practice in the global north, especially today where digital technology, rapid prototyping and agile ways of working all accelerate the speed with which anti-poverty programmes, products, and services can be created and distributed.

The contrast with the global south is not a simple binary one. Many poor and middle-income countries are also experiencing rapid change. And this is the narrative that is often told about 'emerging markets' from Colombia to Vietnam, East Africa to South Asia. It is a story of economic and technological disruption (Economist, 2011; Martin, 2020), and of social and cultural transformation. To illustrate the extent of the latter in 21st-century India, Dheeraj Sinha (2011) evocatively compares two Shahrukh Khan films that launched just 13 years apart (1995's *Dilwale Dulhania Le Jayenge* and 2008's *Rab Ne Bana Di Jodi*). During this time one of the icons of Indian cinema has gone from 'refusing to elope with his girlfriend to asking someone else's wife to run away in search of personal happiness'. As Sinha writes, 'the depiction of relationships and morality in mainstream Bollywood cinema has come a long way – obviously mirroring the tremendous change that India has seen in the last 15 years' (2011: 1).

However, cultural change, like economic change, is growing unevenly, and in areas where poverty is most prevalent and most acute old habits and attitudes are often more rooted. Lofchie (2015: 51) reminds us that 'the over-whelming majority of the African poor are small-scale farmers who combine subsistence production with modest participation in the cash economy. The conditions of life for these farmers, who may still comprise as much as 70 per cent of the population of sub-Saharan Africa, have changed little, if at all, during the past 20 years'. Not only are poor communities often less used to change, they tend to view and value it rather differently to those working on poverty reduction in the global north. Far greater value may be placed on maintaining traditions, whilst innovators are seen much more sceptically than outsiders can easily imagine. The sociologist Pierre Bourdieu (1998: 162) captures this vividly in his account of fieldwork in rural areas of Algeria, where cycles took precedence over innovation and there could be scorn for anyone who strove too eagerly for change:

> So there is mockery too for the man who hurries without thinking, who runs to catch up with someone else, who works so hastily that he is likely to 'maltreat the earth' forgetting the teachings of wisdom
>
> It is useless to pursue the world,
> No one will ever over take it.
> You who rush along,
> Stay and be rebuked;
>
> Daily bread comes from God,
> It is not for you to concern yourself.
>
> The over-eager peasant moves ahead of the collective rhythms which assign each act its particular moment in the space of the day, the year, or human life; his race with time threatens to drag the whole group into the escalation of diabolic ambition, *thahraymith*, and thus to turn circular time into linear time, simple reproduction into indefinite accumulation.[22]

This passage was written in the 1960s, but in many areas of the world its emphasis on the cyclical and traditional is worth absorbing. Development professionals are often focused on disruption and the breaking of cycles, but such cycles are essential to life for many of the world's poorest. This can make it hard for people to embrace new products and services, even if they open up new sources of income. Polak (2008: 142) describes how 'people in poor vil-lages often don't have the eyes to see opportunities under their noses, usually because doing so would require a break with normative cultural expectations'.

Similarly, Rao and Walton (2004: 45) argue that 'for someone born into a social group that faces high levels of social exclusion, discrimination and material poverty, social interactions are geared toward survival and interactions within one's own group. The opportunity cost of a culture of aspiration and change may be high'.

Outsiders like myself have to learn to accept that reluctance to change may have complex and varied roots, one of which we will start to dig into in our next section. We also have to think more rigorously and creatively about how we can make change more attractive and more attainable, and in Chapter 5 I explore the wide range of strategies we can use. One of the messages here is to avoid the temptation to see traditions as simply a brake on innovation or to make the mistake Rao and Walton (2004) highlight where one sees development as 'forward-looking' and culture as 'backward-looking'. The traditions valued by poor communities are often themselves evolving at their own pace and they may also offer the seed of significant and locally useful innovations. Powerful examples of the latter have been shown by writers like Radjou et al. (2012) in the story of 'jugaad innovation'. I explore, particularly in Chapter 3, how we can look for these moments and try to find ways that they may aid more creative and relevant development solutions.

Mistake #5: To downplay the major risks we are asking people to take

Resistance to change touches on our next common mistake, which is to under-estimate the *risks* our new interventions impose on people. Asking someone in a poor community to plant a new kind of seed on their land, receive their payment electronically, take out a loan to develop their business, or encourage their daughters to work outside the home; all of these are risks, with potentially huge downsides. As outsiders we can run all kinds of tests and models to reassure ourselves they are risks worth taking, but for the person taking the risk it can look very daunting indeed. Sat in an office with a spreadsheet, it may seem baffling that a farmer doesn't adopt a new practice *we can just see* will improve their income. But imagine you have a small plot of land and a crop that supplies the majority of your income for the whole year. Now imagine someone asks you to try out a totally new product or technique on it. They are asking you to make an *extremely* brave decision.

In addition, poor people are typically already highly exposed to risks, even before well-meaning people arrive with a new programme or service. These risks range from the dire consequences of becoming ill to the unpredictability of weather in the global south.[23] Life for the poorest is full of uncertainty, with limited scope to mitigate or prepare for downturns. As Banerjee and Duflo argue (2011: 133), 'risk is a central fact of life for the poor, who often run small businesses or farms or work as casual laborers, with no assurance of regular employment. In such lives a bad break can have disastrous consequences'.

Furthermore, when the poor are offered a new programme or product, they don't expect to have much in the way of safeguards to protect them if something goes wrong. A consumer in the global north knows that if they buy health insurance, or some new tools for their business they have some recourse to consumer protection laws and possible compensation. As we will see in the next chapter, the poor can often only rely on exploitation.

All of this can curb the appetite for risk-taking in poor communities. If you live without stable employment, without savings, without government safety nets – and with widespread exploitation – then it takes very significant courage to gamble and embrace risk. When someone offers you a new financial app, a new fertilizer, a new training course, the consequences of it not working are liable to flood your mind; the potential rewards liable to recede. One of the main challenges when we introduce a new intervention is to help people to feel more confident about trialling new solutions and to manage the risks involved. In the course of the book I look at various approaches and tactics for so doing and in Chapter 5 I pull these together into a list of approaches and tools that can be used by practitioners.

Mistake #6: To miss the huge inequalities *within* poor communities

In the pages so far I have often referred to 'the poor' in a way that might imply they are a discrete and homogeneous group. In reality, of course, the different members of any poor community will have very varied identities and very different levels of power, resources, connections, knowledge, and ability to act. The following passage (Narayan et al., 2000: 139) captures some of the myriad inequalities that exist amongst the poorest.

> Worldwide, discrimination on the basis of race, ethnicity, language and religion persists, compounding the isolation of whole communities of poor people. This is true for black people in Brazil, for Roma and Pomaks in Bulgaria, migrant Tajiks in Uzbekistan, indigenous people in Ecuador and minority communities in the northern uplands and the Mekong delta of Vietnam. Religious discrimination is described in the study affecting Hindus in Bangladesh and Protestants in Ethiopia's Dibdibe Wajtu Peasant Association. Traditional social hierarchies exist, affecting lower castes in India, and lower-caste clans in Somaliland and southeast Nigeria. And even language can marginalize groups of people, such as the Khmer communities in Tra Vinh, Vietnam.

Such differences can, though, be easily missed by development outsiders. Too often, solutions are designed as though people in a poor community have consistent needs and equal access. Too often outsiders will 'assume that groups of people (village communities, urban neighbourhood associations, school councils, water user groups) will always work toward a common interest' and gloss over the 'significant problems of coordination, asymmetric information, and inequality' (Mansuri and Rao, 2012: 285). This happens especially when those designing solutions are based a long way from the audience, or when they are new to development. Inequalities often only really emerge when we spend time listening to and interacting with people on multiple occasions and across different contexts. Then we see how, as in rich communities, power and assets are often concentrated along gender lines, distributed unevenly between ethnic, class, and caste groups, as well as according to skin colour, language, religious grouping, occupation, physical and mental health, sexual preferences, or sexual behaviour.[24] Furthermore, there are differences in income; differences which may seem marginal to outsiders, especially when seen on a spreadsheet, but which can have dramatic effects on those with lowest incomes who can find themselves excluded from the social life of their community. Narayan et al. (2000: 35) describe how 'the extremely poor are often rejected, even by those who are also poor'.

Many would argue that tackling these inequalities should be a fundamental and intrinsic goal of development. I would agree and will advance this argument through the course of the book. But the point I want to make here is that even when our projects have other primary aims, we should think carefully about discrimination, power, and inequality. Because if we don't, our projects are less likely to succeed.

First, if we don't identify and design for the vulnerable and excluded members of a community, our programmes may only benefit the *relatively* well off. We will see throughout the book examples of programmes that fail in this way: services that can only be accessed by those poor people who have titles that prove ownership of their land, or the funds to connect the new water supply to their home; apps that require some fluency in the dominant language; empowerment groups that require the confidence to attend a community meeting. There is a constant risk that any new service or resource will end up being shared among the relatively more powerful, rather than according to need, ability, or where they will do optimum good. A very stark example of the latter is shown by Christopher Udry (1996), who found that discrimination against women can prevent communities from getting full returns from vital inputs like fertilizer. His study looked at farming in rural Burkina Faso, where each member of the household farms a separate plot of land, allowing him to test, and then show that the plots farmed by women were systematically given less fertilizer and less labour, leading families to undermine their resources significantly. Banerjee and Duflo (2011: 125) report that 'by reallocating some of the fertilizer plus a bit of labor to the wives' plots, the family could increase its production by 6 per cent without spending an extra penny'.

Second, if we don't take care, new development initiatives can even unintentionally undermine the less powerful, who are not well placed to take advantage of new opportunities and more likely to see their activities and incomes disrupted by change. An example of this takes us back to fishers of Kerala, where later research by Sreekumar (2011) found that although mobile phones had allowed some (mostly male) fishing crews to get a better price for their catch, they had negatively impacted groups of women who made a living buying unsold fish from the beach markets, which they then sold door to door. The women, who were much slower than men to acquire mobile phones, were left out of the new information exchange and found themselves unable to buy the leftover fish at the cheap price they were used to. In the course of time more women acquired mobile phones, and were able to find important benefits, but in the short term they suffered a drop in income.

Thus, a major part of the book looks at discrimination, exclusion, and power relations within poor communities. I try to note their effect throughout, and in Chapter 4 I look specifically at the tactics we can use to reach less powerful groups and to reduce discrimination in the communities where we work. We will see in the pages that follow that in some cases discrimination is actively perpetrated and enforced by more powerful members of a community. On other occasions, though, vulnerable groups learn to *exclude themselves* – a problem that can be both more troubling and difficult to address. Marginalized groups can grow up with narratives that naturalize their lower social status. As Rao and Walton argue, for instance, 'persons born very low in the caste hierarchy deeply internalize this hierarchy and do little to question it, since they lack an ideology of equality' (2004: 34). They may also grow used to being denied services and support and come to assume they aren't going to be the beneficiaries of any new programme. This passage from Narayan et al. (2000: 140) demonstrates with awful clarity how this lowering of expectation can happen. Although the context of the countries described may have changed since time of writing, the structural issues are common across context.

> Tajik refugees in the Kyrgyz Republic do not have passports and so cannot access health care services, employment or loans, and cannot vote in elections. In addition, they face hostility from the local people who say that 'we had enough problems ourselves, and now you're here to add to them'. Problems of discrimination also extend to the classroom. A group of elderly Roma men report that teachers refuse to enrol Roma children in their classes so they don't attend school. In Ecuador an indigenous man complains that 'teachers would also discriminate. They would say, "You are an ass; this is why you can't. You are an animal." Treating us badly in school is a form of discrimination.'

In such instances it's unsurprising people become sceptical about whether outside interventions can really help them.[25] Why go to try the health centre's new nutrition programme when experience suggests you may be pushed to the back of the queue? Why sign up for a new training scheme when it will be dominated by the usual suspects? Unless we are aware of such discrimination within our audience, unless we know which groups have been marginalized, then our interventions may not reach the people who need them most. Even our attempts to consult and design with communities may end up flawed and partial, since when we 'listen to the poor' the first and loudest voices we hear are likely to be those of the more powerful: of men, the dominant ethnic groups, the relatively better off, the traditional leaders.[26] This is a problem that runs through much of the book, feeding into many of its themes and stories. How we can address it, practically, is the focus of the final chapters.

Mistake #7: To assume that outsiders are the experts

Starving people want food immediately. If ever there was a safe assumption, it would surely be this. But Harragin's case study shows how hard it is for an outsider to judge insiders' priorities precisely. The problem is that we development 'experts' still find it hard to shake off our role as experts – however much commitment there may be to 'human-centred design' or 'participative development'. We consult local people, but when it comes to reaching conclusions we privilege professional knowledge. We ask questions in the field, but then record the answers in reports written and read in offices, or books sold to people in rich countries. We recognize poverty is multidimensional, but we still prioritize the goals that currently dominate expert debate. We design solutions that require outside expertise to build and maintain, rather than orientating them around local skills and knowledge. In doing all of this we come close to Edward Said's description of Orientalism with its 'flexible positional superiority, which puts the westerner in a whole series of possible relationships with the Orient without ever losing him the relative upper hand' (2003: 7).[27]

For outsiders to assume expertise is not only ethically problematic, it can be practically destructive too. This is because sometimes – often in fact – expertise in the theory of development is trumped by the local knowledge of those who live on the ground. Polak (2008: 15–16) gives a very clear example of this from his work in Bangladesh, which I will quote in full, since it highlights so clearly how the problem can play out.

> In the 1990s, agriculture experts in Bangladesh were dismayed that small-acreage farmers were applying only a tiny fraction of the fertilizer that their monsoon-season rice crops needed, even though they could triple their investment in fertiliser from the increased rice yields the recommended amount would stimulate. The experts complained about the irrational and superstitious behavior of small-acreage farmers, and set up extension programs and farmer-training programs, but nothing worked ... Finally, somebody asked some farmers why they were using so little fertilizer. 'Oh, that's easy,' they said. 'Every ten years or so around here, there is a major flood during the monsoon season that carries away all the fertilizer we apply. So we only apply the amount of fertiliser we can afford to lose in a ten-year flood'. Suddenly it became clear that the farmers were excellent, rational decision makers and that it was the agriculture experts who had a lot to learn.

The story has a simple message: that an in-depth, accurate knowledge of the local context can be far more valuable than a broad, theoretical understanding of development planning. Expert knowledge may not be perfect, and experts' priorities may not match those of our audience. The goals outsiders set for development aren't necessarily the things our audience most value. To see this in action, we can return one final time to the Keralan fishers. Following Jensen's groundbreaking study, a clear narrative echoed around professional economic and development circles (Economist, 2007; Harford, 2008; LIRNEAsia, 2007). This story was that mobile phones allow poor people to find a better price for their goods and thereby raise their incomes. A lot of the innovation that this story prompted, some of which I was at least peripherally involved in, focused on this single, inviting idea. However, later research showed not only that this premise only held true in certain contexts, but that mobile phones provided fishers with a *much broader range of social and economic benefits than market efficiency and income generation*, including allowing users more time for family life and increasing their sense of security on the water. Sreekumar (2011) concludes that it was in fact security, not improved pricing, that was the most significant benefit in the fishing communities he studied. Srinivasan and Burrell (2013: 10) write that 'fishers and others in the fishing supply chain spoke also in terms of maintaining relationships, with fellow fishers, their auctioneers, or regular buyers, rather than solely in terms of optimizing their incomes'. The problem was that these non-economic benefits were largely ignored in the story told by outsiders, like myself. In so doing, I believe, we unwittingly closed down the scope for other non-financial innovations that might have improved users' lives. Srinivasan and Burrell (2013: 10) see this as a warning 'not to mistake the focus and priorities of disciplines (such as the concern in economics for how information asymmetries affect market functioning) for the interests and priorities of target populations'.

This reflects one particular assumption that outsiders often make, which is that the poor are particularly focused on getting more money and that we should therefore prioritize financial goals over others. It's an understandable assumption – if you have little money you must surely place great value on getting more. But the reality is less clear cut. One of the main conclusions of the huge Voices of the Poor consultation project was that the poor often had non-financial concerns that were at least as important as financial ones. This is clearly captured in the passage from Narayan et al. (2000: 264) below.

> Historically many development professionals have given priority to the material aspect of people's lives. Important as this is, poor people's views of wellbeing, as we have seen, span wide and varied experiences and meanings. The words of a poor woman in Ethiopia illustrate some of the range and balance: 'A better life for me is to be healthy, peaceful, and live in love without hunger. Love is more than anything. Money has no value in the absence of love'. To encompass multiple dimensions, and to make space for poor people's own ideas of the good life means working toward wellbeing for all.

Similarly, Sabine Alkire (2004) describes studies in Pakistan which found even when people are living in acute financial poverty they rate improvements in community cohesion, religious knowledge, levels of education as just as important as improvements in their financial status.[28] For those on the ground poverty is always 'multidimensional', a reality that we will see throughout the book and especially in the following chapter when we explore the contours of life in a poor community. We will also see that outsiders need to be more cautious about judging the choices made by the poor. Outside experts are quick to identify 'poverty traps' – self-destructive patterns of behaviour that insiders don't realize are helping perpetuate their poverty. It is a standard rhetorical trick of development writing to reveal such 'traps', a trick to which I'm not immune. But the expert's point of view is not necessarily the clearest or most informed perspective, as the Bangladesh monsoon example shows. The keen-eyed outsider may miss the local logic that insiders are applying, a logic that may, as in Polak's example, simply trump that of outsiders, who should in fact learn from those on the ground.[29]

How we integrate, use, and value insider and outsider knowledge is a question that runs throughout this book. I will argue that in a pinch the voice of insiders should take precedence, that if there is a difficult decision to be made over a development priority or programme then the choice should ultimately rest with those who have to live with its results. As Sen (1999: 32) writes of one such dispute, 'the pointer to any real conflict between the preservation of tradition and the advantages of modernity calls for a participatory resolution, not for a unilateral rejection of modernity in favour of tradition by political rulers, or religious authorities, or anthropological admirers of the legacy of the past. The question is not only not closed, it must be wide open for people in the society to address and join in deciding'. But in practice this is complex and fluid. What if outsiders believe insiders are dangerously wrong – that their preference to preserve traditions is extremely damaging for their economic prospects, or for the freedom of young people or women? What if insiders are lacking information that might alter their choice? What if dominant groups are using their economic resources and social connections to steer others to the answer they want? These are not questions with easy answers. Participative development is not an objective, technical process, but rather a matter of continual political choices and trade-offs, some of which are extremely uncomfortable to address. An outsider in a rich country may see from their data sheets that reducing fertility rates in a poor country will have 'multiple positive development outcomes', but how far should they go to persuade strangers who have much less power than them to alter their hopes, their plans, their sexual behaviour? We will find such dilemmas surfacing continually throughout the book, nagging at and undermining our neat attempts to design effective and equitable solutions. In Chapter 7 I will turn and face them head on, exploring different ways that we might weigh up and decide between competing priorities and perspectives.

Mistake #8: To not realize that the poor are often busier than the rich

Our last misconception is perhaps the simplest, but no less destructive for that, and it's one I know well. A decade ago I tried to set up a service to help community organizers in poor communities around the world to learn from and support one another. I was hugely excited and energized by the idea. I had met women and men on four continents who were setting up projects so similar I felt they simply had to learn from and help one another. I imagined a group I had met in Recife, Brazil telling youth leaders in rural Indonesia the innovative tactics they were using to keep young children from joining gangs. Meanwhile female social business leaders I knew in southern Kenya would be sharing advice with a group of women entrepreneurs in rural Rajasthan. Of the many mistakes I made, one was especially fundamental and common. I assumed that people would have time for this service I was building. Time to try out and learn a new piece of software; time to search for people they might be able to help, or be helped by; time to invest in building relationships with strangers (like-minded strangers, but strangers nonetheless) in remote regions and countries. Most entrepreneurs, social or otherwise, tend to over-estimate their audience's willingness to devote time to their new inventions. But in the global north we often have a particular misconception about the poor being richer in time than they are in money.[30]

In fact, the opposite is usually true. A comparison of international working hours shows that in general people in poorer countries work much longer hours than people in rich ones. Of countries with data available, Cambodia, Myanmar, and Mexico are the ones with the highest working hours – all over 2,200 hours on average a year. Bangladesh, India, Vietnam, the Philippines, Pakistan, China, Costa Rica, and Thailand are close behind with only South Korea and Hong Kong among rich nations registering over 2,000 hours and European countries, mainly under 1,600 hours.[31] As Narayan et al. (2009: 60) describe, 'in the absence of capital to invest in new technologies and equipment, poor people's primary input is "sheer hard work"'. Furthermore, they continue, 'those people who are worst off, affected by displacement, drought, or conflict, seem to work the hardest'. Whilst many poor people suffer from unemployment and underemployment, this is miles away from idleness. As Mbaye and Golub (2015) write, here specifically about Africa, 'people do have jobs: they are simply too poor not to work. Instead, the problem is underemployment; typically 90% (or more) of the labor force is in the informal sector such as subsistence agriculture and urban self-employment in petty services'. Spend time in a village or poor urban area and you find the underemployed are typically not at leisure but *on call* – whether they are running kiosks on an underused road or waiting in line for a day-wage job that never arrives.[32]

The poor are also obliged to chase multiple sources of income, which further eats into their time. Someone farming their own land, running their own stall *and* working as an occasional day labourer may officially be only 'partially employed', but they can end up spending far more hours working than the average salaried worker in a high-income country. This is far from an unusual pattern. As Banerjee and Duflo (2011: 141) describe, 'one striking fact about the poor is the sheer number of occupations that a single family seems to be involved in: In a survey of twenty-seven villages in West Bengal, even households that claimed to farm a piece of land spent only 40 percent of their time farming. The median family in this survey had three working members and seven occupations'.[33] In addition, the running of a poor household requires intensive work. Getting fresh water or fuel can take hours, not seconds. Travelling to the shops, cultivating your own food in barren or environmentally degraded conditions, and cooking each of your meals from scratch monopolizes large parts of the day – for women and girls especially.[34] When I reviewed two dozen studies on the lives of girls in sub-Saharan Africa, South Asia, and South East Asia, one of the most striking findings was how little time most girls and young women had for themselves.[35]

Hence, we cannot assume that poor people – and especially poor women and girls – have time to experiment with the programmes and services we are creating. My start point now is to assume that people in poor communities are probably busier than me and my colleagues. We need to be respectful in how we ask for their participation and very smart about where and when we introduce our new initiatives to their lives. We need to ensure our services and programmes work around their daily habits. When we invite people to take part in consultations we need to give careful thought about what they gain in return. And we should pause before designing project schedules based around the diaries of those flying in, rather than those working 14 hours a day to keep their families alive.

Moving forward

So why do poor people often reject initiatives designed to tackle poverty? To start to answer this question I have set out eight common mistakes that I have seen myself and others make when designing for the poorest. In so doing we have already begun to tease out some of the ways we can design more sympathetically and effectively. In the chapters that follow I will develop this further to look at what it means in practice to design from the poor's perspective and what new opportunities and what new challenges such an endeavour brings.

- Chapter 2 will sharpen our definition of the audience for development. What is meant when people talk about 'the poor'? Who is and isn't included in this group? What are the boundaries and rhythms of their daily lives?
- Chapter 3 will look more deeply at what we mean by more 'communal cultures' and the opportunities that arise when you design around the stronger social bonds in poor communities.
- Chapter 4 addresses the problems of discrimination and inequality by asking how we reach marginalized audiences without exacerbating tensions between different groups.

- Chapter 5 asks how we can tackle people's scepticism about change, fears about risk-taking (and lack of time) to make new behaviours more inviting and feasible for our audiences.

These chapters set up the final part of the book, which focuses more sharply on the shift to more community-led development. Chapter 6 will examine how we can build on the solutions that already exist within poor communities, whilst Chapter 7 tackles perhaps the most difficult issue in development: how do we transfer control over the development process to communities themselves? Chapter 8 is a short concluding chapter that draws some of the insights from the book into a series of design principles and a set of proposed goals for more community-led development.

Notes

1. World Bank estimates 2016. <http://www.worldbank.org/en/news/feature/2016/02/25/a-year-in-the-lives-of-smallholder-farming-families> [accessed 22 February 2021].
2. They describe how 'it is a small plastic envelope of salts that, when eaten, allow the body to absorb and retain water. Combined with fluid intake, it effectively neutralizes the threat of mortality from the disease. The salts cost a couple of pennies at most, and in many diarrhoea-prone areas of the developing world they are fully subsidized - available for free' (Karlan and Appel, 2011: 42).
3. See Simanis (2012) and Garrette and Karnani (2010) for more detail.
4. The idea of there being a 'demand side' as well as a supply side of development aid is an inviting one, but we will see in the chapters that follow that it can also be problematic. Where, for instance, are the lines between 'stimulating demand' for education and imposing cultural norms on another group of people?
5. See, for instance, Kachra et al. (2012).
6. Writers such as Friedman and Stolterman (2015) see this as a more general failing of design. They cite Donald Norman's criticism of designers who 'claim that fresh eyes can produce novel solutions, but then they wonder why these solutions are seldom implemented, or if implemented, why they fail.' Friedman and Stolterman argue that 'design schools do not train students about these complex issues, about the interlacing complexities of human and social behaviour, about the behavioural sciences, technology, and business' (2015: x).
7. The case has been made that commercial, paid-for solutions can be more sustainable than those provided free by charities and governments (see Easterly, 2006, or for a critical analysis of whether this is true for anti-malarial bednets, see Heierli and Lingerer, 2008). The examples above show that neither approach is failsafe, and that both ultimately rely on understanding and adapting intuitively to the lives of the people who will use them.
8. Not all on the same project.

9. This list is by no means intended to be exhaustive. It's made up of factors I have seen in fieldwork and found corroborated and amplified in other people's research. As such I hope it offers a framework on which to build.

10. Of course, there are differences between countries and regions in the strength and type of communal ties and influence. See, for instance, Kottack (1985) on the different role of extended family in different regions targeted by World Bank projects.

11. In an earlier work on mutual aid in poor communities, Wilkinson-Maposa et al. (2005) expand upon this idea, exploring how this aid transcends and confounds ideas of altruism, because self and others are not strictly separated in the way that altruism implies. Meanwhile, looking at the difference between communal and individual in the context of China, Mills (2011: 73) suggests that 'a Confucian individual is thus one who is *born into obligations*, as opposed to their Western counterpart, who is *born with rights*'.

12. For more on this and a broader critique of human-centred design methods, see Kejriwal (2020). For a discussion of designing for communities versus individuals, see GSMA and Frog Design (2017).

13. Harragin points to how the community traditionally made 'a split between territorial resources and family-owned resources. Grazing and aid are seen as belonging to a territorial group, whereas cattle are seen as being family owned' (2004: 310). When the aid arrived, people judged that it was an asset that belonged to the entire community within an area, rather than to individuals or families.

14. GEM India Research, courtesy of Girl Effect. Similarly in Malawi researchers noted how 'people tend to look at the way the girl behaves in the community, the way she speaks to older people and also the way she dresses. All these will either point to the girl being moral or immoral.'

15. This world is not so distant from ours in time as well as space: Salman Rushdie in his introduction to *Midnight's Children* describes his debt to 'those great Indian novelists Jane Austen and Charles Dickens – Austen for her portraits of brilliant women caged by the social convention of their time, women whose Indian counterparts I knew well' (2010: xii).

16. See Wilkinson-Maposa et al. (2005) and Wilkinson-Maposa (2008) for multiple examples.

17. Thus when Collins et al. reviewed financial diaries among the poor, they found that 'most transactions are carried out with "informal partners" rather than with formal institutions like banks and insurance companies. The partners are often neighbors who seldom keep documentation of agreements, and certainly nothing that would hold up in court' (2009: 46).

18. See Polak (2008) for more on the transformative potential of low-cost irrigation tools.

19. Bagadion and Korten's review of irrigation projects in the Philippines likewise argues that 'existing irrigation groups may be ignored and are wasted as an organizational resource'(1985: 102).

20. The approach shares similarities with – and sometimes draws upon – the Appreciative Enquiry method developed in psychology <https://positive psychology.com/appreciative-inquiry/> [accessed 22 January 2021].

21. Jeffrey, comparing different attitudes to time in India and Europe/North America, draws on the work of the sociologist Raymond Williams, to argue that 'powerful institutions in the West combined the biological notion of development (the life-cycle of an organism) with evolutionary ideas to present a vision of social and economic development as a linear unfolding of progress' (2010: 12).
22. Robb (2007: 91) describes an array of similar maxims in 19th-century rural France where, he writes, 'sayings of the "knowing my luck" variety warned against the folly of trying too hard and expecting too much'.
23. Lofchie (2015: 52) describes how 'for the majority of rural Africans, weather instability, not the trickle-down effects of economic growth, remains the single most important determinant of income fluctuations'. Narayan et al. (2000: 27) highlight how 'weather and environmental problems are common hazards for many poor people around the world'.
24. There were at time of writing over 70 countries where homosexuality remains a crime, with the majority of them low- and middle-income countries. See <http://76crimes.com/76-countries-where-homosexuality-is-illegal/> [accessed July 2019].
25. Narayan et al. (2009: 330) describe how 'Hoff and Pandey (2006) showed that lower castes in India tend to start believing that as hard as they try, they will get unfair rewards for their efforts'.
26. Although, as we'll explore in Chapter 6, the evidence on 'elite capture' is more complicated than this, with some research showing evidence of elite dominated assemblies making decisions that benefitted the poorer and more marginalized.
27. Cole (2016) discusses a recent case of how this can play out in development in the hubris of the 'White-Saviour Industrial Complex'.
28. She writes that 'respondents (men and women, urban and rural, young and old, poor and lower-middle class) identified and valued both poverty-related and sociocultural impacts of development initiatives... both impacts that directly affected their standard of living and ones that had no effect whatsoever on material well-being, but rather affected their relationships or frameworks of meaning' (2004: 190).
29. This problem is not unique to our age. Writing about 18th- and 19th-century France, Robb (2007: 91) describes how 'wealthy men from northern cities pitied the half of France where the prehistoric plough was little better than a hoe - but indispensable on thin and rocky ground. They pitied the huddled masses whose windows were holes in the wall or panes of oil-soaked paper - though many in the warmer south felt no need of glass and spared themselves the cost of window tax'. He goes on to argue that 'This was simplicity rather than deprivation, and even a kind of inoculation against true poverty'.
30. The portrayal of poverty we see in the global north can encourage this idea. Though there are exceptions – notably campaigns for microfinance to support poor entrepreneurs – the global poor have for many years been represented typically as passive recipients waiting for help.
31. See <https://ourworldindata.org/working-hours> [accessed 23 July 2020].
32. For an in-depth account of the frustrating and creative use of 'waiting time' see Jeffrey (2010).

33. Collins et al. (2009: 35) report something similar from their study of household finances. 'The wealthiest farmers will also have secondary jobs such as teaching or own some form of transportation, and the poorer ones will also labor on other people's land or on public works, or seek casual jobs in retail, transport, or in casual self-employment like the cigarette-rollers of India'. Similarly, Narayan et al. (2000: 45) describe how 'to cope with such precarious livelihood conditions, poor people often struggle to diversify their sources of income and food: they work on the land and in quarries and mines; they hunt down temporary jobs and sell an endless variety of goods on the streets; they do piecework in factories and from homes; they patch together remittances; and they cultivate home gardens'.

34. Looking at four low- and middle-income countries (Pakistan, Cambodia, South Africa, and Bulgaria), the World Bank (2012: 81) reports that 'everywhere, women devote 1 to 3 hours more a day to housework than men; 2 to 10 times the amount of time a day to care (of children, elderly, and the sick), and 1 to 4 hours less a day to market activities'.

35. In the words of one respondent 'after school I go to work in the field, so I don't have enough time to study'. (Respondent quoted in India Girl Declarations Consultations. Research commissioned by Girl Effect, 2013.)

References

Abraham, Anita and Platteau, Jean-Philippe (2004) 'Participatory development: where culture creeps in', in Vijayendra Rao and Michael Walton (eds), *Culture and Public Action: An Introduction*, pp. 210–34, World Bank, Washington.

Alasuutari, Pertti (1995) *Researching Culture: Qualitative Method and Cultural Studies*, Sage, Thousand Oaks.

Alkire, Sabina (2004) 'Culture, poverty, and external intervention', in Vijayendra Rao and Michael Walton (eds), *Culture and Public Action: An Introduction*, pp. 185–210, World Bank, Washington.

Bagadion, Benjamin B. and Korten, Frances F., (1985) 'Developing irrigators' organizations: a learning process approach', in Michael Cernea (ed.), *Putting People First: Sociological Variables in Development*, pp. 73–112, World Bank, Washington.

Banerjee, Abhijit V. and Duflo, Esther (2011) *Poor Economics: A Radical Rethinking of the Way To Fight Global Poverty*, Public Affairs, New York.

Bourdieu, Pierre (1998) (1977) *Outline of a Theory of Practice* (trans. Richard Nice), Cambridge University Press, Cambridge.

Camner, Gunnar, Pulver, Caroline and Sjöblom, Emil (2012) *What makes a Successful Mobile Money Implementation? Learnings from M-PESA in Kenya and Tanzania*, [online], GSMA, <https://www.gsma.com/mobilefordevelopment/wp-content/uploads/2012/03/What-makes-a-successful-mobile-money-implementation.pdf> [accessed 8 May 2021].

Chambers, Robert (2014) *Into the Unknown: Explorations in Development Practice*, Practical Action Publishing, Rugby.

Cole, Teju (2016) *Known and Strange Things*, Faber, London.

Collins, Daryl, Morduch, Jonathan, Rutherford, Stuart and Ruthven, Orlanda (2009) *Portfolios of the Poor: How the World's Poor Live on $2 a Day*, Princeton University Press, Princeton.

Cunningham, Gordon (2008) 'Stimulating asset based and community driven development: lessons from five communities in Ethiopia', in Alison Mathie and Gordon Cunningham (eds), *From Clients to Citizens: Communities Changing the Course of their Own Development*, pp. 263–99, Practical Action Publishing, Rugby.

Denzin, Norman K. and Lincoln, Yvonna S. (1994) *Handbook of Qualitative Research Methods*, Sage, Thousand Oaks.

Easterly, William (2006) *The White Man's Burden*, Oxford University Press, Oxford.

The Economist (2007) 'To do with the price of fish', [online], <https://www.economist.com/finance-and-economics/2007/05/10/to-do-with-the-price-of-fish> (posted 10 May 2007) [accessed 24 February 2021].

The Economist (2011) 'Africa rising', [online], <https://www.economist.com/leaders/2011/12/03/africa-rising> [accessed 20 February 2020].

Fairs, Marcus (2017) 'Don't design yet another shelter for refugees, say experts', [online], Dezeen Magazine <https://www.dezeen.com/2017/12/18/dont-design-shelter-refugees-kilian-kleinschmidt-rene-boer-good-design-bad-world/> [accessed 20 November 2019].

Friedman, Ken and Stolterman, Erik (2015) Series foreword, in Manzini, Ezio, *Design, When Everyone Designs*, pp. vii–xiii, MIT, Cambridge Mass.

Garrette, Bernard and Karnani, Aneel (2010) *Challenges in Marketing Socially Useful Goods to the Poor*, [online], California Management Review, Summer 2010, <http://www.societyandorganizations.org/wp-content/uploads/2010/06/Garette-CMR-su10.pdf> [accessed 23 June 2020].

Geertz, Clifford (2000) (1973) *The Interpretation of Cultures*, Basic Books, New York.

GSMA and Frog Design (2017) *mHealth Design Toolkit: Ten Principles to Launch, Develop and Scale Mobile Health Services in Emerging Markets*, [online], <https://www.gsma.com/mobilefordevelopment/wp-content/plugins/plugin_m4d_shortcodes//mhealth/GC_GSMA_FinalBooklet.pdf> [accessed 12 February 2021].

Harford, Tim (2008) 'Mackerel economics', *Business Life*, August 2008.

Harragin, Simon (2004) 'Relief and an understanding of local knowledge: the case of southern Sudan', in Vijayendra Rao and Michael Walton (eds), *Culture and Public Action: An Introduction*, pp. 307–28, World Bank, Washington.

Heierli, Urs and Lingerer, Christian (2008) *Should Bednets be Sold or Given Free? The Role of the Private Sector in Malarial Control*, SDC, Berne.

J-PAL (2017) 'Roll call: getting children into school', [online], <https://jwel.mit.edu/assets/document/roll-call-getting-children-school> [accessed 24 February 2021].

Jeffrey, Craig (2010) *Timepass: Youth, Class and the Politics of Waiting in India*, Stanford University Press, Stanford.

Jensen, Robert (2007) 'The digital provide: information (technology), market performance, and welfare in the South Indian fisheries sector', *The Quarterly Journal of Economics*, 122: 879–924 <https://doi.org/10.1162/qjec.122.3.879>.

Kachra, Ariff, Sarkar, M.B., Kirti, Madhok Sud (2012) 'Nokia life tools: a strategic innovation to tap into India's rural and newly urban population', *Harvard Business Review*.

Karlan, Dean and Appel, Jacob (2011) *More Than Good Intentions: Improving the Ways the World's Poor Borrow, Save, Farm, Learn, and Stay Healthy*, Penguin, New York.

Kejriwal, Geetika (2020) 'Time to change the conversation: beyond human centred design', Unpublished MA Dissertation, Royal College of Art, London.

Kottack, Conrad (1985) 'When people don't come first: some sociological lessons from completed projects', in Michael Cernea (ed.), *Putting People First*, pp. 431–64, World Bank, Washington.

Lafloufa, Jacqueline and Puff, Jefferson (2020) 'Platform and dysfunction', [online], Rest of World, <https://restofworld.org/2020/brazil-favela-chat-groups/> (posted 2 June 2020) [accessed 2 June 2020].

LIRNEAsia (2007) 'Mobile phones and (fish) market performance in Kerala', [online], <https://lirneasia.net/2007/05/mobile-impact-on-fish-markets/> [accessed 23 June 2020].

Lofchie, Michael (2015) 'The political economy of the African middle class', in Mthuli Ncube and Charles Leyeka Lufumpa (eds), *The Emerging Middle Class in Africa*, pp. 36–60, Routledge, London.

Mansuri, Ghazala and Rao, Vijayendra (2012) *Localising Development: Does Participation Work?* World Bank Policy Research Report, World Bank, Washington.

Martin, Eric (2020) 'Goldman Sachs's MIST topping BRICs as smaller markets outperform', [online], Bloomberg, <https://www.bloomberg.com/news/articles/2012-08-07/goldman-sachs-s-mist-topping-brics-as-smaller-markets-outperform> [accessed 20 February 2020].

Mathie, Alison and Cunningham, Gordon (2008) 'Introduction' and 'Conclusions', in Alison Mathie and Gordon Cunningham (eds), *From Clients to Citizens: Communities Changing the Course of their Own Development*, pp. 1–11 and pp. 357–69, Practical Action Publishing, Rugby.

Mbaye, Ahmadou Aly and Golub, Stephen (2015) 'How do we solve Africa's underemployment problem?', [online], World Economic Forum, <https://www.weforum.org/agenda/2015/08/how-do-we-solve-africas-underemployment-problem/> [accessed 23 June 2020].

Mills, Greg (2011) *Why Africa is Poor: And What Africans Can Do About It*, Penguin, London.

Myers, J., Cavill, S., Musyoki, S., Pasteur, K. and Stevens, L. (2018) *Innovations for Urban Sanitation: Adapting Community-led Approaches*, Practical Action Publishing, Rugby.

Narayan, Deepa, Chambers, Robert, Shah, Meera K. and Petesch, Patti (2000) *Voices of the Poor: Crying Out for Change*, Oxford University Press for the World Bank, New York.

Narayan, Deepa, Pritchett, Lant and Kapoor, Soumya (2009) *Moving Out of Poverty Volume 2: Success from the Bottom Up*, a co-publication of the World Bank and Palgrave Macmillan, Washington.

Neumann, Rogerio Arns and Mathie, Alison, assisted by Linzey, Joanne (2008) 'Conjunto Palmeira: four decades of forging community and building a local economy in Brazil', in Alison Mathie and Gordon Cunningham (eds), *From Clients to Citizens: Communities Changing the Course of their Own Development*, pp. 39–63, Practical Action Publishing, Rugby.

Polak, Paul (2008) *Out of Poverty: What Works When Traditional Approaches Fail*, Berrett-Koehler, San Francisco.

Radjou, Navi, Prabhu, Jaideep and Ahuja, Simone (2012) *Jugaad Innovation: Think Frugal, Be Flexible, Generate Breakthrough Growth*, Wiley, London.

Rao, Vijayendra and Walton, Michael (2004) *Culture and Public Action: An Introduction*, World Bank, Washington.

Robb, Graham (2007) *The Discovery of France*, Picador, London.

Said, Edward (2003) *Orientalism*, Penguin, London.

Sen, Amartya (1999) *Development as Freedom*, Oxford University Press, Oxford.

Simanis, Erik (2012) 'Reality check at the bottom of the pyramid', [online], *Harvard Business Review*, <https://hbr.org/2012/06/reality-check-at-the-bottom-of-the-pyramid> [accessed 29 April 2021].

Sinha, Dheeraj (2011) *Consumer India*, Wiley, Singapore.

Sreekumar, T.T. (2011) 'Mobile phones and the cultural ecology of fishing in Kerala, India', *The Information Society*, 27: 172–80 <https://doi.org/10.1080/01972243.2011.566756>.

Srinivasan, Janaki and Burrell, Jenna (2013) *Revisiting the Fishers of Kerala, India*, [online], presented at the International Conference on Information and Communication Technologies and Development, Cape Town, South Africa, <https://markets.ischool.berkeley.edu/files/2013/07/revisiting_fishers_kerala_wp.pdf> [accessed 8 April 2021].

Steyn, J. and Van Greunen, D. (eds) (2014) 'ICTs for inclusive communities in developing societies'. Proceedings of the 8th International Development Informatics Association Conference held in Port Elizabeth, South Africa.

Thompson, John B. (1995) *The Media and Modernity*, Stanford University Press, Stanford.

Udry, Christopher R. (1994) 'Risk and insurance in a rural credit market: an empirical investigation in northern Nigeria', *Review of Economic Studies*, 61: 495–526.

Udry, Christopher R. (1996) 'Gender, agricultural production, and the theory of the household', *Journal of Political Economy*, 104: 1010–46.

Wall Street Journal (2009) 'Dial "M" for "mackerel": can a new mobile phone service in rural India help promote economic empowerment?' [online] <https://www.wsj.com/articles/SB125126978512659859> [accessed 24 February 2021].

Wilkinson-Maposa, Susan, Fowler, Alan, Oliver-Evans, Ceri and Mulenga, Chao F.N. (2005) *The Poor Philanthropist: How and Why the Poor Help Each Other*, Centre for Leadership and Public Values, University of Cape Town, Cape Town.

Wilkinson-Maposa, Susan (2008) 'Jansenville Development Forum: linking community and government in the rural landscape of the Eastern Cape Province, South Africa', in Alison Mathie and Gordon Cunningham (eds), *From Clients to Citizens: Communities Changing the Course of their Own Development*, Practical Action Publishing, Rugby.

World Bank (2004) *Making Services Work for the Poor*, World Bank, Washington.

World Bank (2012) *Gender Equality and Development: World Development Report*, World Bank, Washington.

PART II

Aid through the Eyes of the Poor

CHAPTER 2

Who are 'the poor'? Understanding the audience/s for development aid

Abstract

Who are the users of development aid and what are their daily lives like? This chapter examines different ways that 'the poor' are defined and the complexities and problems within these definitions. Who is and isn't included in these definitions? What important differences do notions of 'the poor' obscure? And how can we arrive at a working definition that we can use in development practice? My own definition includes a granular examination of daily life across poor communities, exploring the everyday rhythms of homes, neighbourhoods, families, working patterns, health, leisure, and consumption.

Keywords: poverty; moving out of poverty; multidimensional poverty; ethnography; labelling

Introduction

Already in this book there have been multiple references to 'the poor', 'poor people', 'poor communities' and 'the poorest'. Expediency means I often reach for these terms throughout the chapters that follow too. But what do they mean? To practise 'international development' is unavoidably to deal in generalizations. But I want to be clear about how I have reached my own generalizations and where I draw the lines. This is to avoid either stereotyping the groups of people I am researching or leaving my readers in the dark.[1] Thus, the purpose of this short chapter is to define and describe more clearly the people who use – and choose not to use – development aid. How is this audience normally defined, who is included in these definitions and, following our focus on the human and the everyday, what are their lives like?

A first, positive point to note is that compared to earlier decades there are fewer people on the planet who are classed as poor. Where in 1990 there were 1.85 billion people living below the global poverty line (set at US$1.90 per person),[2] by 2013 this had dropped to 783 million and by 2017 to 689 million.[3] Since then, the decline has largely continued, although at time of writing there are worrying indications that the COVID-19 pandemic is pushing a significant number of people back into poverty.[4] This general, if sometimes faltering, pattern of declining poverty has played out not just in absolute numbers, but as a proportion of the world's total population. In 1990 35 per cent of humans lived below the poverty line, whilst in recent years it has fallen below 10 per cent.

The story behind this fall, though, is more complicated than the headline figures. First, of the millions who have been 'lifted out of poverty', many haven't been lifted very far. Drèze and Sen (2013) point out that a lot of the poverty reduction in India (from 50 per cent to 34 per cent between 1993–4 and 2009–10) saw people moving from *just below* to *just above* the poverty line. They argue that 'many people are just a little below the official poverty line, so that a small increase in per capita expenditure is enough to "lift" them above the line' (2013: 30). Similarly, headlines may tell us that a third of Africans are now 'middle class', but Ncube (2015) finds that 63 per cent of this 'middle class' have merely moved from earning below $2 a day to earning $2 to $4 a day. Progress to the more stable middle-class levels of $4 to $20 a day is much less common.

This means it is perhaps not surprising if an economic shock like that produced by COVID-19 may push many millions back into official poverty. As Ncube (2015) argues, many no longer officially poor remain 'in a vulnerable position, constantly at risk of dropping back into the poor category in the event of any unexpected shocks'. More broadly – and this applies across economic cycles – the poor *are not a static group*. Even in cases where total numbers of people in poverty are reasonably constant, the people who make up this group will be changing, sometimes very significantly. Some of those just above a line such as $1.90 find themselves slipping just below it and vice versa. One study in Indonesia (cited by Narayan et al., 2009) found that only just over half of 'poor' households at the time of the first measurement were still classified as poor several years later.[5] Another study in Ethiopia (Dercon and Krishna, 2000) found that in *less than a year* 13.7 per cent of poor households had moved out of poverty and 16.4 per cent had moved into poverty. These movements pose significant practical questions if we are designing services and programmes aimed at 'the poor'. Whilst it may seem efficient to narrow down our target audience to those below the poverty line, if we do so we may be missing very large numbers of people who will experience poverty.[6]

We also need to take care that we don't miss people who are living in non-poor households, but who experience poverty on an individual level. Definitions of poverty that are based on income may miss differences within households, since, as we'll explore later, household incomes in some regions are shared much less equitably than in others. A woman living in a region with very high gender discrimination (for instance, an Indian state such as Bihar or Uttar Pradesh) may have the same household income as a woman in the state of Kerala, but considerably less of the food it buys or control over how the money is spent. Poverty can exist acutely in relatively rich households, depending on how the income is shared.

Alongside monetary definitions of poverty we also need to consider the cultural context that shapes how people experience poverty. A woman in

Johannesburg with $3 a day PPP may feel much poorer than a woman in Lilongwe, Malawi, who is earning the same amount. This may not be just her subjective comparison; since in richer environments a poor person will feel more obligation to spend their income on the modern equivalents of Adam Smith's linen shirt – the goods and services that you are expected to buy as part of that community. As Sen (1999: 89) writes, 'the need to take part in the life of a community may induce demands for modern equipment (televisions, video-cassette recorders, automobiles, and so on) in a country where such facilities are more or less universal (unlike what would be needed in less affluent countries)'.

Furthermore, a financial definition, such as $1.90 a day, can only be a start if we see poverty as more than financial status.[7] We have already seen that for those on the ground poverty is not just a lack of money, it is a lack of other important tangible and intangible assets: land, education, political representation, property rights, dignity, control, health, protection of one's local environment.[8] All of these can matter to people as much as, or more than, their income. When poor people themselves are asked to define what constitutes poverty, their criteria are typically much wider-ranging than dollars and cents a day, as reflected in the following definition from Zimbabwe reported by Wilkinson-Maposa et al. (2005: 28). 'They [the poor] have small thatched huts; have inadequate clothes; fail to send their children to school; have insufficient food and are susceptible to hunger; lack draught power and livestock; have little or no money; lack farming equipment; cultivate small pieces of land; have single-parent households; and have little or no happiness'.

It is also striking that the poor's own definitions can include more people than official measures. In the World Bank's Moving Out of Poverty consultation, respondents were asked to map members of their community on a ladder from the best to the worst off, and then to draw on this ladder the line that separated 'poor' from 'not poor'. Narayan et al. (2009: 13) found that their classifications were 'much higher than those that would result from applying the "$1 a day" measure often used [at the time] in international circles as the poverty line'. Similarly, Atkinson (2019) noted that in a household survey in Uganda in 2012–13, 70 per cent of the population classified themselves as 'very poor' or 'poor' compared with just 19.7 per cent identified by the official national poverty line.[9]

The points raised in this brief discussion illustrate, I hope, that the audience for development initiatives can only be partially defined using straightforward income measures.[10] Hence, when I talk about the audience for development as 'poor people' I am using their income as a broad guide, rather than a fixed line. Some people in the audience I'm describing may have crossed the World Bank's current international poverty line, but have not got far above it; some may be at risk of falling back. Some may be in what surveys class as an officially 'middle class' household, but still be excluded from the growing wealth of their household by discrimination of one kind or another. Some may be above the income line, but despite this still experience poverty in one or many of the other ways described.

A billion different people

These substantial caveats made, let's return to the income figure as a helpful, if very approximate, guide. Who are the people who are living with only a few dollars (PPP) each day? Geographically, the great majority live in sub-Saharan Africa and South Asia, and these regions are the focus of the book. However, some inhabit countries better known for rapid GDP growth, such as Brazil and, to a much lesser extent today, China (Sanchez, 2017).[11] More surprising perhaps, is that some high-income countries still have millions of people living below this global line of $1.90 a day, as well, of course, as many more who live below their national poverty lines, which are drawn at higher levels. In recent figures, 1.3 per cent of the US population were identified as living on less than $1.90 a day. Disturbing realities such as this are the subject of a separate body of research around poverty in rich nations.[12] This book, however, is focused on poor people in low- and lower-middle income countries, largely in the global south. This is by far the largest share of the global poor. It is also the audience I know best from research and the people who are most often targeted by development programmes.

Even with these various qualifications, we are still clearly talking about a huge and diverse audience – one that if we do go above the $1.90 line reaches over a billion people. Talking about 'the poor' as a single group is a sweeping generalization, which clearly overrides enormous differences in environment, politics, economy, culture, history.[13] Cornwall (2008) citing Cohen and Uphoff, points out that people would be very surprised to be lumped together as a single group called 'poor people'.[14] And yet trying to detail the diversity of life around the poverty line is a dizzying task, a project that would defeat a lifetime's study and a farcical endeavour for a single book: one reminiscent of Jorge Luis Borges's story 'Exactitude in Science' or Lewis Carroll's imagined pocket map. Chambers (2014: 37) describes this dilemma very clearly, 'the evidence from the 272 sites was varied, demanding interpretations that were qualified and nuanced. Through using the terms "the poor" and "poor people" we were always in danger of implying misleading homogeneity... [But] Pulling in the opposite direction are ethical imperatives for impact. To be remembered, repeated and have an effect, a message is best kept simple and memorable'.

How then do we find a middle ground between ignoring and being overwhelmed by the differences between countries and cultures? I have argued above that one can find structural patterns repeated across cultures and countries. An acute level of risk, the value of cycles versus change, the reliance on one's neighbours, the importance of shared resources: all of these I argued are more common in poor communities in the global south. The authors of large-scale, multi-country studies of poor communities also point to consistent patterns that are more common, if not, of course, precisely the same, across regions. After completing one of the largest ever qualitative studies with low-income people, Narayan et al. (2000: 6) were struck by the structural similarities within people's experiences across very diverse countries:

> From Georgia to Brazil, from Nigeria to Philippines, similar under-lying themes emerged: hunger, deprivation, powerlessness, violation of dignity, social isolation, resilience, resourcefulness, solidarity, state corruption, rudeness of service providers, and gender inequity. The manifestation of these problems varied significantly. We found our-selves, saying, 'We have read this before.' Sometimes even the words and images poor people evoked in describing their reality in very different contexts were uncannily similar.

Thus, my approach is to look for and focus on where common themes exist, but to ground them in local examples of where I have seen them and to be alert all the time to local difference. Where these differences are significant I seek to highlight them. For instance, we will see some themes, such as the communal nature of daily life, are more pronounced in rural communities and some of the approaches I explore, such as total community solutions, need to be adapted to urban or rural realities. Furthermore, I encourage the reader to be open to likely exceptions at every stage. I cannot put it better than Narayan et al. (2000: 23) when they write that 'it would be cumbersome to preface every single generalization with the phrase, "in most but not every single case..." So instead we have written the generalizations that emerge, without constant qualification. We ask the reader to bear in mind that none of the generalizations apply to every location or every poor person. They describe tendencies, but there are always exceptions'.

Life on a couple of dollars a day

So far, I've been attempting to define the audience for development in terms of the boundaries we might place around them – how much money they have, or don't have, which parts of the world they might live in. Another way of defining the audience is by describing the contours of their daily lives: their homes, families, working lives, support networks, daily routines. In this last section I will try to describe, rather than define, poor communities in this way, drawing on a mix of quantitative data and experience of field visits.

I hope that this gives readers with less experience of the field a more grounded perspective of the audience for development aid, one that allows for a certain degree of nuance. The poor people who are shown on screens in the global north tend to live in places of intense, obvious, and easily mediated suffering, places with immediate threats to life, such as war, virulent disease, famine. These are the pictures of poverty that typically make it into rich country media. For many poor people, though, poverty is less dramatic. It is experienced more as a series of constant, debilitating absences – the crops that don't grow, the casual work that dries up, the teachers who don't turn up at the school, the two meals each day that are missed. If you arrived at their house on a sunny day, the family gathered, and enough food to cook an evening meal, you might not see the poverty they experience in the way you would if you visited a refugee camp set up in the wake of war.

So what is life like among the less visible poor? What would the daily world be like if you lived there yourself? First of all, you'd probably find yourself somewhere you wouldn't want to live. As Narayan et al. write (2000), the places of the poor are 'especially risk-ridden from pollution, sewage and crime. Variously steep, low-lying, too close to waterways, or drought-prone, many urban and rural places are vulnerable to the vagaries of weather. Many of the worst deprivations that come with living in these places are seasonal in nature, including property damage by rain, wind, floods and landslides, and unsanitary conditions from flood waters mixed with sewage'.

You probably will, as we saw in Chapter 1, work harder than people in the global north. But you're unlikely to have a guaranteed, stable income. In sub-Saharan Africa, for instance, 89 per cent of workers are estimated to be in informal employment (ILO, 2020). Your main source of income is likely to be farming.[15] But, as we've seen, you may not want to be a farmer. And it's very likely you'll be trying to combine different types of work and income. For instance, when Vodafone Ghana launched a service supplying agricultural and crop price information they found that less than half the regular active users of 'Farmers' Club' made their income solely through farming (Palmer and Darabian, 2017b).

Even if your employment is steady, your income may not be. Labour laws are liable to be weak, so your wages may be withheld or reduced and you may be dismissed with little notice (Collins et al., 2009).[16] Not only do you earn less, you are less sure if you will ever get it. As Collins et al. (2009: 17) point out, 'the "dollar-a-day" view of global poverty... highlights only one slice of what it is to be poor. It captures the fact that incomes are small, but sidelines the equally important reality that incomes are often highly irregular and unpredictable'. They describe, for example, how 'farm labourers get a daily wage when there's work to do; at other times they sit around idle, migrate to towns, or scratch a living from other sources. In the cities and urban townships, self-employed folk like Hamid have good and bad days. Women's paid work in the town, such as maidserving, is often part-time, occasional, or temporary' (2009: 16).

Whether you own land or not will vary greatly by country and region – in Tanzania, for instance, the answer will almost certainly be yes; in South Africa, almost certainly no.[17] Even if you own assets, like your house or your land, these tend to be less secure – again especially if you are a woman. It's quite probable that you lack any official means of proving ownership of your land and house and hence you are vulnerable to government officials, developers or larger landowners attempting to annex both. Narayan et al. (2000: 166) quote a woman in Brazil who captures this threat horribly clearly: 'when a government official comes here and says that we have to leave the area, I freak out. I gather my things ... but don't know where to go ... I don't know if I should take my sons out of school ... if I should pack food so that we don't run out of food on the road ... I feel insecure, lost. At this moment, it is just God and me'.

You will live with limited and flawed infrastructure. Health centres and schools arc likely to be far away (Neumann and Mathie, 2008). If you do make it there, the staff may not be present (Banerjee and Duflo, 2011),[18] or qualified to help you. Researching the Udaipur district of north India, Banerjee and Duflo (2011) found that only around half of doctors had a medical college degree. A study by Das and Hammer (Banerjee and Duflo, 2011) found that unqualified private doctors were likely to ask only one-sixth of the questions that medical experts would expect them to ask when assessing a case. If you are one of the people who works there, you are most likely facing a battle to help, working in an environment that is liable to be overwhelmed and under-resourced.

Life is short. If you are born in sub-Saharan Africa today you can expect an average of 61 years – 20 years less than the 81 you would expect if you were born in the European Union. The stages of life come faster. You are likely to get married young, especially if you are a woman, or strictly speaking a girl, since in many countries you will be married in your teens. Corno and Voena (2020) cite estimates that 700 million people alive today were married before their 18th birthday (56 per cent of whom live in South Asia and 42 per cent in sub-Saharan Africa).

Personal landmarks of marriage, birth, and death are likely to be marked and celebrated intensely and communally. One of the most consistent themes across life in poor communities is the heavy amount of spending on events and festivals (Banerjee and Duflo, 2011; Cunningham, 2008; Rao, 2002). In contrast, your personal, everyday consumption will be extremely low – shockingly low for many readers in the global north. In India, where the national poverty line has traditionally been set lower than in many other countries, Drèze and Sen (2013: 190) paint a picture of what this means for your daily life. The allowance for shoes 'would just about make it possible to get a sandal strap repaired once a month', whilst the amount envisaged for health 'might buy something like the equivalent of an aspirin a day'.[19] The clearest illustration of what you can buy is perhaps a picture – or a series of pictures – in recent work by photographers Stefen Chow and Lin Huiyi, showing the food that can be bought on the budget envisaged by the national poverty line in different countries.[20]

You are increasingly likely to have some access to a TV, a mobile phone, and to the internet, although despite excited talk about a digital planet, the odds are in fact you are still offline. The most recent figures for internet usage listed by the World Bank are 40 per cent in Indonesia (2018), 42 per cent in Nigeria (2017), 34 per cent in India (2017), with much lower levels in South Sudan (8 per cent in 2017), Niger (5 per cent in 2018), and Somalia (2 per cent in 2017).[21] And your access will vary widely depending on your country and state. For instance, TV access in India in 2018 varied from near universal in Tamil Nadu (97 per cent) to a relative rarity (26 per cent) in Bihar and Jharkand.[22] Whilst innovations in digital media may be growing, you are probably one of the over a billion people who don't have proper toilet facilities (Bongartz et al., 2010). If you are a woman this means you may have to get up before dawn to avoid being seen defecating in the open.

With money tight, you are not in a position to bargain. When someone arrives at the farm gate and offers you a small bundle of cash for your crops it's hard to say no, even if you know you are being ripped off (Bolton, 2019). It may be hard to wait to sell through a cooperative if payment takes days or even weeks and you need the money now. 'Poor cultivators across study regions, with their one bag of coffee or clutch of bananas, find themselves in no position to negotiate with bigger buyers. Their immediate cash needs often force them to accept the miserable prices offered or cave in to exploitative terms when taking a loan' (Naryan et al., 2009: 32). The weaker you are, the more open you are to exploitation. Chambers (2014: 40) quotes a group of poor fishermen in Malawi, who tell researchers 'we get some K5, buy some maize for one day's consumption, when it is finished we go again… the problem is that these boat owners know that we are starving. As such we would accept any little wages they would offer to us because they know we are very desperate'.

You grow used to exploitation. Despite your limited cash you may pay higher prices than other citizens. A UNDP report (2004) found that 'in Mumbai, slum-dwellers in Dharavi pay 1.2 times more for rice, 10 times more for medicine and 3.5 times more for water than do middle class people living at the other end of the city on Bhulabhai Desai Road'. The World Bank (2004: 21) describes how 'in Ghana the approximate price paid per liter for water purchased by the bucket was between 5 and 16 times higher than the charge for public supply, even though women and children often had to walk a long distance to purchase the water'.

You are unlikely to have much of a safety net if something does go wrong. Saving is hard; not just because incomes are low, but because you may not have access to fair, reliable, or comprehensible financial services. Although the numbers of unbanked are falling sharply, it is still around 2 billion.[23] And whilst we have seen above how much you may help and be helped by your neighbours, you don't expect much in the way of help from outsiders. People in Europe or North America are sometimes surprised by this fact,[24] but most poor people have never seen overseas aid make a material difference to their lives.[25] This may sometimes be the result of corruption and poor planning, but mainly it is simply a problem of scale: as Narayan et al. (2000: 8) conclude 'even the most successful large NGOs do not reach the majority of poor households'.

In the passages above I have tried briefly to paint a picture of life on a few dollars a day. It is a world full of challenges unknown to most in the global north. It is also often an upside down world, where your skills and your resources are often unacknowledged; you can't get credit because your assets are unregistered; the college certificate you acquired through years of perseverance doesn't translate into secure employment.[26] It is a world of occasional radical change, visible in the nearly half a billion mobile phone users in sub-Saharan Africa (GSMA, 2020) and of stubborn problems, visible in the billion people in the world who don't have proper, safe sanitation. It is a world of widespread self-reliance and understandably cautious expectations from the outside world.

Users, recipients, consumers, people?

There is one final consideration before we end this chapter, which is terminology. The different fields involved in tackling poverty today have often quite different terms for describing poor people. These vary by academic discipline (whether development studies, design, economics, anthropology) and by sector (NGO, government, corporations, start-ups). Depending on the field, the poor may appear as 'recipients', 'users', 'participants', 'respondents', 'consumers', or 'citizens'. I have found that the terms we use can matter, at least subtly, since they do nudge us towards designing certain solutions rather than others. For instance, if we are trying to combat child mortality we might think of our target audience as 'mothers', defined mainly by their relationship with their children. But if, as we'll explore below, one of the most effective ways of keeping children alive is helping their mothers learn to read, then in fact 'women' or 'students' might be better terms to use. When Kilian Kleinschmidt analysed why so many of the solutions aimed at refugees had failed to work he suggests that part of the problem lies in designing specifically for *refugees*. 'They're not a species', he argues, 'there's no need for tech for refugees or design for refugees, or architecture for refugees' (Fairs, 2017). In the chapters that follow, 'the poor' and 'poor people' are the shorthand terms I settle on, but I try to use them with care. When we talk about 'the poor' we can easily slip into thinking of poverty as an inherent quality, something that stays with people for life.[27] I try to remember that these terms describe not a fundamental characteristic of a person, but people's current and hopefully temporary conditions.

Notes

1. See, for instance, Mohanty's (1988) critique of past work on women in low- and middle-income countries.
2. It's worth emphasizing that $1.90 is not the literal number of dollars and cents an individual has to spend; it is the equivalent sum to what $1.90 would buy in that country. Making this 'purchasing power parity' calculation is itself far from straightforward. See Atkinson (2019).
3. <https://www.worldbank.org/en/topic/poverty/overview>   [accessed 24 February 2021].
4. One estimate by the World Bank suggests 100 million people have fallen back below the poverty line. World Bank <https://blogs.worldbank.org/opendata/updated-estimates-impact-covid-19-global-poverty-looking-back-2020-and-outlook-2021> [accessed 2 February 2021].

5. Original study by Lant Pritchett, Asep Suryahadi, and Sudarno Sumarto (2000) 'Quantifying vulnerability to poverty', *Policy Research Working Paper*, World Bank, Washington. Cited by Narayan et al. (2009).

6. This means that in some instances it can be just as efficient to provide a universal benefit, rather than a targeted 'pro poor' one. Narayan et al. (2009) cite a study in China by Jalan and Ravallion that found that over a six-year period the make up of poor households changed so much that had you targeted the group defined as poor in the first year, this would have been no more efficient than simply providing the benefits to all households.

7. Although, as Amartya Sen, one of the leading exponents argues, there is also 'an excellent argument for *beginning* with whatever information we have on the distribution of incomes, particularly low real incomes' (1999: 72).

8. Furthermore, there is not always substantial crossover between financial and other forms of poverty. Alkire (2018: 10) gives the example of how in Bhutan in 2012 12 per cent of people were income-poor and 12.6 per cent were multidimensionally poor and yet only 3.2 per cent were poor by both measures.

9. Atkinson suggests that self-classified poverty can be affected by two opposing biases. In the first instance some people may become so accustomed to poverty, and so accepting of poverty, that they don't recognize that they themselves are poor. In the second instance people officially above the poverty line may regard themselves as poor if they believe their peers' income is rising faster than theirs. He suggests the former is particularly likely to occur in remote areas, where it may be harder to make comparisons with the relatively rich (2019: 33–4).

10. See Atkinson (2019) for further discussion.

11. China has eradicated poverty at extraordinary rates, but with a population of over a billion, even a small proportion of people in poverty runs into millions. The World Bank estimates that 25 million people lived on less than $1.90 a day (Sanchez, 2017).

12. See Philip Alston's UN report on poverty in the USA, <https://www.ohchr.org/EN/NewsEvents/Pages/DisplayNews.aspx?NewsID=22533> [accessed 24 June 2020].

13. Writing about the African continent, Dowden (2008: 52) describes how 'the European Union has only 23 languages. Africa has at least 2000, and between 6,000 and 10,000 political or social entities, each of which once had its own governance and legal system, its leadership and customs and culture'.

14. The original article is Cohen, J. and Uphoff, N. (1980) 'Participation's place in rural development: seeking clarity through specificity', *World Development*, 8: 213–35.

15. 1.3 billion people in developing countries make their living primarily from agriculture <https://www.gsmaintelligence.com/research/?file=29e480e55371305d7b37fe48efb10cd6&download> [accessed 11 April 2021].

16. Collins et al. (2009: 44) found that whilst in South Africa 'labor laws are more rigorously enforced, and when households do manage to find a

waged job, they tend to have a fairly reliable source of income'. In India and Bangladesh, 'a formal sector job… doesn't necessarily translate to more reliable income'.

17. In their comparison of the assets owned by households earning less than $2 a day, Banerjee and Duflo (2011) found that the proportion who owned land varied enormously, from 91 per cent of rural Tanzanians to 19 per cent of rural Ghanaians to 5 per cent of rural South Africans. Similarly, Banerjee et al. (2015) show how land ownership is much lower in some Indian states (such as Bihar) than in others.

18. Banerjee and Duflo (2011) cite a World Bank survey carried out in Bangladesh, Ecuador, India, Indonesia, Peru, and Uganda that found a 35 per cent absentee rate among health workers.

19. The authors suggest 'destitution line' is a better description than poverty line. This, they argue, reflects the fact that 'poverty-line standards were set decades ago, at a time when even bare subsistence was far from assured for a large majority of the Indian population'.

20. See <https://www.chowandlin.com/thepovertyline> [accessed 24 June 2020].

21. <https://data.worldbank.org/indicator/IT.NET.USER.ZS> [accessed 24 June 2020]. The Pew Research Center's 2018 global survey found 24 per cent of Indians owned a smartphone (and 64 per cent owned a mobile phone of any kind), 39 per cent of Nigerians had smartphones (and 83 per cent owned a phone of any kind), 42 per cent and 70 per cent in Indonesia and 60 per cent and 93 per cent in South Africa. <https://www.pewresearch.org/global/2019/02/05/smartphone-ownership-is-growing-rapidly-around-the-world-but-not-always-equally/> [accessed 24 June 2020].

22. <https://www.statista.com/statistics/1177498/india-tv-penetration-by-state/> [accessed 27 February 2021].

23. The World Bank report that 'the number of people worldwide having an account grew by 700 million between 2011 and 2014. 62 percent of the world's adult population has an account; up from 51 percent in 2011. Three years ago, 2.5 billion adults were unbanked. Today, 2 billion adults remain without an account. This represents a 20 percent decrease' <http://www.worldbank.org/en/programs/globalfindex/overview> [accessed 11 April 2021].

24. This is partly because people in the global north can over-estimate the amount spent on aid. De Haan (2009) writes that 'Opinion polls show that US citizens overestimate the amount of aid given by their government by as much as 15 times according to one [survey] and 40 times according to another'.

25. Talking to poor people in 47 countries, Narayan et al. (2000: 8) describe how for the majority of the poor 'their lives remain unchanged by government interventions'. Analysis by Wilkinson-Maposa et al. (2005) of the help that poor people receive found that help given by neighbours and family members far exceeded help from formal organizations such as NGOs.

26. In 2017 the *Times of India* reported that 60 per cent of engineering graduates did not have a stable job <https://timesofindia.indiatimes.com/home/education/news/60-of-engineering-graduates-unemployed/

articleshow/57698133.cms> [accessed 13 February 2021]. See Honwana (2012) and Jeffrey (2010) for detailed accounts of youth unemployment in Africa and South Asia respectively.

27. As Narayan et al. write, 'there is nothing intrinsically wrong with creating an empirical category based on a characterization of the fraction of the population having a certain experience. Yet no one would think of "the pregnant" as identifying a stable set of *individuals*. We all recognize pregnancy as a transitory condition that is an experience or situation of individuals at certain points in their lives' (2007: 23–4).

References

Alkire, Sabina (2018) 'The research agenda on multidimensional poverty measurement: important and as-yet unanswered questions', *OPHI Working Paper* 119, University of Oxford, Oxford.

Atkinson, A B. (2019) *Measuring Poverty Around the World*, in John Micklewright and Andrea Brandolini (eds), Princeton University Press, Princeton.

Banerjee, Abhijit V. and Duflo, Esther (2011) *Poor Economics: A Radical Rethinking of the Way To Fight Global Poverty*, Public Affairs, New York.

Banerjee, Anindo, Preece, Rohan and Chandrasekharan, Anusha (2015) 'Breaking the barriers to information: community-led land mapping in Bihar', in T. Thomas and P. Narayan (eds), *Participation Pays: Pathways for post-2015*, pp. 5–23, Practical Action Publishing, Rugby.

Bolton, Laura (2019) *Economic impact of farming cooperatives in East Africa*, Institute of Development Studies, Brighton.

Bongartz, Petra, Musyoki, Samuel Musembi, Milligan, Angela and Ashley, Holly (2010) 'Tales of shit: community-led total sanitation in Africa', *Participatory Learning and Action*, 61: 27–51.

Chambers, Robert (2014) *Into the Unknown: Explorations in Development Practice*, Practical Action Publishing, Rugby.

Collins, Daryl, Morduch, Jonathan, Rutherford, Stuart and Ruthven, Orlanda (2009) *Portfolios of the poor: How the world's poor live on $2 a day*, Princeton University Press, Princeton.

Corno, Lucia and Voena, Alessandra (2020) 'Institutions & political economy economic shocks and the age of marriage in sub-Saharan Africa and India', [online], Vox Dev, <https://voxdev.org/topic/institutions-political-economy/economic-shocks-and-age-marriage-sub-saharan-africa-and-india> [accessed 27 February 2021].

Cornwall, Andrea (2008) 'Unpacking participation: models, meanings and practices', *Oxford University Press and Community Development Journal*, 43: 269–83 <https://doi.org/10.1093/cdj/bsn010>.

Cunningham, Gordon (2008) 'Stimulating asset based and community driven development: lessons from five communities in Ethiopia', in Alison Mathie and Gordon Cunningham (eds), *From Clients to Citizens: Communities Changing the Course of their Own Development*, pp. 263–99, Practical Action Publishing, Rugby.

Dercon, Stefan and Krishna, Parmila (2000) 'Vulnerability, seasonality and poverty in Ethiopia', *Journal of Development Studies*, 36: 25–53 <https://doi.org/10.1080/00220380008422653>.

Dowden, Richard (2008) *Africa: Altered States, Ordinary Miracles*, Portobello, London.

Drèze, Jean and Sen, Amartya (2013) *An Uncertain Glory: India and Its Contradictions*, Princeton University Press, Princeton.

Fairs, Marcus (2017) 'Don't design yet another shelter for refugees, say experts', [online], Dezeen Magazine <https://www.dezeen.com/2017/12/18/dont-design-shelter-refugees-kilian-kleinschmidt-rene-boer-good-design-bad-world/> [accessed 20 November 2019].

GSMA (2020) *The Mobile Economy Sub-Saharan Africa 2020*, [online], <https://www.gsma.com/mobileeconomy/wp-content/uploads/2020/09/GSMA_MobileEconomy2020_SSA_Eng.pdf> [accessed 17 February 2021].

de Haan, Arjan (2009) *How the Aid Industry Works: An Introduction to International Development*, Kumarian Press, Sterling.

Honwana, Alcinda (2012) *The Time of Youth: Work, Social Change and Politics in Africa*, Kumarian, Virginia.

ILO (2020) *World Employment and Social Outlook: Trends 2020*, [online], International Labour Office, Geneva, <https://www.ilo.org/wcmsp5/groups/public/---dgreports/---dcomm/---publ/documents/publication/wcms_734455.pdf> [accessed 30 April 2021].

Jeffrey, Craig (2010) *Timepass: Youth, Class and the Politics of Waiting in India*, Stanford University Press, Stanford.

Mohanty, Chandra Talpade (1988) 'Under Western eyes: feminist scholarship and colonial discourses', *Feminist Review*, 30: 61–88 <https://doi.org/10.1057/fr.1988.42>

Narayan, Deepa, Chambers, Robert, Shah, Meera K. and Petesch, Patti (2000) *Voices of the Poor: Crying Out for Change*, Oxford University Press for the World Bank, New York.

Narayan, Deepa, Pritchett, Lant and Kapoor, Soumya (2009) *Moving Out of Poverty Volume 2: Success from the Bottom Up*, A co-publication of the World Bank and Palgrave Macmillan, Washington.

Ncube, Mthuli (2015) 'Introduction', in Mthuli Ncube and Charles Leyeka Lufumpa (eds), *The Emerging Middle Class in Africa*, pp. 1–9, Routledge, London.

Neumann, Rogerio Arns and Mathie, Alison, assisted by Linzey, Joanne (2008) 'Conjunto Palmeira: four decades of forging community and building a local economy in Brazil', in Alison Mathie and Gordon Cunningham (eds), *From Clients to Citizens: Communities Changing the Course of their Own Development*, pp. 39–63, Practical Action Publishing, Rugby.

Palmer, Tegan and Darabian, Nicole (2017b) *Farmers Club: A Mobile Agriculture Service by Vodafone Ghana*, [online], GSMA, <https://www.gsma.com/mobilefordevelopment/wp-content/uploads/2017/06/farmers-club-mobile-agriculture-service-vodafone-ghana.pdf> [accessed 27 February 2021].

Rao, Vijayendra (2002) 'Experiments in participatory econometrics: improving the connection between economic analysis and the real world', *Economic and Political Weekly*, 22: 1887–91.

Sanchez, Carolina (2017) 'From local to global: China's role in global poverty reduction and the future of development', [online], Speech to Taobao Village Summit, <https://www.worldbank.org/en/news/speech/2017/12/07/from-local-to-global-china-role-global-poverty-reduction-future-of-development> [accessed 26 February 2020].

Sen, Amartya (1999) *Development as Freedom*, Oxford University Press, Oxford.
UNDP (2004) *Unleashing Entrepreneurship: Making Business Work for the Poor*, UN, New York.
Wilkinson-Maposa, Susan, Fowler, Alan, Oliver-Evans, Ceri and Mulenga, Chao F.N. (2005) *The Poor Philanthropist: How and Why the Poor Help Each Other*, Centre for Leadership and Public Values, University of Cape Town, Cape Town, South Africa.
World Bank (2004) *Making Services Work for the Poor*, World Bank, Washington.

CHAPTER 3

My village's name will be up in lights: designing for communal cultures

Abstract

Life in poor communities is typically more communal than in the global north. There tends to be greater sharing of resources and mutual support. Social scrutiny and peer pressure can be more intense. These factors can inhibit people's willingness to experiment with new aid solutions. But if we design with these factors in mind they can also be the source of innovative and effective interventions. These include sharing economy services, microfinance, and total community approaches such as CLTS. We will also see the enormous potential for word of mouth, both on the ground and in combination with digital media. Using case studies from my own fieldwork and from successful programmes across regions, we will see the rich potential that comes from acknowledging the collective aspects of daily life, whilst questioning the simple binary between 'communal' and 'individual'.

Keywords: sharing economy; community-led total sanitation; microfinance; word of mouth; social media

Introduction

Outsiders from the global north are prone to ignore, or at least downplay, the intensely communal nature of life in poor communities and to frame the goals of development in overly individualistic terms. This was first on my list of reasons why development initiatives may fail to engage their intended users. In this chapter I start to explore what happens when one *does* pay attention to the collective aspects of life in poor communities. What kinds of problems does one encounter, but also what opportunities? What interventions have already been produced by thinking this way, and what new possibilities might emerge?

In this chapter I will explore, for instance, how microfinance, sharing economy services and 'total community' solutions all tap into the higher levels of social cooperation and social control that can sustain poor communities. I look at the importance of personal recommendation in poor communities and trace the potential for, and challenges of, building word of mouth and peer influence. Throughout, I will introduce case studies from my own and other's fieldwork. Doing so will show the value of thinking more communally, but also, I hope, the problems of drawing too stark an opposition between the 'individualistic' global north and the 'communal' south. In place of this simple binary I will try to explore communal and individualistic in more dynamic and nuanced terms, ones that reflect the rich and changing reality of life on the ground and how this inevitably varies across location.[1]

It's also important to recognize the double-edged nature of communal ties. Sometimes, as above, they can act as a catalyst for development. Other times, they may impede the adoption of new ideas. People's acute awareness of their community – and what this community may think – can discourage them from pursuing new initiatives that might improve their income or wellbeing. We saw above, for instance, the potentially transformative effects of mobile phone ownership. Yet I remember clearly in the early days of mobile phones how much people could worry about how they would be perceived for being one of the first to own a phone. As one respondent told me, 'if someone has a phone that can do all these new things people will start to talk about them, where did they get the money, what are all these new things they are searching for?'[2] Narayan et al. tell a story from fieldwork in Bangladesh that illustrates this tension clearly:

> When her husband fell sick and could no longer pull rickshaws, Beauty suggested that they open a tea stall, as there was none in the village. 'Keeping a chair, table, and two benches in front of our house, my husband started a tea stall. He sold only tea and biscuits at that time. Now from oil to soap to all necessary goods are available in our shop,' she said with much pride. A loan from Grameen Bank helped. Beauty now manages the tea stall herself. Following their example, five other tea stalls have opened in the village. *In the past, people spoke down to her for being a woman and sitting in the open without purdah.* 'Now everybody says that due to Rashid's wife his family is leading a better life now' (2009: 65 – my italics).

I have heard very similar stories echo around many of the villages, *kampungs* and *chawls* that I have visited in fieldwork. In communities with strong traditions, slow social and economic change, and neighbours living cheek by jowl, a new behaviour may easily garner suspicion or even outright antagonism. This can be the case – sometimes is especially the case – if the new activity helps people raise their incomes.[3] Some people, like Beauty, have the determination to experiment in the face of criticism and mistrust, but many others understandably do not. The well-meaning outsider brandishing a transformative new technology or social programme can easily fall at this first hurdle.

In this chapter we will look at a number of ways that we can work *around*, but also work *with*, the strong social ties that bind and support people in poor communities. Because in the right circumstances these same social pressures can also accelerate the development of solutions to poverty. Peer pressure, social scrutiny, and reciprocity can foster innovations that take root in low-income communities and make development programmes more intuitive and effective. In the following sections I will look at some of the questions I believe it's useful to ask to make this success more likely. They include:

- How do we allow people to share our interventions (rather than own them personally)?
- How do we identify and preserve the resources that are already being shared within the community?
- How do we allow people to adopt a new behaviour en masse, rather than as individuals?
- And how do we harness the power of personal ties to create positive word of mouth?

Designing to be shared

In my early days of fieldwork I often embarked on what I imagined was a simple exercise. I would ask respondents to show me what, if any, technology they owned and to talk me through how they used it day by day in a typical week. I would soon find myself becoming frustrated. A young man would reveal only at the end of the visit, that the phone he'd been describing for several hours as 'his' was really his father's. His father would then further clarify that his own phone was currently being borrowed by his friend, so he was using one borrowed from a cousin who ran a local phone stall. But we're interested in your 'personal technology', we would try to insist.[4] Jamal Khadar describes a similar experience when working for the charity Girl Effect. 'We would recruit girls who "owned" phones or "shared" phones as if they were two discrete categories. You could spend the first 30 mins trying to understand who had the phone, who used it, what rights they had and still not be clear'.

In recent years there has been much hyperbole around the idea of the 'sharing economy',[5] hype that has normally put the global north at the centre of the story (Forbes, 2019). And yet, as I falteringly discovered, communal consumption has deeper and wider roots in many lower-income communities. Poor people may often share resources, including financial resources, in ways that would surprise many outsiders. Narayan et al. (2009: 83) describe how 'families manage their portfolios of assets jointly. All family members, including children, typically contribute to the household's support, whether by working to earn money or by getting an education to prepare for future work'. Similarly, Lofchie (2015: 49) writes of how in many African countries, extended families will pool resources, 'treating the flow of cash from all their activities as a common resource so that when one source of livelihood diminishes, others absorb the slack'.

Even when new services and goods appear, the tradition of sharing will often endure and evolve. Polak (2008: 59) describes how 'in most rural cultures, when a family installs a low-cost hand pump, the neighbors are welcome to use it too'. This facility for sharing extends into urban settings and the new digital worlds too. During fieldwork in poor communities in Brazil, I have regularly found myself in 'the house that has wireless' – the *slightly* richer household whose owners could afford a WiFi router, and who would then rent out their access to others at a discount price, or pass it on free of charge to close friends / those who couldn't afford it.

The logic of sharing shouldn't be romanticized as purely selfless mutuality. In a world of scant resources, you *work these resources harder*, getting them into the hands of more people, finding ways to keep them in action as close as possible to 24/7. Wilkinson-Maposa et al. (2005: 47) capture this cultural logic with great clarity, arguing that 'under conditions of poverty, the bias is against resources lying idle, being reserved, or put aside and is in favour of resource use and application'. Sharing is therefore constant, habitual, something with multiple motivations – from altruistic to the more underhand. Teenagers in poor areas become sophisticated internet and social media users without having their own data, or even phone. 'You challenge the one who has a phone and if you win the game, they have to give you data to use' one respondent told us. Another non-phone-owning social network user described another common technique: 'I have set up Hike and WhatsApp on my auntie's phone and talk to my friends on that ... she doesn't know because she doesn't know how to use it'.[6]

Once you think about sharing as an engrained part of life, you find yourself asking questions like: 'do we really need to get this solution into *every* home?' And 'how do we design something that will have *as many owners as possible*?' Or 'how can we create a service that different users can use *at different times*, to make it truly 24/7?' In the global north the success of an innovation is often measured in the number of units produced. But when the audience for aid is instinctively used to sharing assets, you should ask the question the other way around: what is the *smallest* number of things we need to produce in order to be used by everyone? The numbers of people who are unbanked, are living without access to the internet, or clean water, or latrines look a little less daunting if you find a way for everyone who gets access to share it with another, or several others.

Sharing resources can have multiple benefits for development. First, it can bypass the 'sceptical neighbours' problem described above, since an intervention that is clearly *designed to be shared* is far less likely to attract accusations of individual one-upmanship. There can also be significant environmental benefits. Writing in 2011 (when Uber was barely out of its beta phase), Chandran Nair (2011: 131) set out a vision of communal and sustainable transport in South and East Asia where 'travellers for short as well as long journeys could arrange their travel by booking into networks of local taxis and buses, train or light rail networks, even bicycle hires, that allow them to make journeys as quickly – maybe even more quickly than they could with private cars'. Retamal and Dominish (2017) meanwhile argue that goods-sharing has the potential to boost domestic economies in the global south. It's unsurprising then that a number of explicitly 'sharing' services has recently been launched in low-income countries. One service, Hellotractor, allows farmers in parts of sub-Saharan Africa to rent tractors to and from one another. A service called Sarura in Rwanda creates shared crop storage facilities for farmers and cooperatives, with the aim of reducing spoilage and making collection more efficient. Ride-sharing services that are specific to the travel habits of local people are also appearing, including Safemotos (motorbikes) and Gawana (long-distance car trips) in Rwanda, and Jugnoo (autorickshaws) in India. There remain, though, important questions over who owns and profits from any new sharing services. A service that allows farmers to share vehicles or equipment may save those users money and improve their outputs, but if it is operated by a company who pay low wages and distribute profits outside the communities where they are used, then the net contribution to reducing poverty may be low or even inverse. Retamal and Dominish (2017) point to more socially progressive examples from the global north, such as Fairmondo – a cooperative version of eBay – or Juno – a ride-sharing platform which reserves 50 per cent of its equity for drivers – rather than the better-known corporate names who are most often associated with the label of the sharing economy.

There are also occasions where a development solution can *only* work if it reaches everyone. Iskander and Bentelab-Maes (2008) give a striking example of initiatives to bring electricity to rural areas of Morocco. Many residents were trapped in a cycle of increasing land loss and desertification: without electricity they couldn't run pumps to reach deep-lying water and were over-harvesting wood to meet their energy needs; this meant growing deforestation, which in turn meant even lower water levels. Looking at the problem *individually*, the relatively better-off members of the community might have invested in private generators. Or an electrical provider could have introduced supply to those homes who could have afforded it. But what the community realized was that electricity would only break the current destructive cycle if it was *universal*. This was because only then would the poorest be able to stop over-harvesting wood and thus stop reducing the water supply. As Iskander and Bentelab-Maes explain, 'in order for this virtuous relationship between electricity and the protection of water supplies to hold firm, *all villagers* had to have access to electricity, regardless of the ability to pay' (2008: 166 – my italics).

Protecting existing shared resources

This brings us to a second question that outsiders should ask more often, which is how to preserve the resources that are already shared by a community. As well as sharing physical goods – bikes, tractors, plant equipment, phones, internet access – the poor also often rely heavily on *shared natural resources* in a way that has almost disappeared from life in the global north. This is especially the case in rural environments, where poor people often heavily depend on communal 'goods' in the broadest sense of the word: lakes, rivers, wells, forests, grazing land. Mansuri and Rao (2012: 178) describe how 'the poor are often more dependent than the nonpoor on access to natural resources', such as lakes, rivers, wells, and forests. These are things over which no one can unproblematically make an individual decision or claim individual ownership.

In addition, the assets that people do own individually may be very dependent on the assets owned by others. A plot of land may be owned by one person or family, but its value is very likely to rely on how neighbours protect, irrigate, and plant their own land. So if an outsider wants to help any individual landowner they may have to help their neighbours simultaneously. Mathie (2008) gives a good illustration of this in practice in southern India where community groups worked cooperatively on each family's plot of land, creating embankments, levelling soil, and improving water collection on each individual family's territory, recognizing that in so doing they were making their own individual plot more productive. She describes how 'under this system, each participating family's land would benefit from increased productivity because land that had not been productive in the past, due to lack of water or excess soil erosion, could now be farmed' (2008: 218).

These shared or mutually dependent resources are things that outsiders from the global north can easily miss or misconceive. Too often when helping design a new solution I have found myself focusing on how it improves the incomes and immediate welfare of individual people in the community, and have missed the ways we may be jeopardizing or depleting the sharing economies that already exist. A good example of this can be seen in the early reaction to the Keralan fisher research, which focused on the potential for maximizing the prices gained by individual fishers, or boats of fishers. What was downplayed in the original story, but highlighted in later research, was that for many fishers maintaining communal stocks could be an equally important concern as individual, immediate profits. Sreekumar (2011) describes how traditional, small boat fishers in Kerala would suspend fishing during the monsoon, partly because their boats struggled in the rough seas, but also because of 'an ecological sensitivity to the fact that the fish spawn during that time'. As larger trawlers proliferated, these boats started to fish through the monsoons. The fish workers' union responded with 'clamors for a total ban on trawlers entering the coastal waters during the monsoon season', writes Sreekumar, 'a demand it won through long and arduous agitation'.

The potential for unwittingly eroding communal resources is clearer still when we consider that some of these resources are much less tangible and visible than forests or shoals of fish. The things that poor communities share also include the huge reserves of time and goodwill that we saw earlier in the many examples of informal childcare, education, security, and home care. It can be easy to introduce programmes that unintentionally undermine these assets. For instance, a programme to encourage employment among young people or women needs to consider basic questions of what else they are doing with their (often limited) time and what non-financial assets they may be contributing to their community. Can we be sure that our new resources are not undermining the resources that already exist? An audit of shared resources in the community is a vital task, even if it is complex and time-consuming. In Chapter 7 we will explore some of the challenges in more detail.

Total community approaches: adopting en masse versus as individuals

The third question is whether you can introduce your intervention to a whole community of people simultaneously, en masse. This is not an approach often taken in the global north, where huge time and energy is instead devoted to modelling how innovations diffuse over time and to identifying different types of 'early adopters'.[7] But in the context of aid it is an approach worth considering, because whilst strong social norms can discourage individual experimentation, the flip-side of this is that new behaviours can spread very rapidly if a community reaches a joint consensus.

One of the most attention-grabbing examples is an approach called 'Community-Led Total Sanitation' (CLTS). It addresses one of the least glamorous but most important problems facing many poor communities today: the lack of proper toilet facilities that leads to millions of people defecating in the open (Bongartz et al., 2010). It employs a combination of behaviour change and community design, and has been used by NGOs including Plan, World Vision, Water Aid, and UNICEF. The pioneers of CLTS emphasize that their approach targets communities, not individuals (Bongartz et al., 2010), and this is particularly critical to the problem they are tackling, since stopping some, or even most members of the community from defecating in the open isn't enough.[8] The 'total community' approach has several aspects:

- First, it requires working with all of, or at least all sections of, a community.
- Second, it seeks to reveal uncomfortable truths and present them starkly to the community to debate and respond. This is also the case with Praxis' equally frank and methodical approach to land reform (Preece et al., 2015), which we'll explore in Chapter 7.
- The third aspect of the approach builds heavily on the reciprocity we have seen often exists within poor communities, by targeting better-resourced members to help the more vulnerable. Bongartz et al. (2010: 30) describe how 'when communities realize that open defecation is a collective issue, the poorest people do not need outside assistance but are supported by those who are better off in their community'.

This combination of inclusivity and frankness has led to dramatic changes in communities which previously had been resistant to change. Chambers (2014: 77) writes that 'communities who defecate in the open, when facilitated to see the realities of what they are doing... are so disgusted that they resolve to do something about it. This can take immediate effect, and can lead whole communities to making themselves Open Defecation Free (ODF) in weeks or months, after many years of teaching and instruction have had little or no effect'.

I am cautious of absorbing or applying the lessons of CLTS uncritically. The spirit of egalitarian, collective endeavour that CLTS relies upon is extremely hard to engineer – as we will address directly in Chapter 7. In addition, CLTS had its initial success in rural areas, where communal living was more straightforward. A team could work in one distinct village, with a geographically defined group, who could be easily identified, gathered, and encouraged to support and monitor one another. This does not apply so neatly in a city, as shown in Myers et al.'s account (2018) of applying CLTS to urban locations. Community members are less likely to know one another well, or to identify strongly with their community and they tend to have less time to gather collectively. Urban areas can also have much higher numbers of short-term residents who are less invested in the community and 'busy lifestyles, based on the cash economy of urban dwellers, can mean low attendance at triggering' (2018: 13). But this does not mean that the social ties of shared identity, reciprocity, and social monitoring are absent altogether, as work by Wilkinson-Maposa et al. (2005) and Mathie and Cunningham (2008) has also shown.[9] Myers et al. describe how 'people may have strong ties that are not based on geographic proximity: for example, people may not know their neighbours well but are closely linked through a church, fellow market traders, ethnicity, where they originated, or a savings group' (2018: 39). Thus, they found that a 'total community' approach can be maintained to some degree in urban areas by working with these subgroups in parallel. Myers et al. give the example of a project in Mauritania, where 'triggering at different sites was conducted almost simultaneously and the city was treated as an overall unit. Competition between the different sub-units was encouraged' (2018: 48). By working in this coordinated way with more diffuse subcommunities, collective action was taken and they report a further 32,000 people now living in an ODF environment.

Another example of how strong social ties can be used as an accelerator rather than a block on innovation is microfinance. One reason it has traditionally been hard to offer financial services to poor people is that most have little if anything in the way of credit history or formal assets – the things that suppliers use to assess potential customers.[10] A principal innovation of microlenders was to work with the knowledge that *did exist*: the social ties and public scrutiny across many poor communities. As Karlan and Appel (2011) describe:

> Clients know one another better than the bank knows any of them. Group members can monitor one another because they buy from the same distributors and sell at the same outdoor markets and they see one another at church. So they hear about it when someone spends their loan money on a new TV…They know if someone suddenly starts taking days off from work. And since they *all* have something to lose (namely, the possibility of borrowing again in the future), each member has a material incentive to keep all the others in line (2011: 117).

Muhammad Yunus, the founder of Grameen Bank, sees these social dynamics as fundamental to the success of the approach he pioneered. He writes that 'the positive social pressure created by the group and the centre does a lot to encourage borrowers to remain faithful to their commitments' and that 'when Grameen members are surveyed about why they repay their loans, the most common answer is, "because I would feel terrible to let down the other members of my group"' (Yunus, 2007: 58).

However, sceptics like Karlan and Appel ask whether microfinance solves the problems that stopped banks from lending to poor people, or has simply *shifted* these problems onto poor people themselves. It is, they point out, the borrowers who must pay back if their associates default. The popular micro-credit model also places a significant cost in time on the borrower, who must travel to regular group meetings – and dedicate mental and emotional energy to financially profiling their neighbours and friends. In addition, group borrowing can encourage the poorest in any group to over-stretch themselves. These poorer borrowers might individually choose to borrow very small sums; however, once they join a group there is an incentive to borrow at least as much as the average loan. (Why share the risk for the whole sum loaned if you are borrowing only a tiny fraction of this sum?) This reminds us that whilst there are opportunities to be found in the communal nature of life in poor communities, we can't assume that communal solutions are always optimum or problem-free. In the case of microfinance, Karlan and Appel (2011) point out that Grameen, the originators, have now been running a loan service based on individual liability for over a decade, and that it has been a striking success.

Selling village to village: the potential and problems of building word of mouth

The close ties and regular face-to-face interactions found in many poor communities make word of mouth a particularly important and powerful tool when designing and marketing solutions to poverty. Many development success stories have relied significantly on word of mouth. Under-estimating it is, conversely, a major reason why new initiatives fail to interest and engage poor audiences. It is an approach that is particularly important to consider in rural communities, but not exclusively so. Myers et al. (2018: 37) give the example of the motorcycle riders in urban Nigeria, known as *okada*, who 'transport hundreds of passengers every day and so can play a useful role in advocating for CLTS'. Urban stall-holders were, we will see, essential to the spread of mobile money in East Africa. 'Word of mouth' is such a widely used term it may seem to need no explanation. There are, though, two slightly different aspects to word of mouth that I want to draw out and explore here in turn.

The first is personal recommendation: when a new service, programme or behaviour is recommended by people you know. Of course personal recommendations are valued the world over and generating recommendations is an old staple of marketing. But if, as many poor people do, you live in a community with strong social ties where you rely heavily on your neighbours, and where it is important not to deviate from the social norm, then recommendations by your peers can be *particularly* resonant. In a survey by McKinsey consultants (McKinsey, 2012) personal recommendations were rated as twice as important for Chinese respondents and three times as important for Egyptian respondents as they were for American or British respondents. There are obviously questions to be asked of self-reported data of this kind (for example, Egyptian respondents might simply be more willing to admit to the influence of their peers). However, a similar story is also suggested by field trials. Karlan and Appel (2011: 52), for example, describe how peer recommendation had a significant effect on adoption of farming insurance and that 'in-person marketing visits became a third more effective when the insurance salesman was introduced by a known and trusted agent from a local microfinance bank'.

This example draws out a second aspect of word of mouth that particularly plays out in poor communities, which is getting advice in person and face to face. Some of the most successful pro-poor products and services have involved word of mouth of this kind, introducing themselves on the ground, village by village. Grameen again is a famous example, making wide use of face-to-face marketing, including solar power agents, telephone saleswomen, and a network of local bank representatives, to reach tens of millions of poor Bangladeshis (Yunus, 2007). Polak's IDE managed to sell over one and a half million treadle pumps with a marketing campaign that took the product out to village after village. This included a travelling cinema screening a movie in which the pump had a starring role.[11] A *Lancet* study by El Arifeen et al. (2013) identifies the vital role played by a network of village health workers and their intensive on-the-ground campaign in achieving Bangladesh's dramatic health improvements. Sanitation, nutrition, and take-up of ORT have all improved to the degree that Bangladesh leads its neighbours and many other better-off countries in these areas. Immunization rates rose from 2 per cent in 1985 to 82 per cent in 2010.[12] Commercial companies, who normally operate with huge media budgets and high-tech communication channels, have developed similarly effective initiatives to reach low-income customers. Unilever in India, for instance, trained rural women to become local sales agents, a network that grew to over 70,000 representatives, selling to more than 4 million households in 162,000 villages.[13] In the early part of the century Coca-Cola almost doubled its sales in rural India with a campaign that combined TV advertising with face-to-face sales at tens of thousands of weekly markets and local fairs.[14] A few years later Nokia established mobile phones as a mass market service (the company at one point was selling over 70 per cent of the country's phones) with a huge emphasis on village-to-village selling. Per Braginski, who worked for the company at this time, describes how 'the financial cost and the social cost of getting on a bus, maybe for hours along unpaved roads meant many people wouldn't get phones if they had to go to the store. The store had to go to them' (personal communication, 2021).

What then are the ingredients of a campaign of this kind? A first aspect is the value of what might be called experiential learning, the chance to see and use new services in action yourself. This is because learning in poor communities tends to occur through experience and practice. You learn by seeing something in action and by doing it yourself, not through abstract discussion. This is a theme we will pick up and explore in much more depth in Chapter 6.

A second important, if sobering, lesson is that these campaigns are hard work. Whilst they may seem low-key, even old-fashioned compared to the possibilities of digital media, face-to-face networks require significant amounts of time, resources, and persistence to create and maintain. El Arifeen et al. (2013) illustrate this clearly, noting that among the community healthcare workers they researched in Bangladesh the drop-out rate was 12 per cent when measured in 2008 and had been as high as 44 per cent at some earlier points. Maintaining the team was a continual and demanding process. This point is emphasized by Drèze and Sen (2013: 64) when they compare the results in Bangladesh with the more partial success of similar programmes in India. They conclude that 'India, of course has also initiated programmes of this sort, but it still has much to lean from Bangladesh, both about the required intensity of these communication and mobilization efforts, and about the need to overcome the social barriers that often stand in the way'. Braginski argues that the importance of these mobilization efforts are often underplayed, especially by actors in the global north, who assume that once they have developed a solution to a problem they can rely on a network of distribution that in fact rarely exists. 'In Europe and North America, people are used to a whole network of logistics that will connect their idea to their audience, but in these contexts you often have to build it yourself... If your solution doesn't have a route to the audience it isn't really a solution' (personal communication, 2021).

If building and maintaining a network is hard, one thing that can help us here is to think about where the roots of such a network may already exist. Who are the potential allies, the people within communities who may already have an inclination and incentive to promote and spread your service, programme, or product? The stall-holders who added M-Pesa to their wares and *okada* riders who spread sanitation messages are excellent examples of third parties who acted as ersatz 'extension agents'. Rather than having to line up and train a network of field agents, we can ask who is already in our field. This is again what IDE did when marketing treadle pumps in rural areas. Their approach was to identify people in each village who were selling related products and then discuss with them the business case for selling the new pumps. Village by village, IDE built up over two thousand local dealers, who between them sold over a million units. This quite quickly became a self-sustaining network, since once 'these dealers were able to sell twenty five treadle pumps a year with a margin of 12 per cent, they made enough money to sustain themselves' (2008: 148). Other organizations have identified and built similar franchises to reach remote audiences in this more personal way.

Tata Motors launched a mini-truck called 'Ace' across rural India by training local mechanics to be able to guarantee service on common problems. As Khanna and Palepu (2010: 137) describe, 'instead of building an expensive new network of service centers, the company trained local mechanics and gave them tools to take care of common problems'.

We should also consider the power relations involved in these networks of intermediaries and the potential for those on the ground to be exploited. Mann and Nzayisenga (2015) look at the case of mobile phone intermediaries in Rwanda who, like the M-Pesa agents cited above, helped spread mobile phone coverage through the country. They argue (2015: 16) that 'while the telecommunication companies are building long-term, highly profitable infra-structures for both delivering content and services and accessing potentially valuable data about Rwanda's population and economy, the credit sellers are primarily gaining short-term financial benefits and some long-term skills and expertise'. They note the minimal or non-existent training given to the credit sellers and the precarity of their incomes that relied on commission. When building up, or building on, networks of intermediaries we need to think carefully about who gains and who loses what from the network.

We can also look at how to make use of movement within regions where we are working. Faced by the figure of 638,365 separate villages in the Indian Census,[15] it can be easy to despair at the possibilities of ever reaching remote rural audiences, but when you look at the level of interaction that can take place between rural and urban audiences, the reality is more promising. For instance, Banerjee and Duflo (2011) found that in the rural area around the Indian city of Udaipur, 60 per cent of families had at least one member who was working in a city during the previous year and that only 10 per cent of these trips were for longer than three months. Rural communities are not as cut off from urban influence as might first seem and when seeding new services or behaviours, we can identify and target those people who are linking urban and rural in this way.

Finally, we should consider how face-to-face approaches can be enhanced by the growing reach of digital and broadcast media. In the last two decades media access has spread rapidly in many low-income countries and exposure overall is far greater than when BRAC, IDE or Unilever began their work.[16] Furthermore, research shows that mass media can have profound effects on social habits in rural communities. A 2007 study by Jensen and Oster (2007) in India found that as cable TV spread across rural India, women's status and power improved on a number of measures, including higher enrolment at schools, reduced levels of domestic violence, and smaller family sizes. Perhaps the most famous case is a study in Brazil by La Ferrara et al. (2012) which showed that family sizes among poor Brazilians declined in line with the growth of cable TV and specifically the transmission of telenovelas. The authors suggest that because the stories focused on upper-middle class characters with no or few children,[17] poorer audiences gradually reassessed their own assumptions about what made a normal or ideal family size.[18] The authors claim that the expansion of Globo 'can account for about 7 per cent of the reduction in the probability of giving birth over this period'. In reaching this conclusion the authors looked for other evidence that suggests TV's social power, such as the finding that parents in areas of Globo coverage were far more likely to give their child a name shared by a major telenovela character (33 per cent versus 8.5 per cent in non-Globo areas). They also found that the effect was stronger for women who were a similar age to the main characters portrayed that year, and stronger also when the series portrayed a storyline of upward social mobility.[19]

However, access to digital media is still very far from complete in the world we are exploring. It is estimated, for instance, that the majority of people in Africa are not yet online.[20] Access to TV and digital tends to be lower in rural areas and in poor countries and districts. For instance, whilst Facebook usage has grown rapidly in India, it is concentrated in certain, typically richer, states (so, for instance, Maharashtra has over six times as many users as Bihar or Odisha) and usership skews to men and boys, who make up around two-thirds of users.[21] Thus, face to face remains an important means of communication. As one respondent in recent research with community activists in West Africa told us, 'many people – in displacement camps, rural areas, they don't have access. But they're still organising ... Digital can't reach everyone – some people need physical contact'.[22]

Furthermore, even if we can reach people in the literal sense of getting them to hear our radio message or watch our online video, this doesn't mean the message will be absorbed in the same way as if they encountered it face to face. Dowden (2008) argues that AIDS prevention campaigns in Africa have often struggled because they remained confined in people's minds to the abstract world of media, rather than permeating into everyday, local life. He describes how 'in Botswana AIDS is called the radio disease – people hear about it on the radio but they do not necessarily connect it to their daily lives. Many people I spoke to in Africa said they had decided to practise safe sex only after someone close to them had died. They had not taken AIDS education programmes seriously' (2008: 332–3). A report by GSMA and Frog Design (2017) argues that even when the new service you are providing is itself digital, face-to-face activity can be vital, particularly during the registration phase where people may be uncertain about the value of the offer and inexperienced in using the technology. They describe how 'face-to-face user engagement, such as through [Ugandan NGO] Living Goods' community health promoters, can create a human bond to overcome trust issues in markets that are rife with misinformation'.

The ideal approach is to think of media and face to face not as alternatives but as complementary approaches, which we can use alongside each other and blend together. A classic example of this is Victor Papanek's *Batta-Koya* ('Talking Teacher') distributed in sub-Saharan Africa in 1973 (Clarke, 2015). This was a simplified version of a cassette player with minimal controls on which people could play tapes with public health messages in their local language. The aim was to replicate the oral tradition of learning in rural communities, whilst managing to reach dispersed groups of people who spoke over 200 different dialects. A much more recent example (Palmer and Darabian, 2017a) can be found in Malawi, where, as in many poor countries, agricultural extension officers play a potentially vital role, providing farmers with advice on how to increase their yields and adapt to changes in climate and soil. The problem is, Palmer and Darabian describe, that the ratio of officer to farmer is between 1–1,500 and 1–3,900 depending where you are in the country, meaning huge numbers of farmers were being left out of this word-of-mouth programme. The Malawian government tried initially to get round this problem by identifying 'lead farmers' (more progressive, respected in their community) and training them to act as a bridge between official services and their peers. However, this only increased the scale of the programme to a small degree and so in recent years a mobile phone company, Airtel, have developed a phone service, which supplies information to these influencers, who then disperse it during face-to-face meetings of farmers' groups. Once again, this example encourages us to think about how media can *combine with and expand* the power and reach of word of mouth, rather than simply replacing it.

Beyond 'communal versus individualistic'

I have sought in this chapter to do two things: to explore the opportunities that spring from the stronger communal ties in poor communities, whilst also trying to steer away from a simplistic story of 'communal' and 'individualist' cultures. In my experience, poor communities in the global south tend to lean consistently, if not, of course, uniformly, towards the former. Life is lived in greater public view. Social norms exercise a more powerful grip. Neighbours and friends support each other more through a network of reciprocal ties. Information that arrives through personal contacts carries particular weight, and decisions are liable to be taken more collectively. In all these ways, daily life in a poor community typically has a different emphasis from life in most rich country settings. 'Emphasis' and 'typically' are the terms to bear in mind here, though. The differences are not categorical; there are exceptions, and the balance of individuality and communality is fluid not fixed.

We also need to be careful not to aggrandize the potential for more communal approaches. First, we have seen that there are powerful forces, in particular the growth of digital media and the spread of consumer goods, that are pushing many poor people towards more individualistic habits, assumptions, and aspirations. We can't assume that people who are used to sharing resources will continue to want to do so. In their study of the 'sharing economy', for instance, Retamal and Dominish (2017) note in middle-income Thailand and Vietnam that the appetite for shared solutions is competing with a strong desire for more individualistic consumption.

Second, there can be a tendency among outsiders, myself included, to romanticize the communal. This is perhaps particularly the case today as those in the global north seek ways to restore social capital to their own communities. Manzini (2015: 14) describes, for instance, how 'mutual help between neighbours is mainstream in a Rajasthan village in India, where it is part of a living tradition, but it may be radically new in a middle-class neighbourhood in London or Milan'. We need to be clear-sighted about the potential drawbacks of communal solutions, such as, in the case of microfinance, the burdens and pressures it can place on some users. We will return to this theme in Chapter 6.

Third, we should recognize that not all members of a community may be as able to benefit from the communal solutions that most easily emerge. Social capital is highly unequally distributed. Social ties work to constrain some people and support others. For example, shopping clubs and cooperatives are two ways that poor communities have used their strong social ties to their advantage. The former address the common problem that poor people often buy household goods in very small quantities and hence pay a much higher price per unit cost. They do so by bringing poor people together to pool funds and buy in bulk from stores with bigger discounts. Cooperatives work in a similar way for producers, allowing farmers to buy fertilizer, seeds, equipment collectively at a better price. But the benefits of clubs and cooperatives may often go mainly to those who are relatively better off and connected. Work by Rao (2002) suggests that shopping collectives often aren't accessed by those at the very bottom of the economic chain. Similarly, I have often seen that the poorest and most vulnerable farmers in a region are less likely to be members of a cooperative. Reviewing past studies, Muradian (2013) concludes that 'cooperatives tend not to serve the poorest of the poor (the smallest growers)' whilst ILO research in Kenya, Uganda, and Tanzania found women's representation on cooperative boards was on average just 17 per cent (Bolton, 2019). This reminds us that when we design for a group we need to think about who is left outside, or at the margins of, such groupings; who does not benefit from the communal. This is an issue to which we will turn in our next chapter.

Notes

1. One of the most obvious and basic differences is between the urban and the rural; the social ties that we explore in this chapter tend to be stronger in, though as we will see by no means exclusive to, rural settings.
2. Fieldwork, Rajasthan, 2008.
3. Envy and resentment of others' successes are hardly unique to poor communities, but they may be more destructive in communities that rely on mutual self-help and where anyone who falls out of this network may be dangerously exposed.
4. Personal communication, 2021.
5. The 'sharing economy' is defined as 'sharing assets – physical, financial and/or human capital, between many without transferring ownership, via a digital platform to create value for at least two parties'. 'Digital sharing for global growth: sharing resources, building economies', Dalberg Global

Development Advisers (2016). Retrieved from <https://www.digitalsharing economy.com/> [accessed 26 June 2020].
6. Fieldwork, Mumbai, 2016.
7. I have been involved in creating a number of such models, such as one for the ROAR youth research project in the UK. See Marketing Week <https://www.marketingweek.com/youth-watch/> [accessed 26 June 2020].
8. Or as Bongartz et al. (2010: 29) more bluntly describe, 'as long as even a minority still defecates in the open, all members of a community are in danger of "eating each other's shit"'.
9. In other work, Wilkinson-Maposa et al. found that reciprocity continues in urban environments and just has different focus, with city dwellers giving and lending money, whereas in rural areas people were more likely to share labour and resources (Wilkinson-Maposa et al., 2005). Similarly, Mathie and Cunningham (2008) show that community groups can provide an intense level of group identification in urban as well as rural areas.
10. This is an area that is changing rapidly. See, for instance, reports by GSMA <https://www.gsma.com/mobilefordevelopment/digital-identity/>. A number of businesses and NGOs are exploring ways of building digital economic profiles in poor countries, which are based on land owned and farmed, mobile money transfers, and social network analysis. See <https://www.jumo.world/stories/> or <https://tala.co.ke/2020/10/02/what-determines-my-tala-loan/> [both accessed 22 February 2021].
11. Word of mouth was also central to the success of the drip irrigation devices that Polak developed. Despite their potential to transform incomes by allowing farmers to grow vegetables during the traditionally dead off-season, initial take-up was poor. Polak (2008: 22–3) writes that 'our Pokhara field staff convinced the Kathmandu office staff, who convinced me, that we would never be able to sell low-cost drip systems until we trained farmers how to use these systems to grow off-season vegetables. We introduced field-based training programs in intensive horticulture, and sales took off quickly. It never would have happened if our field staff hadn't kept talking to our customers'.
12. El Arifeen et al. (2013: 2016) write that 'workers going from house to house to teach women to make the oral rehydration solution from ingredients at home is perhaps the most well known example of how community health workers played a part in the widespread dissemination of an innovation that was adapted to the local context and introduced to each household'.
13. See <https://sellingwithpurpose.unilever.com/?p=43> [accessed June 2019].
14. India Brand Equity Foundation, 'How Coca Cola conquered rural India' <https://www.ibef.org/pages/4489> [accessed June 2019].
15. Indian Census Board 2001. <https://censusindia.gov.in/Data_Products/Library/Post_Enumeration_link/No_of_Villages_link/no_villages.html> [accessed 26 June 2020].
16. India, for instance, at time of writing had 290 million users of Facebook and 440 million users of TikTok, <https://socialmediadata.com/social-media-by-country/> [accessed 12 April 2021].
17. When they analysed 115 of the highest-rated novellas, they found that 72 per cent of the main female characters under 50 had no children and 21 per cent had just one child.

18. The fact that Rede Globo had a near monopoly on major telenovelas and that the channel was gradually rolled out state by state over a long period of time created a natural experiment in which researchers could track the correlation between the arrival of cable TV and family size. They found that fertility rates dropped in Brazil from 5.8 births per woman in 1970 to 4.4 births per woman in 1980 to 2.9 births per woman in 1991 to 2.3 births per woman in 2000, and that Globo coverage correlated with a 6 per cent decline from the mean for women aged 25–34 and 11 per cent for women aged 35–44.
19. To explore other possible unobserved determinants, the researchers also looked at fertility rates prior to Globo's arrival (to see if the rollout might follow fertility patterns already under way), but concluded that 'there is no decline in fertility before the year in which Globo enters, while fertility sharply declines one year after Globo enters'. La Ferrara et al. (2012) also point to qualitative research by Herzog in the 1990s, describing how researchers 'asked the group subjects, adult women of middle and lower-class backgrounds, to portray the families that are more frequently displayed on television by using available photographs, drawings, and printed material. They asked the same subjects to portray the family of common people using the same material. The results were clear. Television families are small, rich, and happy. The families portrayed as common people are poor, contain more children, and the faces reveal unhappiness'.
20. See <https://internetworldstats.com/stats.htm> [accessed 12 February 2021].
21. See <https://www.statista.com/statistics/717615/india-number-of-facebook-users-by-age-and-gender/> and <https://www.soravjain.com/facebook-users-statistics-india-infographic/> [accessed 26 July 2020].
22. Fieldwork conducted by Jamal Khadar for Plan International, Senegal. May 2019.

References

Banerjee, Abhijit V. and Duflo, Esther (2011) *Poor Economics: A Radical Rethinking of the Way To Fight Global Poverty*, Public Affairs, New York.

Bolton, Laura (2019) *Economic impact of farming cooperatives in East Africa*, Institute of Development Studies, Brighton.

Bongartz, Petra, Musyoki, Samuel Musembi, Milligan, Angela and Ashley, Holly (2010) 'Tales of shit: community-led total sanitation in Africa', *Participatory Learning and Action*, 61: 27–49.

Chambers, Robert (2014) *Into the Unknown: Explorations in Development Practice*, Practical Action Publishing, Rugby.

Clarke, Alison J. (2016) 'Design for development, ICSID and UNIDO: the anthropological turn in 1970s design', *Journal of Design History*, 29: 43–57 <https://doi.org/10.1093/jdh/epv029>.

Dowden, Richard (2008) *Africa: Altered States, Ordinary Miracles*, Portobello, London.

Drèze, Jean and Sen, Amartya (2013) *An Uncertain Glory: India and Its Contradictions*, Princeton University Press, Princeton.

El Arifeen, Shams, Christou, Aliki, Reichenbach, Laura, Osman, Ferdous Arfina, Azad, Kishwar, Islam, Khaled Shamsul, Ahmed, Faruque, Perry, Henry B. and Peters, David H. (2013) 'Community-based approaches and partnerships: innovations in health-service delivery in Bangladesh', *The Lancet*, 382: 2012–26 <https://doi.org/10.1016/S0140-6736(13)62149-2>.

Forbes Magazine (2019) 'The sharing economy is still growing, and businesses should take note', [online], <https://www.forbes.com/sites/forbeslacouncil/2019/03/04/the-sharing-economy-is-still-growing-and-businesses-should-take-note/> [accessed 26 June 2020].

GSMA and Frog Design (2017) *mHealth Design Toolkit: Ten Principles to Launch, Develop and Scale Mobile Health Services in Emerging Markets*, [online], <https://www.gsma.com/mobilefordevelopment/wp-content/plugins/plugin_m4d_shortcodes//mhealth/GC_GSMA_FinalBooklet.pdf> [accessed 12 February 2021].

Iskander, Natasha and Bentaleb-Maes, Nadia (2008) 'The hardware and software of community development: migrant infrastructure projects in rural Morocco', in Alison Mathie and Gordon Cunningham (eds), *From Clients to Citizens: Communities Changing the Course of their Own Development*, pp.161–80, Practical Action Publishing, Rugby.

Jensen, Robert and Oster, Emily (2007) *The Power of TV: Cable Television and Women's Status in India*, [online], NBER Working Paper 13305, <http://www.nber.org/papers/w13305.pdf?new_window=1> [accessed 26 June 2020].

Karlan, Dean and Appel, Jacob (2011) *More Than Good Intentions: Improving the Ways the World's Poor Borrow, Save, Farm, Learn, and Stay Healthy*, Penguin, New York.

Khanna, Tarun and Palepu, Krishna (2010) *Winning in Emerging Markets*, Harvard Business School Press, Cambridge.

La Ferrara, Eliana, Chong, Alberto and Duryea, Suzanne (2012) 'Soap operas and fertility: evidence from Brazil', *American Economic Journal: Applied Economics*, 4: 1–31 <https://doi.org/10.1257/app.4.4.1>.

Lofchie, Michael (2015) 'The political economy of the African middle class', in Mthuli Ncube and Charles Leyeka Lufumpa (eds), *The Emerging Middle Class in Africa*, pp. 36–60, Routledge, London.

Mann, Laura and Nzayisenga, Elie (2015) 'Sellers on the street: the human infrastructure of the mobile phone network in Kigali, Rwanda', *Critical African Studies*, 7: 26–46 <https://doi.org/10.1080/21681392.2015.974136>.

Mansuri, Ghazala and Rao, Vijayendra (2012) *Localising Development: Does Participation Work?* World Bank Policy Research Report, World Bank, Washington.

Manzini, Ezio (2015) *Design, When Everyone Designs*, MIT, Cambridge Mass.

Mathie, Alison (2008) 'People's institutions as a vehicle for community development: a case study from southern India', in Alison Mathie and Gordon Cunningham (eds), *From Clients to Citizens: Communities Changing the Course of their Own Development*, pp. 207–35, Practical Action Publishing, Rugby.

Mathie, Alison and Cunningham, Gordon (2008) 'Introduction' and 'Conclusions', in Mathie, Alison and Cunningham, Gordon (eds), *From Clients to Citizens: Communities Changing the Course of their Own Development*, pp. 1–10 and pp. 357–69, Practical Action Publishing, Rugby.

McKinsey (2012) 'Winning the $30 trillion decathlon: going for gold in emerging markets' [online], <https://www.mckinsey.com/business-functions/strategy-and-corporate-finance/our-insights/winning-the-30-trillion-decathlon-going-for-gold-in-emerging-markets> [accessed 26 June 2020].

Muradian, Roldan (2013) 'The potential and limits of farmers' marketing groups as catalysts of rural development', Paper Presented to UNRISD Conference, 6–8 May 2013, Geneva.

Myers, J., Cavill, S., Musyoki, S., Pasteur, K. and Stevens, L. (2018) *Innovations for Urban Sanitation: Adapting Community-led Approaches*, Practical Action Publishing, Rugby.

Nair, Chandran (2011) *Consumptionomics: Asia's Role in Reshaping Capitalism and Saving the Plane*t, Infinite Ideas, Oxford.

Narayan, Deepa, Pritchett, Lant and Kapoor, Soumya (2009) *Moving Out of Poverty Volume 2: Success from the Bottom Up*, a co-publication of the World Bank and Palgrave Macmillan, Washington.

Palmer, Tegan and Darabian, Nicole (2017a) *'Creating Scalable, Engaging Mobile Solutions for Agricultur*e, [online], GSMA, <https://www.gsma.com/mobile fordevelopment/wp-content/uploads/2017/07/create-scalable-engaging-mobile-solutions-agriculture.pdf> [accessed 27 February 2021].

Polak, Paul (2008) *Out of Poverty: What Works When Traditional Approaches Fail*, Berrett-Koehler, San Francisco.

Preece, Rohan, Joseph, Stanley, Sarangan, Gayathr and Bharadwaj, Sowmyaa (2015) 'Knowledge base: towards a community-owned monitoring system', in T. Thomas and P. Narayan (eds), *Participation Pays: Pathways for post-2015*, pp. 41–61, Practical Action Publishing, Rugby.

Rao, Vijayendra (2002) 'Experiments in participatory econometrics: improving the connection between economic analysis and the real world', *Economic and Political Weekly*, 22: 1887–91.

Retamal, M. and Dominish, E. (2017) *The Sharing Economy in Developing Countries*. Prepared by the Institute for Sustainable Futures at the University of Technology, Sydney (UTS) for Tearfund UK.

Sreekumar, T.T. (2011) 'Mobile phones and the cultural ecology of fishing in Kerala, India', *The Information Society*, 27: 172–80 <https://doi.org/10.1080/01972243.2011.566756>.

Wilkinson-Maposa, Susan, Fowler, Alan, Oliver-Evans, Ceri and Mulenga, Chao F.N. (2005) *The Poor Philanthropist: How and Why the Poor Help Each Other*, Centre for Leadership and Public Values, University of Cape Town, Cape Town.

Yunus, Muhammad (2007) *Creating a World Without Poverty: Social Business and the Future of Capitalism*, Public Affairs, New York.

CHAPTER 4

Knots and cages: the myriad problems of reaching the excluded

Abstract

Although 'the poor' are often categorized as a single audience, significant inequalities exist within poor communities and whilst these are often hidden they profoundly shape the way that different people are and aren't able to access aid programmes and services. This chapter examines the way that certain groups are marginalized by their location, by poor targeting of programmes, by the exploitation of their peers, and by learning to adapt their own expectations to exclude themselves. It then offers practitioners a range of pragmatic and disruptive tactics for making their initiatives more inclusive. These include both more indirect methods, such as identifying resources that benefit the more marginal and more direct ones that confront issues of power head on. Whilst the chapter gives a particular focus to issues of gender, it emphasizes throughout the importance of thinking about discrimination in intersectional terms.

Keywords: marginalization; exclusion; gender; intersectionality; ethnicity

Introduction

In the eight years since I began this book the problem of discrimination in poor countries, and especially of gender discrimination, has moved from the margins to mainstream. Not long ago researchers from the Voices of the Poor project wrote there 'may be no other domain that suffers such neglect by governments, international agencies and the private sector as gender relations' (Narayan et al., 2000: 276–7). Today, I find myself talking to three separate international NGOs about gender empowerment projects in the space of six months. This change in focus and conversation is hugely welcome. However, as we will see, progress on the ground remains slow. The term 'inclusivity' may appear in more development documents, but it still often slips into the background during daily development work. Even where it remains a focus the challenges of addressing discrimination are complex and deep. In this chapter we will explore the reality of making development more inclusive, including the severe difficulties we face, and the trade-offs we are forced to make. It is an area of growing hope and possibility, but one with few simple answers.

The chapter has two broad aims. The first is to explore why issues of power and discrimination are so important, even for those working on projects that aren't explicitly about equality. I look at discrimination as both an intrinsic problem and as something that stops us achieving other development goals, such as improved health, education, and incomes. In the second section I explore the tactics we can employ to reach less powerful groups and to work against, or at least around, discrimination. This quickly leads into the complexities we face when tackling engrained and often overlapping forms of inequality. An initiative gets more girls into school, only to find they are reading textbooks reinforcing patriarchal attitudes' social norms. An attempt to extend land rights to more women ends up entrenching inequalities between different classes.

This reflects how discrimination in poor communities – as in rich ones – occurs on many lines. These include gender, ethnicity, caste, class, sexuality, religious affiliation. Of these many strands, gender discrimination is the particular focus in this chapter. It is a choice made for several reasons. First, it is one of, if not the most pervasive forms of inequality across poor communities.[1] After interviewing over 20,000 poor people, Narayan et al. wrote that one of the most common themes in their lives was that 'gender relations are troubled and unequal' (2000: 2). Second, gender discrimination is an issue that I have encountered frequently in my own fieldwork. I have seen repeatedly how it can breed misery, stir family tensions, blunt personal ambitions, and cause and reinforce other social ills. Third, it is an area where there is wide and growing research material to draw upon.

Through this chapter, however, other examples of discrimination surface all too regularly. Indeed, a central message is that power relations within poor communities can only be understood from an 'intersectional' perspective, which takes into account inequalities between classes, castes, religious groups, ethnicities, and other social lines. Thus, whilst gender is centre-stage, the questions raised help illuminate other areas of discrimination and encourage other forms of inclusive development.

Why inclusivity is critical

For some readers inclusivity will be a central tenet of their work. For others it is more peripheral. For the latter, my aim in this section is to illustrate why discrimination and inequalities should be important considerations on any project. For the former, I'm aware I may be preaching to the converted (and some readers may wish to move on to the more solution-focused sections below). But I believe there is value in pausing briefly to unpick the different rationales for pursuing inclusivity. If we pursue equality because we value it for its own sake we may arrive at a different place than if we see it as a route to better health outcomes or higher incomes.

The first reason why inequality and discrimination are important considerations is very straightforward: that in any poor audience there will be certain sub-groups of people who need more help, because they have less than others. This is consistently the case with women in poor communities. Women and girls almost always earn less money – the gender pay gap in sub-Saharan Africa is calculated to be 68 per cent and in South Asia 66 per cent. They own far fewer assets too. A World Bank gender report (2012: 18) found that women almost everywhere own less land than men. In Brazil just 11 per cent of registered landowners were women, in Kenya only 5 per cent. Research by Oduro, Baah-Boateng, and Boakye-Yiadom (Oduro and Nabalamba, 2015) found that nearly twice as many men as women own their own home (30 per cent versus 16 per cent). Identifying these structural differences lets us think more clearly about where we target resources.

Not only do some groups start with less, some groups will also need more in the way of input to get the same output – a bigger share of development resources in order to make the same development progress. For instance, someone excluded by gender or ethnicity may need more time, money, and support to finish school or launch a business than a young man in the same poor community who comes from a dominant ethnic group. This is easy to overlook when we are designing for a very poor audience – all of whose needs may seem to outsiders to be very great. But if we are going to serve everyone, including the more vulnerable, we need to accept that we can't give everyone the same degree of resources and expect them to achieve the same outputs. As Nussbaum (2003: 35) argues 'in a nation where women are traditionally discouraged from pursuing an education it will usually take more resources to produce female literacy than male literacy'.

The third reason for focusing on marginal groups is that if we *don't* do so, our initiatives simply may not reach them. A project that doesn't take discrimination into account is liable not to benefit those who need it most. Or as Thomas et al. (2015: 66) argue, 'the presence of infrastructure in a village does not necessarily guarantee its equitable use by all households in a village'. We saw in Chapter 3, for instance, how agricultural extension services can allow poor farmers to transform their incomes by drawing on new techniques and inputs and selling to new markets. Yet the crops supported by these extension services are much less likely to be ones grown by women and girls (Edström and Shahrokh, 2015). Similarly, poorer members of farming communities are often less likely to be reached: 'only the big farmers get the new information, the officers do not reach us here' as one respondent told my colleagues during recent research in Sri Lanka (GSMA, 2018). Likewise, marginal groups are less likely to be reached by support programmes, such as state social benefits (Narayan et al., 2000). Even a celebrated initiative like the National Rural Employment Guarantee appears to have done less for marginal audiences.[2] I've visited many Indian communities where people could point to new wells, roads, sanitation projects built by local people in this way and yet Mansuri and Rao (2012: 126) write that across communities the better informed and better off were 'more likely to obtain the full benefits of the program in terms of wages, the timing of payment, and hours worked'.

This kind of exclusion may occur overtly – with certain groups deliberately pushed out by other members of the community. But exclusion can happen in subtler, less easily identifiable ways. For instance, schools, health centres, and government offices may not just be further away from lower-class or lower-caste homes, these important services may have fewer lower-class or lower-caste workers staffing them, making them less *socially* as well as physically accessible. When we think about inclusivity we need to consider these less obvious, more intangible barriers.

The final reason for focusing on marginal or vulnerable groups is that it gives you more bang for your development buck. There is growing evidence that initiatives aimed at excluded groups can have a bigger impact and better results, both in terms of boosting economic returns (World Bank, 2012) and improving wider development outcomes.[3] Research shows, for instance, a clear correlation between the status of women in a community and the birth weights of children (Drèze and Sen, 2013). There is also a convincing story of causation: that communities where women are given less respect also give women less food, leading to children born at lower weights and with lower levels of health (Drèze and Sen, 2013: 94). It has been argued specifically that female access to education correlates with marked improvements in their children's health and their own educational achievements. The World Bank (2012: 5) claim that 'in Pakistan, children whose mothers have even a single year of education spend one extra hour studying at home every day and report higher test scores'. Meanwhile, Sen (1999) cites work that shows increased female literacy significantly reduces deaths in childhood, and is dramatically more effective in doing so than increasing male literacy, or improving families' incomes. I quote from Sen's conclusions at length, because they are so arresting:

> Murthi, Guio and Drèze's statistical analysis indicates that, in quantitative terms, the effect of female literacy on child mortality is extraordinarily large... For instance, keeping other variables constant, an increase in the crude female literacy rate from, say, 22% (the actual 1981 figure for India) to 75% reduces the predicted value of under-five mortality for males and females combined from 156 per thousand (again the actual 1981 figure) to 110 per thousand. The increase in male literacy over the same range (from 22 to 75 percent) only reduces under-five mortality from 169 per thousand to 141 per thousand and a 50% reduction in the incidence of poverty (from the actual 1981 level) only reduces the predicted value of under-five mortality from 156 per thousand to 153 per thousand (1999: 198).

These examples reflect how tackling discrimination can have 'instrumental' as well as intrinsic value. Increasing women's access to education not only addresses the social ills of discrimination itself, it can also save children from dying – more effectively it seems than raising incomes. As we will see shortly below, this can also provide us with an argument to make to people on the ground. Parents may be more willing to keep daughters in school, if they can see this will lead to better jobs and higher household income. I have some reservations, though, about making the case for inclusivity too reliant on its 'instrumental' value. First, if we value equality *because it leads to higher incomes or better health* we risk undermining the intrinsic value we place on equality. Hickel (2014: 1362) argues that this slippage is already occurring and he laments a discourse where 'basic rights and human dignity for poor women in the global South are never considered worthwhile goals in and of themselves – they must always be justified according to corporate interest and economic outcomes'. The second issue is that we set ourselves up for a rather tricky problem if the correlation between equality and other goals no longer holds, or even reverses. Imagine that data shows that in some contexts female illiteracy actually led to *higher* growth, *higher* incomes, or *better* health outcomes; would we choose to accept, or promote this discrimination? I find it hard to picture anyone in development making the case for pro-growth gender discrimination, but the more we frame equality in instrumental terms, the further down we must climb if our efficiency argument collapses. Whilst the positive secondary effects of inclusivity shouldn't be ignored, I believe we should regard tackling discrimination and social injustices as goals in their own right and look to base our interventions on this premise.

How do we promote inclusivity: strategies and tactics from the field

If we accept, then, that inclusivity matters, the rest of the chapter examines ways that we can pursue it in practice. These ways, we will see, vary widely – from long-term cultural change programmes to small-scale nudges and from highly targeted work with the excluded to the challenges of addressing tensions across a whole community. This wide-ranging exploration is very deliberate, because the way discrimination manifests varies so significantly across country, region, and even local district. We need to be very alert to context and to think about how we adjust our approaches and pick the tools that work in each situation. The following example from BBC Media Action research in central India (Gambhir and Kumar, 2013: 38) illustrates this reality clearly.

> In Madhya Pradesh people in two communities reeling from severe drought for the past eight years had not seen much development and felt that the future impact of environmental changes would be quite high. Yet they were very different in their responses. One community was heterogeneous with people of multiple castes living in separate hamlets, and access to resources including water was based on the caste membership. The lower caste people in the community did not have access to water pumps. The community did not work together to deal with water shortages and the community and its panchayat leaders did not seem particularly willing to work together to find solutions. The other community, just 15km away, was smaller and more homogeneous, but

people were responding to water shortages. This community had only one radio, which a resident nicknamed 'Khabrilal' (person who provides information) listened to and then mobilized his friends to participate in a rural radio competition, developed by Development Alternatives, India. He began to use organic manure on crops and this successful experiment won him the competition. Subsequently more people in the village began to adopt this technique. A community led by a young girl who demonstrated the use of waste water from household chores to grow and nurture a kitchen garden in a water-scarce community was the runner-up.[4]

This, in my experience, is not uncommon. I have found myself visiting a community with deeply engrained caste, ethnic or gender tensions and then travelled only a mile or two down the road to find a community actively engaged in solving these problems. What would work in the first community would be inappropriate in the second and vice versa.

A major consideration often concerns how *overt* our attempts to tackle discrimination and inequality need to be. Sometimes, inclusivity can be pursued quite quietly in the background, for instance, by just adjusting the types of crops that an extension programme includes, or by informing communities about the growth in female employment opportunities. On other occasions, it may require us to confront issues of power and privilege, to deal with aggressive resistance and to manage damaging tensions within a community. In the pages that follow I will therefore explore inclusivity under these two broad headings:

- First, I look at *indirect* ways of reducing discrimination and inequality, tactics that allow us to help the marginalized without necessarily making this aim overt, or engaging directly with power struggles within a community.
- Second, I look at more *overt and negotiated* ways of reducing discrimination and inequality. I explore what happens when relatively more privileged groups try to co-opt or undermine our inclusivity initiatives. I look at the benefits of applying an intersectional perspective in order to avoid inadvertently entrenching other forms of discrimination and to build alliances across a community. I examine how 'dominant groups' can participate in inclusivity interventions as active partners.

Inclusivity by stealth: indirect ways of tackling discrimination

In some contexts, as we will see below, discrimination has to be tackled head on. There are though, more indirect approaches we can take, which are worth considering at the outset of any project. A good example of this 'inclusivity by stealth' approach comes from work in northern India led by Jensen (2013), which sought to change parents' attitudes to female education. The study didn't try to tackle parental discrimination directly; rather it sought to encourage parents to change their own minds, by giving them information about the jobs available for women in the local area. To test their hypothesis, the research team ran recruitment programmes for call-centre jobs in 40 rural villages in northern India (where it was assumed that awareness of these jobs was typically low). They then compared behaviour and attitudes in these villages with 40 control locations in the same four states, who were given no new information. Jensen found that in the 'test' villages girls aged 5–11 were 5 per cent more likely to be enrolled in education – closing 60 per cent of the gender gap between the numbers of boys and girls in education. Young women in these villages were also 10–13 per cent more likely to expect to work than their peers in the control villages.[5] The percentage of 15–21 year olds (the peak age for marriage in rural India) who had got married or had had children was also 5–6 per cent lower. In these villages girls also weighed more, suggesting parents were taking more care of them. This case study shows how significant gender disparities can be addressed without an explicit gender-based campaign if we can think somewhat laterally about the root causes of the discrimination.

Another indirect approach involves simply identifying, and then prioritizing those aspects of development that particularly empower excluded groups in our community – versus those that benefit more dominant parties. For instance, Van Domelen (2007) found that in many cases at the time of her analysis, irrigation and microfinance interventions helped relatively well-off and powerful citizens more than they did the poorest.[6] In contrast, an ILO (2012) study found that the expansion of electricity supply could have a disproportionately positive effect for impoverished women. Applying this kind of analysis at a local level at the start of a project may help us design interventions (for instance, low-cost solar power) that will help the less powerful without necessarily needing to be explicitly positioned in this way.

Inclusivity can also be about ensuring our initiatives reach the spaces that the most vulnerable inhabit. We have seen that women and girls in some communities may have little chance to travel beyond a very small geographical area and a very limited number of locations. Kishor and Gupta (2004), for example, found that in some of the most restrictive states in the north of India (such as Jammu and Kashmir, Assam, Uttar Pradesh, Nagaland, and Odisha), only 20 per cent or fewer of women were allowed to go without permission to the market or to visit friends or relatives. Similarly, Narayan et al. (2009: 80) report that 'across a wide swath of societies, from India, Afghanistan, and Bangladesh to Mexico, Malawi, and Tanzania, women express anger at restrictions on their movement. Some compare their experience to living like "a bird in a cage"'. Hence a small, but important, way we can increase inclusivity is by thinking carefully about the spaces in which our intervention will be used and discovered. Does our solution require people to interact in public spaces (a marketplace, a village meeting room)? Who will and won't be comfortable there? Are we reaching people who live remotely and rarely move beyond their village? The NGO Girl Effect crystallized this in an ambition to get their

Ni Nyampinga magazine not just to the most rural part of Rwanda, but to the most remote houses within these provinces.

To ensure inclusive access we also need to think not just in terms of *who* consumes it, but *how* they consume it. To take a glaring example, the numbers of girls in school has been improving in many low-income countries and in this sense 'access to education' has been widely celebrated as a development success. However, enrolment data doesn't tell the full story of access – or exclusion. More girls may be in schools, but this does not mean they will be taught the same way, receive the same support, or be set the same goals. Stern and Clarfelt note, for instance, that 'in many schools, girls are predominantly responsible for cleaning, sweeping, monitoring the classroom, rearranging desks, and interacting with adults in comparison to boys' (2015: 56). Their research also found that in many countries textbooks depict women in more passive and domestic roles. To achieve real equality of access we need to address these more subtle ways that girls are excluded from education. For instance, Stern and Clarfelt (2015) cite a teaching guide developed in India to help teachers and students to think more critically about how gender is depicted in educational materials, whilst the charity Plan has developed a score-card to help teachers reflect on how they teach boys and girls and whether there are differences. Inclusivity is not just about equal numbers of people accessing a service, it means ensuring parity in the *experience* of the service.

Tackling discrimination directly

Thus far, there has been limited friction in the story of how to promote inclusivity. The methods and case studies I've examined have tended to work by stealth. They rely on supplying information that nudges people to make a less prejudiced decision; they find ways to fine-tune the physical and social environment to make it easier for disempowered groups to realize their potential. Often inclusive development runs less smoothly than I have described so far. Sometimes, as we will explore shortly, it requires a more direct intervention in power relations; sometimes our attempts at inclusivity are met by resistance.

Resistance to inclusive development can take many forms. On occasions, previously dominant members of the community may react to a scheme by trying to take over and benefit from it themselves. A classic example is a programme in Kenya that tried to employ the targeting tactics outlined above, by offering agricultural training and inputs specifically to poor and poorly educated female farmers (Mansuri and Rao, 2012). Researchers found that the scheme, which gave participants an average of $34 (the equivalent of almost 15 per cent of a typical farmer's total assets) attracted many new female members to the groups. At first glance, this seemed a good result for inclusivity and for the targeted approaches we have explored just above. The problem was, in fact, many of the new users were better paid and more educated than the intended beneficiaries; some of them were also men. Meanwhile, significant numbers of older female members left the groups. This is a risk that outsiders need to bear in mind when targeting initiatives; that as Mansuri and Rao warn, 'an increase in external funding can displace the most vulnerable people by inducing greater participation by the more educated, wealthy, and young' (2012: 133). The issue is further complicated by the fact that such takeovers can happen in ways that are hard to detect. For instance, a study in India, Sri Lanka, and Ghana by Bernhardt et al. (2017) found that female entrepreneurs given microloans often diverted some of their funds to their partners' businesses. Their research shed light on earlier studies that had found loans to male entrepreneurs had a higher return than those made to women. It was not the case, as some had argued, that male entrepreneurs were using the money better, but rather that female entrepreneurs would fund their male partners – but not vice versa. The authors also found that when women were the only entrepreneurs in a household they had as good a return on investment as men. This illustrates how carefully we may need to guard against dominant group takeover.

On other occasions, dominant groups react by seeking to *undermine* rather than exploit the new intervention. Abraham and Platteau (2004) describe a project in the Republic of Congo, which gave new gill nets to one particular poor community on the shores of Lake Kivu. This inclusive and targeted project was resented by people living in nearby villages, who 'did not hesitate to steal gill nets from the beneficiaries'. Worse, some 'went so far as systematically catching juvenile fish with the apparent purpose of sabotaging the (future) productive performance of gill net operators, regardless of the cost entailed for themselves' (2004: 220). Cornwall (2000) cites an empowerment project in Uganda, which triggered the 'indignance of older men as women involved in a PRA process began to challenge them' and then turned into 'beatings and other forms of abuse that came in the wake of efforts to empower women and enable them to exercise voice'.[7] This reminds us of the real risks involved. 'Inclusivity' is one of the warmest of words, but practising inclusivity in development can be a dangerous undertaking – not for those who do it professionally, but for those who live with its results.

How, then, do we deal with resistance of this kind? A first point to note is that resistance may often be more intense if initiatives are seen to originate outside the community, or even to be imposed by outsiders. Reporting on programmes in Kenya, Edström and Shahrokh (2015: 31) warn that rejection is more likely 'when such calls for reform are seen as an imposed agenda from outside their communities'. They also note that 'in India, men's rights' groups have emerged to oppose structural changes to improve the status of women, such as in the form of legal reforms. These changes have sometimes been challenged as a result of a "foreign influence of feminism"'. This is one of the many strengths of the more insider-led approaches that I explore in the last two chapters of the book: that they explicitly avoid imposing solutions and assumptions from the outside.

The second point to note is that resistance can be passive, or even simply latent, and yet still very destructive. In 2016 I worked on a project to encourage girls in urban Nigeria, India, and Indonesia to make more active choices over education, work, and family. We were working with the Geena Davis Institute's principle that 'if she can see it, she can be it'. Or, in less pithy terms, that girls who see a richer range of role models will develop richer ambitions for their own lives. There is certainly evidence that role models can have the exact impact we hoped to achieve (Brannen, 2012). But the more fieldwork we did, the more we found these urban girls were already aware of role models, already had richer dreams. And, in fact, the more we showed them these opportunities, the more we were simply highlighting the real problem: that their families wouldn't permit them to pursue the dreams they already had. 'It's not real', one respondent told us, 'If I spoke to my grandmother about starting a Facebook group to discuss this [gender issues], she'd ask why I didn't just go and get married'. 'This isn't us', other respondents told us in one group discussion. 'At home there are so many restrictions that we can't do these things ... too many people who will talk about us if we tried'. In this instance resistance wasn't active, but it was powerful. These older relatives did not need to speak or act to resist our interventions. Their assumed reaction was already undermining our plans.

The value of intersectional thinking

The fact that those resisting gender empowerment were other women leads us to a third, and I'd suggest critical, way to think about resistance, which is to understand it in 'intersectional' terms. By this I mean that we need to think about how *different forms of power overlap* in the communities we are working in, to see how gender, for instance, intersects with age, ethnicity, sexuality, religion, disability, literacy, and income. Gender is not, as Mohanty (1988) reminds us, 'an already constituted, coherent group with identical interests and desires, regardless of class, ethnic, or racial location or contradictions'. Instead, gender is part of a nexus of other power relations. So, for instance, women in a community may in general have less power than men, but there will be other forms of power that will benefit *some women* more than others. Older women, like the grandmothers we heard about above, may be more invested in, and benefit more from, existing domestic roles. Richer women may be able to grow the crops that agricultural extensions support, or to have land that can benefit from irrigation services. Women from a dominant ethnic group may feel more confident joining a new entrepreneurial initiative; those with more access to education, more comfortable with an app we have designed in the dominant local language.

Thinking in this intersectional way has a number of advantages. First, it reduces the risk that as we seek to address one kind of inequality, we inadvertently reinforce others. This is a common problem, as we have already hinted at and it is worth pausing to illustrate with a few examples. These include a scheme in Mozambique to help more women acquire land, but which ended up exacerbating inequalities between richer women, who had the money, connections, and confidence to take advantage of the scheme, and poorer women, who did not (Edström and Shahrokh, 2015). Another case is a pilot scheme in Indonesia's celebrated KDP programme that mandated half the places for women, but which ended up inadvertently reinforcing class differences. Van Domelen (2007: 45) recounts how 'voting was more likely to favor the village elites, and poor women were less likely to have their preferences reflected in the final choice'. In 2019 I had my own experience of this problem whilst helping my colleague Jamal Khadar and the charity Plan International (2020) to identify and support female-led activism and community work in West Africa. We found that the young women we identified, especially when relying on desk research, tended to come from comparatively wealthy families and had more access to education. Representation from poorer girls, from ethnic minorities, and from LGBT+ audiences was low. Great care was needed to ensure that support for the girl-led groups did not reinforce other hierarchies and forms of inequality.

The second benefit of an intersectional perspective is that it pushes us to be precise about where the roots of discrimination lie. The World Bank (2012) claim that almost two-thirds of the girls globally who are out of school are from ethnic minority groups in their own countries. The same report contains numerous other examples of intersectional discrimination: for instance, the proportion of women in Vietnam giving birth without pre-natal care is twice as high among ethnic minority groups as among the majority Kinh women; illiteracy rates in Guatemala are 60 per cent among indigenous women, double those of other women and 20 percentage points higher than indigenous men. Meanwhile, Edström and Shahrokh (2015: 26) note how 'sizeable gender pay gaps are compounded where poverty combines with other factors of social exclusion, such as ethnicity, caste, remoteness, race, disability, or sexual orientation'. Looking for, and reflecting on, these correlations between different forms of power and discrimination is useful because it immediately poses useful questions about the order and emphasis given to different factors (here gender and ethnicity) in our targeting and messages. Where, for instance, might tackling ethnic discrimination improve gender outcomes more effectively than starting with gender? Or vice versa?

Lastly, intersectional thinking helps us to explore ways of building wider coalitions of support for inclusive development. If we look beyond the binary of men versus women, for instance, to questions of class, ethnicity, or age, are there certain men who are naturally more supportive? Are there ways of framing our initiative that would unite men and women as a common group? One example of this I encountered early in my career was a group of men in rural India who were initially resistant when women in the area started running their own businesses, but who had become more supportive over time. This is because the women's activities had come to be seen as part of a broader story of the rise of *their community* versus traditionally richer and higher-caste neighbours. 'They are showing that *we* the poorest can do it', as one respondent described it (Fieldwork, Rajasthan, 2010). These men's allegiance to their area, class, and castes overtook the initial stance they took as men versus women, threatened by growing female power. As Hamaus and Edström (2015: 152) argue, 'intersectionality' also provides the exit route out of this patriarchal trap, as men's gender-based interests and identities can be overridden by other relational interests or identities – such as class, race, sexuality, ethnicity, etc. – or can possibly be transcended by broader beliefs in social justice for all.

Understanding inclusivity from the resister's perspective

The discussion above has started to hint at a rather uncomfortable but potentially productive idea: that we should take time to understand the perspective of those who may or do resist inclusivity and who perpetrate discrimination. This isn't an easy or inviting thing to do. Our instinctive reaction to people who constrain the ambition of their granddaughters, or exploit their poorer neighbours is often anger, or disgust. I have certainly felt these emotions myself. But unless we understand the motivations for marginalization and oppression, we may have limited chance of making progress. In the case of gender I have encountered a few people who discriminate against women and girls out of crass stupidity or malice. But I have come across many more who do so for reasons that can be understood – if not to any degree condoned – and reasons which vary widely. I have met men who discourage women from developing their business ideas because they feel frustrated with their own lack of progress at work.[8] I have met family elders who've stopped young women going to college because they are scared about their safety. I have met young men who can only characterize women as obedient wives, or shameless vamps, not just because they have limited imaginations, but because they have been discouraged from interacting with the opposite sex and their main experience of women comes from movies.

The purpose of unpicking these causes and motivations is *not to excuse* the behaviour, but to see how we might detonate it. In the examples above, we may want to consider how to help provide reassurance that women are safe to travel, how to give boys and girls more opportunity to interact securely, how to improve economic opportunities for men, or to challenge the portrayal of gender in media. On this last point, for instance, Smith et al. (2016) found that of 493 characters in popular Indian films only a quarter were female and in no film was a woman an active co-lead character. Of the male characters in the Indian films, 70 per cent were portrayed as employed, compared to 39 per cent of female characters. Women in these (largely PG) films were almost three times more likely than men to be filmed in sexy attire.[9]

It also leads us to think about how the dominant group themselves might benefit from reducing discrimination. In the case of gender, patriarchal norms and assumptions can damage men as well as women. (Or as Juliette Kristensen, of Goldsmiths College, describes it, 'the patriarchy is shit for everyone'.) Edström and Shahrokh (2015) argue that the notion of men's dominant social role as a provider not only limits women's opportunities at work but is also very damaging to men's psychological wellbeing. They argue that challenging this assumption can harmonize male–female relationships by taking pressure from men. Research by the non-profit Girl Effect in northern Nigeria shows how gender stereotypes constrain both male and female identities. They note how 'a man who is less educated/wealthy than his wife, or is seen to be doing "women's work" such as going to the market or running errands is called a "*Mijin Hajiya*" – a derogatory term for a kept man. Girls do not find this an attractive trait for a husband'.[10] The more one probes into the mechanisms behind gender discrimination, the more a simple model of oppression is replaced by something closer to R.D. Laing's 'knots', where 'dominant' and 'marginalized' groups are tied together in mutually destructive habits. Unravelling this mess often requires the active participation of both parties.

There are a number of encouraging approaches that show what this active participation can look like. In each case people who might potentially have resisted inclusive development are brought into the process of positive change.[11] The first is illustrated by a study by Ahmed in Bangladesh and cited by Edström and Shahrokh (2015). The project deliberately looked beyond binary male/female divisions and focused instead on how openness to change differed across the audience. During the research Ahmed drew out three broad groups of men in the sample:

1. 'More oppressive men'. These were men who were often hostile to gender empowerment initiatives and who, for example, 'showed violent responses to women's achievements related to microcredit programmes'.
2. 'Mixed men', who were willing to support their female relatives, but only with boundaries that the men set themselves.
3. 'High-minded men', who were men that had positive attitudes towards gender equality and wanted to support greater rights for women.

It was this last group of 'high-minded' men that Ahmed identified to help lead a change of norms within the community. His work highlights the value of segmenting attitudes within the potentially resistant group, rather than treating them as a single body.

The second example suggests the potential for 'social norms' as a means of bringing potential resisters on board. This study by Bursztyn et al. (2018) was conducted in Saudi Arabia, which has among the lowest female employment rates in the world (below 15 per cent). The researchers hypothesized that it was not a simple case of men resisting female employment. Their more subtle theory was that the majority of men actually support greater female participation, but simultaneously *under-estimate* the number of other men who agree with them. To test this premise they conducted an experiment with 500 men in Riyadh, who were asked to respond to a number of statements about women in the workforce. Half the men were then shown other participants' responses, whilst a control group were not. All were recontacted three to five months later. The researchers' initial hypothesis appeared to be confirmed. Across the sample, 72 per cent of men had under-estimated other men's acceptance of female participation. And the act of revealing to men that other men shared their views had a tangible effect. Where men had seen others' views their wives were now 5 per cent more likely to be working outside the home, whereas in the control group the rise was just 1 per cent. The authors conclude that 'providing information to update misperceptions about certain beliefs and social norms' may be a possible way to encourage women to work outside the home.

The third example comes from a number of successful programmes aimed at children and adolescents. Stern and Clarfelt (2015) report a programme called GEMS, first introduced to 6th- and 7th-grade students in low-income public schools in Mumbai. Outside facilitators ran discussions on gender roles, inequality, violence, as well as physical and emotional changes at puberty. Stern and Clarfelt (2015: 63) report that children in these schools were 'four times more likely to report gender-equitable attitudes, three times more likely to support higher education for girls, and more than twice as likely to oppose violence'. The programme has since been expanded to thousands of schools in Maharashtra and to secondary school students in Vietnam. It shows the potential efficacy of tackling discrimination from a young age, but also reminds us of the potentially long time-frames we need to consider when addressing engrained social problems.

Moving forward: 3D thinking and navigating dilemmas

The aim of this chapter has been to simplify and to problematize: simplify in the sense of making clear the vital importance of inclusivity in development; problematize in the sense of highlighting the major challenges of pursuing it in practice. The problems I find only intensify once we become lost in the daily difficulties of development work. Once immersed in a gender empowerment project, it can be hard to maintain the kind of 3D intersectional thinking that I've advocated above. With tightly defined goals and even tighter deadlines the subtlety of different power relations can get muddied and we are drawn back to simpler binaries like male versus female, or higher- and lower-income groups. To try to maintain more subtle, intersectional ways of thinking I have made a list of questions that I find useful to return to through the course of a project. These include:

- Why have we identified a particular group as marginalized or excluded? What are the measures on which they are not able to participate? In what ways are they likely to be left out?
- What differences are there within the marginalized group? How do other factors (including class, ethnicity, caste, gender, sexuality, religion) affect their experience of the issues and their ability to bring about change?
- Where are there examples of multiple exclusions and deprivations?
- What alliances and conflicts can we see within the group we see as marginalized?

- How might different people within this group benefit or lose from the change we aim to bring?
- What role can we give the groups we see as dominant, beyond problem, or gatekeeper? What active roles might we envisage and why would people adopt them?
- What are the different reasons why people in the dominant group are oppressing or marginalizing others? What do they stand to gain from this? How conscious or unconscious is this?
- Where would the dominant group want, or benefit from, change?
- What differences are there within the more dominant group? Who is most open to change?
- Where is there already change occurring within the dominant group and what is driving this?

The second thing we encounter in practice is constant dilemmas. We have just seen, for instance, how targeting more dominant actors, such as men and boys, can be effective in increasing gender equity. But if we want to make development more inclusive, is it not perverse to do so by investing in the relatively privileged? The answer is partly, I'd argue, a matter of what works: i.e. is investing in boys and men likely to lead to better results? But I believe we also need to think carefully again about the purpose of inclusivity. What are we ultimately trying to achieve? Imagine we discovered that in the region where we are working we could reduce domestic violence or improve women's nutritional intake more if we invested in boys' education rather than if we invested the same amount of resources in education for girls. Should we take this 'more effective' path? Our response is likely to depend on whether we see education as a means of achieving other goals, such as improving infant health and reducing gender violence, or whether we prioritize equality of education for its own sake. It is also likely to depend on how we value participation in development. If we believe that active participation and agency are essential aspects of development, do we prioritize female education, even if educating boys might be the more effective immediate instrument?

There are rarely simple or universal answers to such dilemmas (and we will return to how we can approach such choices in the last chapter of this book). What I think is important is to be aware of our own prejudices and assumptions – and how these frame how we see inclusivity. Earlier, I quoted a young woman who told us that she won't go to college because her grandmother and aunts won't let her. As a middle-class British man who grew up with strong female, and feminist, role models and who now spends part of his time teaching in higher education, my reaction is probably easy to imagine. All that the speaker is going to lose flashes in front of my eyes. What I don't see anything like so quickly is what she gains through her relationship with her extended family; what she might lose were she to go against their wishes; what else she learns and values learning outside of formal education. If I am going to be anything close to helpful I have to find a way to open my eyes to this.[12]

This brings us back to some of the tensions we explored in the previous chapter and the risk that outsiders from Europe and North America end up imposing an individualistic idea of empowerment on more collectivist cultures. Hickel (2014: 1356) criticizes many recent gender empowerment initiatives for this tendency, where they 'rely on assumptions about "freedom" that are particular to the Western liberal tradition, which focuses on achieving individual authenticity and self-mastery'. He warns that this may lead outsiders to undermine important communal behaviours and structures in the pursuit of an individual freedom that they in fact value more than the people they are hoping to help.

I would be wary of drawing such a blunt opposition between west and east, or north and south. But I believe Hickel's concerns need considering. Outsiders like myself who come from less communal cultures can be prone to seeing relationships and tensions in development as occurring between individuals. We are quick to identify where one person has had his or her rights infringed and to look for the goals and priorities people have *as individuals*. We need to approach this with care, taking more time to ask, in Nussbaum's words, 'whether the individual is the only bearer of rights, or whether rights belong, as well, to other entities, such as families, ethnic, religious, and linguistic groups, and nations' (1997: 274). This should influence both the methods we use to elicit opinion and how we interpret and weigh the views we hear. For instance, can we assume – as outside researchers tend to do – that the preference that a young woman states when sitting among her extended family is less authentic than the one she gives when interviewed alone?

The outcome of such reflections is not always straightforward. Trying to determine whether we are *uncovering* someone's desires to pursue their individual dreams, or *imposing* such a desire onto them takes us into deep philosophical waters. The ineffability of consciousness, or the extent to which we can comprehend the experience of another human being lie far beyond my expertise and word-count.[13] What I do know is the stakes involved in work of this kind are high. Narayan et al. (2009: 295) recount one story that captures the tensions we face here, and which I will quote in full.

> Melise, a 35-year-old woman in Chiksisi, Malawi, is among those who spoke of earning respect from her husband – but not without initial resistance. Her husband initially refused to let her take a loan for brewing and selling beer. 'He said that if I take the loan, I will become promiscuous. He beat me over this issue. What made me determined more than ever was the fact that I was not his only wife. I had discovered that he had another wife from Mozambique whom he married before me'. Melise went ahead and took the loan over her husband's objections, using the money to buy a bale of clothes to sell in the local market. The business earned her good money and, eventually, respect from her husband. 'He started being nice to me and started telling me that we should sit down and strategize on the way forward'.

How do we react to this story? Do we focus on the end-result of raised incomes, seemingly improved marital relations, and a successful female entrepreneur? Or on the hiatus during which one human being was repeatedly beating another for daring to make her own decisions? We outsiders can normally debate and measure our interventions from a safe distance, but behind the metrics used in development books and presentations are individual stories like this one. This is why when it comes to judging the risks of development work and its success and failures it should be insiders who have the strongest voices and the casting votes. We will return to this theme, and the myriad problems of making it a reality, many times in the pages that follow.

Notes

1. Of course, major differences can be seen across country and region. The OECD's survey of gender inequality (which looks at factors such as early marriage, inheritance rights, violence towards women, access to resources, and civil liberties) ranks Brazil 8th out of 86, India 57th, and Nigeria 79th. See <http://genderindex.org/ranking> [accessed 26 June 2020]. Similar differences can be seen in the UN's GDI and GEM measures, which compare male/female life expectancies, school enrolments, literacy, and incomes, and find more than 50 places between Brazil and India.
2. This is a major Indian government intervention that pays underemployed and unemployed people to work on community projects. See Drèze and Sen (2013) for an introduction to the scheme and its workings.
3. See, for instance, World Bank (2012: 35) for an account of the Mama Lus Frut scheme, where it was found that paying women directly for their work both empowered female farmers and improved the efficiency of collection. Another example comes from Naryan et al., who cite evidence suggesting that creating *equal* access to employment leads to a much bigger rise in incomes than simply increasing access to employment per se (2009: 118).
4. Narayan et al. (2000: 119) give a similar example of two villages in Andhra Pradesh, which have very similar types of infrastructure, climate, employment opportunities, and yet totally different levels of social cohesion and relationships between caste groups. They note how in one community 'over the past 10 years, social stratification seems to have declined sharply in Malkapur, and at the time of data collection the community was characterized by solidarity and unity', whilst only a few miles away they say 'social stratification is pervasive in Dhampur. Groups are demarcated strictly on the basis of their caste membership (untouchables, lower castes, backward castes, and upper castes) as well as their religious identity and education levels'.
5. The number saying they expected to work before marriage stood at 43 per cent versus 30 per cent in control villages; the number saying they expected to work after marriage but before having children was 30 per cent compared to 19 per cent, and the number expecting to work after their children have married was 34 per cent compared to 29 per cent.
6. See Van Domelen (2007: 36) for a full table of interventions.

7. Original study cited is Mukasa, G. (2000) 'Dealing with gender difference: the case of Redd Barna Uganda', MA Dissertation, Institute of Development Studies, University of Sussex.
8. For instance, Edström and Shahrokh (2015: 27) write that 'in a context of socioeconomic change, the breakdown of social and political institutions, and deepening poverty – widely held, and socially constructed expectations and norms of men as breadwinners and household heads fall into question. This is especially significant in a context of increased unemployment and low income, with men from poor and marginalised groups most affected by a "crisis of masculinity" ... Manifestation of this sense of insecurity has been observed as sexual control, aggressiveness, and violence against women to restore male dominance'.
9. This problem is far from unique to South Asia. The analysis of US and UK films found only 30 per cent in each case had a female co-lead and similar differences to India in how men and women were dressed. China, Japan, and Australia had the highest percentage at 40 per cent.
10. Girl Effect, research in Nigeria, 2013.
11. Other examples include a campaign called MenCare that has run in over 20 countries, including low- and middle-income countries such as Rwanda, Indonesia, Brazil, and South Africa. Hassink and Baringer (2015: 47) describe the range of activities, which include 'training healthcare workers to recognise and support men's positive roles in their partners' health; facilitating conversations with young men and women about sexual health and gender roles; running group counselling sessions with men to help prevent future violence against female partners; and launching community-wide campaigns'.
12. We should also be aware of how in the not-too-distant past, outsiders have used apparently benign interventions, such as encouraging female empowerment, to justify their own destructive agendas, like the imposition of colonial rule. Lila Abu-Lughod (2002) writes that 'many who have worked on British colonialism in South Asia have noted the use of the woman question in colonial policies where intervention into sati (the practice of widows immolating themselves on their husbands' funeral pyres), child marriage, and other practices was used to justify rule'. Similarly, she describes in early 20th-century Egypt, 'a selective concern about the plight of Egyptian women that focused on the veil as a sign of oppression but gave no support to women's education and was professed loudly by the same Englishman, Lord Cromer, who opposed women's suffrage back home'.
13. I find myself feeling like the heroine of *The Portrait of a Lady*, forced to listen to Madame Merle: 'fond of metaphysics, but reticent of making a bold analysis of the human personality'.

References

Abraham, Anita and Platteau, Jean-Philippe (2004) 'Participatory development: where culture creeps in', in Vijayendra Rao and Michael Walton (eds), *Culture and Public Action: An Introduction*, pp. 210–33, The World Bank, Washington.

Abu-Lughod, Lila (2002) 'Do Muslim women really need saving?' *American Anthropologist*, 104: 783–90 <https://doi.org/10.1525/aa.2002.104.3.783>.

Bernhardt, Arielle, Field, Erica, Pande, Rohini and Rigol, Natalia (2017) *Household Matters: Revisiting the Returns to Capital among Female Micro-Entrepreneurs*, [online], J-PAL Working Paper, <https://www.poverty-action. org/sites/default/files/publications/5187_Household-Matters-evisiting-the-Returns-to-Capitalgender_paper_Field_et.al_2017.pdf> [accessed 25 February 2021].

Brannen, Conner (2012) *Raising Female Leaders*, [online], J-PAL Policy Briefcase, <https://www.povertyactionlab.org/sites/default/files/publication/2012.03.28_Powerful_Women.pdf> [accessed 26 June 2020].

Bursztyn, Leonardo, González, Alessandra L. and Yanagizawa-Drott, David (2018) 'Misperceived social norms: female labor force participation in Saudi Arabia', [online], NBER Working Paper No. 24736, <https://www. povertyactionlab.org/evaluation/effects-misperceptions-social-norms-female-labor-force-participation-saudi-arabia> [accessed 23 May 2019].

Cornwall, Andrea (2008) 'Unpacking participation: models, meanings and practices', *Oxford University Press and Community Development Journal*, 43 <https://doi.org/10.1093/cdj/bsn010>.

Drèze, Jean and Sen, Amartya (2013) *An Uncertain Glory: India and Its Contradictions*, Princeton University Press, Princeton.

Edström, Jerker and Shahrokh, Thea (2015) 'Poverty, work and employment', in J. Edström, A. Hassink, T. Shahrokh and E. Stern (eds), *Engendering Men: A Collaborative Review of Evidence on Men and Boys in Social Change and Gender Equality*, pp. 24–38, EMERGE Evidence Review, Promundo-US, Sonke Gender Justice and the Institute of Development Studies.

Gambhir, Varinder and Kumar, Prerna (2013) *How the People of India Live with Climate Change and what Communication can do*, [online], BBC Media Action, <https://downloads.bbc.co.uk/rmhttp/mediaaction/pdf/climateasia/reports/ClimateAsia_IndiaReport.pdf> [accessed 24 June 2020].

GSMA (2018) *Digital Identity for Smallholder Farmers: Insights from Sri Lanka*, [online], <https://www.gsma.com/mobilefordevelopment/wp-content/uploads/2018/03/DigitalIdentity_SmallholderFarmers_SriLanka.pdf> [accessed 22 February 2021].

Hamaus, Julia and Edström, Jerker with Shahrokh, Thea (2015) 'Public and political participation', in J. Edström, A. Hassink, T. Shahrokh and E. Stern (eds), *Engendering Men: A Collaborative Review of Evidence on Men and Boys in Social Change and Gender Equality*, pp. 151–65, EMERGE Evidence Review, Promundo-US, Sonke Gender Justice and the Institute of Development Studies.

Hassink, Alexa with Baringer, Laura (2015) 'Fatherhood, unpaid care and the care economy', in J. Edström, A. Hassink, T. Shahrokh and E. Stern (eds), *Engendering Men: A Collaborative Review of Evidence on Men and Boys in Social Change and Gender Equality*, pp. 39–53, EMERGE Evidence Review, Promundo-US, Sonke Gender Justice and the Institute of Development Studies.

Hickel, Jason (2014) 'The "girl effect": liberalism, empowerment and the contradictions of development', *Third World Quarterly*, 35: 1355–73 <https://doi.org/10.1080/01436597.2014.946250>.

ILO (2012) *Global Employment Trends for Women*, [online], <http://www.ilo.org/wcmsp5/groups/public/---dgreports/---dcomm/documents/publication/wcms_195447.pdf> [accessed 26 June 2020].

Jensen, Robert (2013) *See Tomorrow's Jobs, Invest in Girls Today*, [online], J-PAL Policy Briefcase, <https://www.poverty-action.org/sites/default/files/publications/Jobs-for-Women-See-Tomorrows-Jobs-Invest-in-Girls-Today.pdf> [accessed 26 June 2020].

Kishor, Sunita and Gupta, Kamla (2004) 'Women's empowerment in India and Its states: evidence from the NFHS', *Economic and Political Weekly*, 39: 694–712.

Mansuri, Ghazala and Rao, Vijayendra (2012) *Localising Development: Does Participation Work?* World Bank Policy Research Report, World Bank, Washington.

Mohanty, Chandra Talpade (1988) 'Under Western eyes: feminist scholarship and colonial discourses', *Feminist Review*, 30: 61–88 <https://doi.org/10.1057/fr.1988.42>.

Narayan, Deepa, Chambers, Robert, Shah, Meera K. and Petesch, Patti (2000) *Voices of the Poor: Crying Out for Change*, Oxford University Press for the World Bank, New York.

Narayan, Deepa, Pritchett, Lant and Kapoor, Soumya (2009) *Moving Out of Poverty Volume 2: Success from the Bottom Up*, a co-publication of the World Bank and Palgrave Macmillan, Washington.

Nussbaum, Martha C. (1997) 'Capabilities and human rights', *Fordham Law Review*, 66: 273–300.

Nussbaum, Martha C. (2003) 'Capabilities as fundamental entitlements: Sen and social justice', *Feminist Economics*, 9: 33–59 <https://doi.org/10.1080/1354570022000077926>.

Oduro, Abena and Nabalamba, Alice (2015) 'Gender' in Mthuli Ncube and Charles Leyeka Lufumpa (eds), *The Emerging Middle Class in Africa*, pp. 149–69, Routledge, London.

Plan International (2020) *Girls' and Young Women's Activism and Organising in West Africa*, Plan International, Dakar.

Sen, Amartya (1999) *Development as Freedom*, Oxford University Press, Oxford.

Smith, Stacy L., Choueiti, Marc, and Pieper, Katherine (2016) *Gender Bias without Borders: An Investigation of Female Characters in Popular Films Across 11 Countries*, [online], Geena Davis Institute on Gender in Media, <https://seejane.org/wp-content/uploads/gender-bias-without-borders-full-report.pdf> [accessed 9 April 2021].

Stern, Erin with Clarfelt, Alice (2015) 'Education', in J. Edström, A. Hassink, T. Shahrokh and E. Stern (eds), *Engendering Men: A Collaborative Review of Evidence on Men and Boys in Social Change and Gender Equality*, pp. 54–73, EMERGE Evidence Review, Promundo-US, Sonke Gender Justice and the Institute of Development Studies.

Thomas, Tom, Kader, Moulasha and Preece, Rohan (2015) 'Lost policies: locating access to infrastructure and services in rural India', in T. Thomas and P. Narayanan (eds), *Participation Pays: Pathways for post-2015*, pp. 63–84, Practical Action Publishing, Rugby.

Van Domelen, Julie (2007) 'Reaching the poor and vulnerable: targeting strategies for social funds and other community-driven programs', *Social Protection Paper No 711*, World Bank, Washington.

World Bank (2012) *Gender Equality and Development: World Development Report*, World Bank, Washington.

CHAPTER 5

Selling the new: making change more attainable and attractive

Abstract

A combination of factors can make it difficult for poor people to embrace change: the risks development programmes ask people to take are often very significant; individuals and communities lack the agency to effect change; and the routines of life in poor communities are often very engrained, making it harder to engage with new behaviours. Development practitioners need to think more creatively about how to make change both more inviting and more practical. This chapter shows a number of ways to do this, drawing on practice and expertise from other disciplines, such as design, marketing, and behavioural economics. It explores methods of building individual and collective agency, how we can change perceptions of risk, and the importance of how we time our interventions. It highlights the surprising roles that aesthetics and entertainment can play in making solutions more intuitive and appealing and the value of hands-on or 'experiential' forms of learning.

Keywords: risk; agency; behaviour change; experiential learning; aesthetics

Introduction

To escape poverty people normally must embrace change. But if we look from the poor's perspective, there are good reasons to regard change suspiciously. The poor are very exposed to risk. They have few safety nets if something goes wrong. They have often suffered exploitation and corruption and they may be understandably wary of outsiders' motives. Furthermore, many development initiatives ask the poor to wait a long time for their pay-off. If I use this app to monitor and prepare my soil I might not see a return *for months*? If I sign up to keeping my son in school he might be richer in *five or ten years*? Behavioural science tells us that humans everywhere struggle to delay gratification, but when your immediate financial situation is difficult, a long-term pay-off feels even less motivating.

The previous chapters have shown us some important ways in which change can be made more practical and appealing. By designing more communal solutions and understanding the complexities of reaching marginalized people we can work 'with the grain' of life in poor communities. In this chapter I want to hone in and examine a number of more defined and practical ways we can encourage people to be comfortable with change and to trial our new initiatives. These are all approaches that have had some success, either in my own, or others' work. They are far from infallible and they are highly context specific, but they give us *options* we can use when planning and implementing a new initiative. I will briefly introduce them now:

- The first section investigates ways that we can help poor people to *mitigate the risks* they face when adopting our programmes and products.
- The second section looks at how we can build people's confidence in their ability to pursue and achieve new objectives, to *build their sense of agency* over their own future.
- The third looks at the ways we can make change more comfortable for poor audiences through small *tactical nudges and adjustments* to our designs – for instance, to ensure they fit with season and schedules within the community.
- The fourth section looks at the importance of *making our ideas more tangible*, examining ways that we can encourage learning by doing and hands-on interaction. I look at the challenges of designing for audiences who may have lower levels of written literacy but often higher levels of practical and craft skills.
- The final section explores the importance of *entertainment and aesthetics* in increasing people's appetite for change – factors that are often under-estimated when thinking about poor audiences.

It's obvious, I'm sure, that these five approaches are quite different from one another. They range from addressing deep psychological barriers to thinking tactically about how we design communication materials. I see them as a set of tools to choose from and combine according to the context in which you are working, rather than a programme to apply as a whole. In some cases, for instance, we may be able to 'nudge' people into experimenting with a new behaviour with a relatively small change to the situational factors that surround them. In other cases we may need to focus on engrained psychological barriers and help people to change how they see themselves and their own capacities. Rather than becoming wedded to a single approach, we should consider the specificities of each new context and weigh up how far the distinct tactics might work here and now.

Mitigating risk

When we ask poor people to trial a new programme, product, or service we are asking them to take a risk. It may seem a small risk to us, the creators, but it is a risk nonetheless. And life in a poor community is often already so filled with risks that people's appetite for new risk-taking is often blunted. This is a fundamental tension that many development initiatives struggle to solve. To see how destructive it can be, let's take a very common example, one which I've seen play out in the lives of many farmers I have met in countries around the world. Anna Schickele (2016: 1) describes it very clearly in a paper for J-PAL, which I will quote at length:

> In order to cope with unpredictable weather, farmers often plant low-risk, low-return crops instead of investing in more profitable crops that are more sensitive to weather. In India, farmers may plant sorghum, a low-risk crop, instead of groundnut, a higher-risk cash crop. Furthermore, farmers wary of bad weather may hesitate to make other investments in their farms, such as increasing fertilizer use. As a result, the threat of extreme weather can trap farmers in a cycle of low productivity.

'Trap' is precisely the right word here. To escape poverty these farmers need to take one or more calculated risks: to plant riskier but higher-return cash crops; to invest in fertilizer and other inputs. And yet they are understandably unwilling to do so. With little savings or social safety net to fall back on, why would you take the chance of losing your crop to the changeable weather? An obvious solution to this problem – and one which many people have explored – is insurance. If farmers can be encouraged to take out insurance, they can then take the risks on new crops and inputs more safely. And indeed J-PAL's work has found that when farmers *do* take out weather insurance they are more likely to avoid the destructive trap Schickele describes, since they feel emboldened to plant higher-risk but more profitable crops and in turn they make more money.

The problem is that our solution to risk (insurance) is *a risk in itself.* If you live on a few dollars a day then you are wary of spending your meagre income on anything new, especially the unproven and rather abstract promise of an insurance payout – versus the obvious attractions of, say, some food to eat. When you talk to farmers about the idea of insurance many question whether payouts will actually be made. Their scepticism can mount, as sometimes happens, when some farmers experience drought even as the nearest measuring station records rain. From the farmer's point of view it is understandable that take-up of weather insurance remains very low in many poor communities.

What can we do then when we reach this kind of double bind? Schickele's (2016) paper identifies some ways to start the chain of positive risk-taking, looking at interventions that have helped set it under way. The first trick is not complex: it is to reduce the financial costs involved in the risk. Thus, a study she cites in Ghana found that when the price of insurance was reduced to a third below the market price, coverage rose from 18 per cent to 45 per cent. Another study in India found a 75 per cent discount pushed take-up to 60 per cent.[1] Sometimes to ask the poor to take a risk, we may need to be prepared to offer substantial financial incentives.

There are also, though, more subtle ways of encouraging this form of positive risk-taking. One is to increase the amount of control and visibility available to the user. Schickele (2016) argues that the structure of weather insurance could be changed, so that payments are based on whether someone has experienced actual drop in yields, rather than on the evidence of extreme weather. This would address concerns that base stations may not accurately reflect individual circumstances.

The *timing* of interventions is also a way of making experimentation with new ideas more appealing and manageable. Work by Mani et al. (2013) suggests that people's critical reasoning declines in moments of acute poverty, making it less likely they can assess risks accurately. The researchers found that after farmers had been paid for their harvest their cognitive reasoning skills were significantly better than those who had not yet been paid. They conclude that when people are suffering from immediate and acute poverty it leaves them with less mental capacity for assessing new ideas or making critical assessments of them. One very successful trial in Kenya (Schickele, 2016) found that farmers were much more likely to buy insurance if they could pay for the product at harvest time, with the premium *deducted* from the yield of their harvest, rather than actively paid up front. This relatively small tactical shift increased adoption dramatically from 4.6 per cent (for the full price up front payment product) to 71.6 per cent with the deduction.[2] Not only did it make payment terms easier, it also made the risk feel less daunting; signing up for a future deduction is likely to seem less intimidating than making an immediate payment. These small tactical changes to design made a big difference – a premise we'll explore in more detail in the next section.

Last, it can help to look at the broader social and economic dynamics that are affecting our audience's attitudes to risk. Most obviously, attitudes to risk will fluctuate according to economic highs and lows and political in/stability. But we should be alert to how more micropolicies can shift attitudes to risk. For instance, there is evidence (Lichand, 2010) that when governments introduce Conditional Cash Transfer programmes this increases levels of entrepreneurial risk-taking among poor people. Lichand suggests that 'because they are guaranteed to receive the transfer irrespective of what happens with their business, from success to bankruptcy, individuals could be more willing to engage in risky activities.' National and regional policy choices may lie far beyond the control of our own work, but we should still take into account their likely effects.

Helping to build 'agency'

Oscar came to meet us at the end of the road. Giving us directions to his house would have been futile – like telling someone who had never seen a video game how to succeed at Pokémon. He was waiting for us at the end of the asphalt, where the official city ran out and the buses stopped running. A lot of the kids to whom he introduced us along the way rarely crossed that line, he explained. When he had run a trip into the city last month, they had returned a little wide-eyed with the stories of elevators and sky scrapers. 'There is an invisible wall that surrounds the community', he tells us. At Oscar's home he invited us onto the roof. Like a lot of Brazilians he was building his house level by level, and from the top of floor 2, surrounded by bricks and bags of cement, he pointed out two schools to us: the one surrounded by trees two miles away where he used to work as a warden; and the one where his kids went to school. He sometimes feels like he should go back to college and finish his studies, but 'I think about it and just can't picture myself in a classroom... I know that I'm contradictory because I can't face going to school, but I'm always telling the kids they have to go!' If his faith in education is total, his faith in educators is much more partial. He and the other leaders of the community have had a number of run-ins with their school's Principal, who has been disparaging about the prospects of children from the favela. Fed up with being dismissed and patronized, they downloaded the Brazilian Constitution from the web and referred her to the rights it grants to all children. She has started treating them rather differently since then (Fieldwork Sao Paulo 2009).

Building 'agency' may seem an airy goal for development, compared to, say, building schools or hospitals. And yet these psychological traits are strongly associated with escaping poverty. When Narayan et al. (2009) analysed why certain people had crossed the poverty line, they found a significant association between people's confidence in their abilities and their actual ability to raise their incomes. They describe how in Bangladesh, for instance, a '2-unit increase in individual control is associated with a 15 percent increase in the probability of moving out of poverty' (2009: 29). Of course we can't be sure which way the relationship works – it could be that when incomes rise self-confidence rises as a result, rather than vice versa. Narayan et al.'s conclusion, though, is that the relationship is two-way; just as rising incomes boost confidence, so confidence can affect people's ability to improve their income and wellbeing.

Others with extensive field experience agree. Paul Polak, who interviewed over three thousand poor farming families across Asia, Africa, and Latin America, concluded that a lack of agency was often critical, arguing that 'many people have become so used to being poor that they have lost hope about anything changing' (Polak, 2008: 142). Polak illustrates his argument with a story, in which he took a group of farmers from a poor Maharashtrian village to meet an entrepreneurial farmer who was living only a few kilometres away. He recounts how the latter agreed to teach the farmers what he knew, 'but they were reluctant to take advantage of the opportunity. They listed a litany of obstacles that were real enough, but the farmers seemed to lack enough entrepreneurial spirit to overcome these obstacles' (2008: 142). A man as spirited and entrepreneurial as Polak cannot help letting a sliver of frustration slip into his description. But he is also sensitive to why such passivity creeps in. Without money it is harder to choose freely. And without the habit of making active choices, a sense of powerlessness can grow.

The poor themselves also reference agency as a vital requirement for moving out of poverty. Narayan et al. (2009: 130) write that 'people in our study repeatedly stressed the importance of personal agency. Over and over, they said that self-confidence, a sense of control over one's own decisions, and a sense of "I can do it" are what allows a person to move up' (2009: 130). The authors conclude that 'psychological self-efficacy is often the most important precursor to action, and the magnitude of effects reflected in our quantitative data confirms the importance of personal agency and aspirations in poverty escapes' (2009: 171). Agency is also, as writers such as Alkire (2009), Nussbaum (2003), and Sen (1999) have long argued, not just an instrument for progress, but an intrinsic good.

If empowerment and agency matter, how then might we think about building these qualities? I will look at some methods we can employ in one moment. First, I want to pause and reflect briefly on what it is exactly we are building. 'Agency' and 'empowerment' have become widely used terms in development, but they are defined in quite varied – and sometimes vague – ways. In a review of these concepts, Alkire notes over 30 different definitions of empowerment by different development scholars and she suggests that agency is 'inescapably plural in concept' (Alkire, 2009: 456). Alkire's own definition of agency, however, captures succinctly what I am interested in here, which is as follows: 'a person's ability to act on behalf of what he or she values and has reason to value'.

I'd argue that the second part of the definition ('what she values and has reason to value') is particularly vital for our purposes. For there is a risk that as outsiders we design initiatives to boost people's ability to pursue goals they actually don't care much about. A woman may not be involved in household spending decisions because she is bullied out of them by her husband, or because she's more interested in exercising her agency elsewhere. As Alkire points out, 'people may prefer *not* to be bothered with certain decisions but delegate them to others' (2009: 464). We may decide that ultimately we want to try to persuade people to care more about these areas, but we need to be clear that this is what we are doing and consider the ethical and practical challenges that come with trying to change people's minds – issues we will return to in Chapter 7.

Coming to the question of *how* we build agency, an important first step is to identify how far a lack of agency is actually an issue in the context where we are working. Fatalism can be a major problem in poor communities, as the examples above reflect, but it is far from all-pervasive and it tends to correlate with certain, logical factors. First, it can be a more serious issue when a community is facing threats that originate from far outside their own community. For instance, a BBC Media Action survey in India (Gambhir and Kumar, 2013) found that 69 per cent of respondents believed that *no response* they made to climate change would make a difference to the problem.[3] Second, the problem is unsurprisingly more serious among the socially and economically excluded, such as the long-term under/unemployed. The sociologist Alcinda Honwana (2012) cites data suggesting that 39 per cent of unemployed young people in Africa had given up actively searching for a job.[4]

She argues that growing numbers of young people on the continent are stuck in a passive state she terms 'waithood', one where 'the possibilities for long-term self-projections are foreclosed [and] young people have few expectations beyond the present' (2012: 29–30).[5]

How, then, might we help people to address a lack of agency when it does occur? An important initial consideration is whether one takes an individual or communal approach.[6] Do you try to increase individuals' own self-confidence, or to build a sense of confidence among a whole community? A good example of the former is explored by Ashraf et al. (2016), who looked at whether agency-building initiatives could address one of our recurring problems: how to help girls to stay in school. The project took place in Zambia, where girls are three times more likely than boys to drop out. The researchers hypothesized that helping girls to gain the confidence and skills to negotiate with their parents could help address this divide, and to test this premise they recruited girls from 29 schools in Lusaka and assigned them to one of three groups. The first group took part in lessons in negotiation and interpersonal communication.[7] The second group had no extra activities assigned, whilst the third were invited to a girls' 'safe space' to spend time with other girls and a local female coach.[8] Researchers found that several months after the programme girls in the negotiation groups had higher school attendance rates, better exam scores, and lower pregnancy rates. These girls also had a better understanding of negotiation tactics when questioned about these directly. In comparison there was no improvement in these measures among the control and 'safe space' groups. There was, though, a caveat to these findings. The researchers found that the programme had a much stronger effect on girls with higher educational abilities. In contrast, girls with lower aptitude for education were less likely to learn to negotiate to stay in school. This highlights a potential pitfall of individual agency-building. If we don't consider people's differing ability to take advantage of the initiative we can end up perpetuating, or even increasing inequalities within the audience.

An alternative approach, then, is to look at how we can increase people's *collective* sense of agency. Given the highly communal nature of life in many poor communities, the degree of shared resources and mutual self-reliance, such a focus can often make sense. Mathie and Cunningham emphasize this point in their review of community development success stories, noting how 'many of the cases also illustrate individual agency as it relates to collective agency' (2008: 3). One pioneering methodology here is the Asset Based Community Development approach, or ABCD (Cunningham, 2008; Mathie and Cunningham, 2008; Neumann, 2008). It involves starting every project by focusing not on the problems in a community, but on the strengths and assets that the community has and on progress that the community has made. These assets and successes may be barely recognized, not widely known or celebrated, but discussing and then capturing them in a form that people can see and return to helps members of the community recognize their individual and collective potential to make changes. Detailing the results of this exercise in the Tigray region of Ethiopia, Cunningham describes how it began with a process of asset identification, which captured 'individual skills, the various formal and informal associations in the community... and the community's physical assets and natural resource base'. He notes how 'once all the diagrams, inventories, and maps had been hung in the farmer's training centre, community members took pride in showing them to visitors – particularly to members of nearby communities' (Cunningham, 2008: 276).

Building collective agency can also mean building a community's sense of what they can demand from outside actors. In fieldwork I have often heard people talk about their powerlessness in relation to formal agencies, especially local government. 'We are ignored; we don't know the right people and we don't know how the system works', is how one respondent in rural India described the problems of their village to me (Fieldwork, 2010). A major reason why poor people can feel powerless in this way is that they are unaware of their rights as citizens – to education, health, social security, protection. As Narayan et al. write, 'Poor people are acutely aware of their lack of information and lack of contacts to access information. Across countries, poor men and women discuss how these put them at a disadvantage in their dealings with public agencies, NGOs, employers, traders and lenders, and contribute to their feelings of powerlessness' (2000: 237).

A number of projects have sought to tackle this by raising poor people's awareness of their status as citizens, who should expect and can demand better services as a matter of right. This can often mean creating practical tools that help hold government to account. Narayan et al. (2009) cite a programme in Bangalore to introduce 'citizens report cards', aimed at 'revolutionizing the manner in which city residents relate to service providers' (2009: 261). Another example of citizen reviewing is described by Drèze and Sen, who claim that 'Thailand has made huge and rapid progress in universal coverage of healthcare for all through radical health initiatives, helped by interactive reviews of the problems encountered by citizens at the receiving end' (2013: 18). Banerjee and Duflo (2011) give another example from Brazil, where, since 2003, 60 local governments are drawn at random in a televised lottery to have their accounts audited. The results are then put online and publicized in local media. Whilst not an obvious high water mark in entertainment television, it is having a measurable effect on how people vote. Politicians who had received negative reports just before an election were 12 per cent less likely to be voted back in. Those who had a good audit just before an election were 13 per cent more likely to be returned. Banerjee et al. ran a similar study in poor areas of Delhi and found similar results (Banerjee and Duflo, 2011).

Tactical nudges – making change friction-free

Mitigating risk and building a sense of agency sound like grand projects, which potentially could take years, or even in the latter case generations, to achieve. What the previous sections have shown, though, is that both can sometimes be achieved by relatively small measures – changing the time of year that insurance is sold, giving people report cards to score their local government's service performance, for example. In the last decade there has been a lot of discussion about the potential to solve major social problems using small but creative innovations of this kind (Thaler and Susstein, 2008; Heath and Heath, 2011; Karlan and Appel, 2011). Advocates suggest that wide-scale behaviour change can be achieved if we understand people's everyday habits and assumptions very acutely and design small, tactical nudges that subtly – and often unconsciously – push people towards making 'better' choices. In this section I want to explore some of the ways that this line of thinking is being applied to poverty reduction and the lessons that we can draw from work so far. How might small, tactical interventions encourage people to embrace change and adopt new programmes and products? What are the limitations of this approach?

I began the book with the surprising difficulty of introducing clean water initiatives. One way of responding to the challenge would be to try to persuade people to perceive the risks and benefit differently – to tackle engrained beliefs about water usage and to reassure people about the safety and value of chlorination. Another course is to look at very small practical design interventions that change people's behaviour, without requiring them first to change their minds. Banerjee and Duflo (2011) cite a famous example of the latter developed by Michael Kremer. It addressed one of people's major barriers to chlorinating their water, which is how to gauge a dose that is high enough to make the water safe, but not so high it wastes money, or makes the water taste horrible. Kremer's solution was to install 'one turn' chlorine dispensers next to village wells, which provide the right quantity of chlorine with every turn. This simple intervention was, Banerjee and Duflo write, 'the cheapest way to prevent diarrhoea among all the interventions for which there is evidence from randomized trials' (2011: 66).

Small behavioural interventions have been explored around another of our signature problems: encouraging families to keep girls in school. We've seen that the problem lies partly in deep-set cultural attitudes towards gender. But research shows that there are also simpler, physical causes and potentially smaller, tactical solutions. Studies in Pakistan and Afghanistan (both countries with persistently low female enrolment) show that if girls live near a school they are *much* more likely to attend. In Pakistan 500 metres difference in distance can affect female enrolment by 20 percentage points (World Bank, 2012). Another study run in both countries showed that girls who lived next to a school were just as likely as boys to attend it (World Bank, 2012). Researchers theorize that it is parents' fears about girls travelling to school that is keeping attendance down and that if these fears could be assuaged, attendance would rise. This would appear fertile ground for smart tactical interventions that make the school journey visibly safer for girls. A study of female employment in Ecuador (cited Robb, 2002) provides a useful parallel for how such practical approaches could work; when street lighting was improved and guards added to government buses the number of women working out of home rose significantly. Change here did not rely on confronting the complexities of cultural attitudes to gender and employment, but on making some relatively small changes to the physical infrastructure of the city environment.

We saw above that one effective tactical change is often adjusting the *timing* of interventions so that they fit more naturally with the cycles within poor people's lives. The weather insurance case above is a classic example. Another study in Zambia (cited Robb, 2002) found that school fees were currently being demanded at a time of year that caused maximum economic stress for households. Simply by changing the time of payment, the government was able to remove financial pressure on the poorest and make it more likely for children to remain in school. A study in Kenya by Duflo et al. (2011) showed that farmers were significantly more likely to invest in a voucher that would give them fertilizer in the future if it was sold to them just after the harvest when they had money available.

There is obvious appeal in this story that has been unfolding. Development is a world of constrained budgets and enormous, intractable problems. So the prospect of clever, small-scale disruptions with outsized impacts is naturally alluring. But there are limitations to this approach too. The first, most fundamental problem, is that they work in some contexts much better than others. They are a useful tool, but not the whole toolbox. The examples above were effective because they addressed problems rooted in behaviour more than knowledge. The farmers in Kenya didn't appear to need a lot of persuasion to be convinced to use fertilizer, they just needed it to be more practical to buy it. Duflo et al. (2011: 1) write 'at harvest time, when farmers have available cash, they may not be motivated to buy fertilizer, and pre-purchasing it may be inconvenient. Later in the season, when it is time to apply fertilizer to crops, farmers may find that they do not have enough money left to buy it'. This assumption is reinforced when we learn that farmers reverted to their previous habits once the programme was ended.[9]

The problem is that in other contexts a behavioural intervention may not be enough. For instance, I've conducted research on female employment in Nigeria and India that identified similar findings to the Ecuador study just cited. Here, too, fear of crime discouraged young women from working outside the home. But the reasons women didn't take up external work also included long-standing cultural assumptions about gender roles, which many women had tacitly absorbed and enforced themselves. Recall, for instance, the stereotype of the *Mijin Hajiya* or 'kept man' described in the previous chapter. Here, as in Edström and Shahrokh's work, 'patriarchal constructions of men as providers, such as the male "breadwinner's" role have significant implications on the gendered construction of paid and unpaid work within households, markets, and communities' (2015: 25). With many of the women we met, a small, practical intervention of the kind that worked in Ecuador was less likely to be transformational on its own.

I am also wary about the magical thinking that can sometimes accompany the stories being told around behavioural interventions. Take, for instance, Save the Children's small, lateral intervention in Vietnam that involved cooking and eating shrimp and sweet potato leaves, which led to a very significant improvement in children's nutrition. This case study has been widely cited as an example of the power of small-scale interventions and of creative approaches to solving poverty, one which led to 65 per cent of children from participating families being better nourished (Heath and Heath, 2011). This is obviously an excellent result and one based on thorough research – and a large number of very well-coordinated face-to-face interventions. However, not every problem can be cracked in such a dramatic fashion. An NGO recently told me a sweet potato story that is more representative of the realities of development work. They believed they had identified an effective way to reduce sight loss amongst rural farmers in a region of Africa where white sweet potato was a major food crop. The NGO knew that this had far less beta-carotene than orange sweet potatoes. If they could just get farmers to switch from white to orange, then their Vitamin A intake would rise significantly and sight-loss rates would fall. It seemed a simple solution and a straightforward task for communication. In practice it was nothing of the sort. Farmers, who for years had grown the same crop, were unsure about the new variety being offered and sceptical about the magical-sounding correlation between orange vegetables and long-term macular health. The NGO had to revisit their plan and consider how to overcome these barriers to adoption. Whilst there are occasional dramatic sweet potato leaf moments, more often progress is of the orange sweet potato kind: humbler and more iterative, a process of listening and observing, revising, and reworking to try to find a solution that works.

The last caveat takes us back to the question of agency. In most of the case studies above change has been encouraged through sleight of hand – by making it easy for people to change their behaviour with minimal effort – rather than through an explicit and open discussion of the merits of change. Improved street lighting, automatic deductions, and post-harvest vouchers made it easier for women to go to work and farmers to buy insurance and fertilizer. They do so without any of these individuals having to reflect on the merits (or otherwise) of this change. Advocates of the behavioural approach point to this as a strength of the method; it makes it more efficient in time and money than consciously persuading people. Furthermore, the examples above may all seem to have positive outcomes: in each case they are helping people to earn more money. But we have seen already the problems that come from outsiders judging what is 'good for' poor audiences. It's not impossible to imagine contexts where the women 'nudged' into work actually saw their quality of life decline as they are obliged to combine their new work with the vast majority of domestic tasks in the home. In fact, Chapter 4 showed how this precise problem can occur. If we focus all our energy on nudging someone's behaviour and not on understanding their individual experiences and opinions, it is much more likely that we will meet with unintended consequences. We need to be cautious, I would argue, about behavioural interventions that accelerate change without engaging people consciously in a conversation about this change.

Designing tangibly

Ignacio's family are no longer poor, but the neighbourhood is. The third time that thieves broke into his house, Ignacio had had enough. It took nearly a month's work, he emphasises, but he now has a home-security system of which he is proud. Made from scratch, but boasting six different cameras, controlled from his phone and from the two old TVs in his house, it is a masterpiece of DIY engineering. Hence our surprise when we ask him, offhand, if he can look up something for us on the internet. This hugely intelligent and resourceful man sits uncomfortably at the computer for 30 seconds. It feels much longer. The mouse hovers uncertainly. Then he stands up, calls out for his young son for help. 'Computers are impossible', he tells us, 'things always seem to be hidden under one thing or another' (Fieldwork Brazil, 2009).

Wilson lives nine miles from the nearest town, nine miles of untarmaced road away. Wilson goes there during harvest time, the five weeks or so in which he makes three-quarters of his annual income, withdrawing hundreds of dollars at a time. There aren't many robberies in this part of East Africa, he says, but you never know. I am watching him nodding sceptically as the local facilitator outlines the idea of payments directly to his mobile phone; they would be safer, save him time, reduce the temptation to spend too quickly. I try to maintain a neutral, but encouraging face. At the back of my mind though is the story I've just heard that farmers who have recently switched to mobile money payments have being going into banks with their phones, asking to withdraw it all as cash, counting it and then paying it in again. They wanted to check it was there, my colleague explained (Fieldwork Tanzania, 2017).

The meeting with Ignacio took place during a long-running project to develop digital services for low-income audiences and in particular to find ways of giving poor people better access to digital information. The day at his house helped crystallize my growing realization that my colleagues and I were presenting our 'helpful' online information in ways that were singularly unhelpful to our audience. Far too often our ideas mirrored the offices and colleges that I knew, rather than the worlds that the intended users inhabited. The software we were envisaging employed indexes, folders, and pages: a structure instinctively familiar to us from books, paperwork, and 'knowledge work'. When our users encountered our ideas they often seemed incredibly abstracted; and they were, because they were the products of an incredibly abstract culture.

The majority of development work unfolds in ways that reflect life in the global north: it is done on Post-it notes, lecture notes, flow diagrams, PowerPoint presentations, journal articles, and books such as this one. Development work in the north leans towards abstraction, long written descriptions, conceptual modelling, often dense quantitative data. It is practised by people who talk about silos and pipelines but who would be hard-pressed to draw, let alone make, a basic grain storage unit or a simple check valve. The worlds of the poorest are not simpler but they are, in general, more oriented around physical things. Much of people's daily work is manual.[10] The majority of people's knowledge comes from learning through doing. Books and written material are rarer, and written literacy, lower,[11] whilst artisanal skills are often far more developed and refined. People's aspirations also lean towards the concrete and the immediate: as Kottack writes (1985: 438), 'their goals are not abstractions such as "learning a better way, progressing, increasing technical know-how, improving efficiency"... Rather, their objectives are concrete, limited, and specific: increasing yields in a rice field, amassing enough food and cash to host a ceremony, getting a child through junior high school'. This reality is reflected in the following comments from a man in rural Ethiopia talking about the impact of participative development in his community and quoted by Cunningham (2008: 287):

> To date, we have carried or driven six members to the clinic in time to prevent their deaths. We have replaced two oxen and three cows. We have also been able to give money to one member to build his home. Initially, we began our savings by contributing 20 cups of grain each and five ETB during the rainy season. The grain was used by the members in times of need. They were expected to give back double what they took at the next harvest period. We now have 30 quintals of grain saved. At the end of each season, we sell the remaining grain to make a profit for the group.

This is how a lot of development plays out on the ground: in grain stores and rainy fields, on the trips along bumpy roads carrying neighbours to a distant clinic. It may involve complex questions of identity and agency, but its experience and currency is physical. I am not going to make the case here for the value of practical versus theoretical knowledge. Books like Crawford's *The Case for Working With Your Hands* (2010) and Sennett's *The Craftsmen* (2008) do this more than effectively. What I want to explore is how as outsiders we can suspend our learned inclinations to abstraction and make our interventions more intuitive to people who inhabit less abstracted worlds. How do we present ideas in more visual ways? How do we allow for hands-on learning? How do we work around problems with written literacy and make more use of insiders' skills?[12] In this next section, I will outline four broad ways we can do this:

- Prioritizing hands-on experience.
- Translating ideas into visuals.
- Distilling messages into practical guidelines.
- Building on people's existing physical habits.

First, we should try to develop opportunities for people to learn about our programmes through *hands-on experience*, to create opportunities for people to learn through using. When new ideas are introduced in this way, the results can be transformative. Chambers gives an example of how children with limited formal education can learn complex technological skills when given the chance for hands-on interaction, describing, for instance, 'children in rural Ethiopian villages given solar-powered laptops without instructions who have shown they can teach themselves through playful learning' (2014: 127).[13] A recent report by ISEAL highlights how agricultural training can work much more effectively through using 'demonstration plots' where farmers can see new inputs and techniques in action, rather than in abstract training guides. The Haller Foundation in East Africa use a 1,000 square metre demonstration plot where, they say, farmers 'are able to learn from this "finished article" and replicate it on their own nearby plots'. They report that 'we've seen this to be a highly effective way of motivating behaviour change amongst smallholders, showing them the tangible difference that Haller's techniques can have on crop production'.[14]

Second, we should look at how we use *visual material* in places where writing might typically be expected. Banerjee and Duflo (2011) describe how introducing a more visual voting system had a marked effect on participation and political choices in Brazil. The country had previously been using a reasonably complex paper ballot, where you had to write in the name of your chosen candidate. This was replaced with an electronic voting system, where you saw a picture of the candidate before you confirmed your vote. This saw the number of invalid votes reduced by 11 per cent, and, significantly, the profile of successful candidates changed too. The authors describe how 'the newly enfranchised voters were poorer and less educated; the politicians they elected were themselves poorer and less educated; and the policies they chose were more likely to be targeted to the poor' (2011: 247). Neumann et al. give another example of how a focus on visuals can have remarkable results. They describe how outside healthcare professionals trained members of the Palmeira community in north-eastern Brazil to conduct important health monitoring and education initiatives with their neighbours with no need for high levels of literacy. Instead of using text the outsiders used 'a sophisticated visual tool with simple pictures and symbols [that] was designed so that health data could be recorded by all these volunteers, regardless of literacy levels'. They describe how this 'helped people develop skills to monitor children's health and deliver basic care, whilst simultaneously raising awareness about the social, environmental, and economic factors affecting children's health' (2008: 47).

In other instances it can be a matter of *distilling material into shorter and more practically focused guidelines*, stripping out the theoretical and abstract and orientating advice around daily life. For example, a study by Drexler et al. (2014) showed how important, but potentially very abstract, accountancy training was much more effective when it was synthesized into shorter and practical 'rules of thumb'. The researchers ran a trial with over a thousand low-income business owners, who had previously expressed interest in having more training. The sample was divided into three groups: one that received no training, one that was given six weeks' traditional accounting training, and a third that was given very simple 'rules of thumb' training over five weeks. At the end of the trial participants who learned the rules of thumb were more likely to report separating business and personal accounts, keeping accounting records, and calculating revenues compared to participants who had received no training, *or those who had had the formal training*. The 'rule of thumb' group also appeared to be applying the accounting tools to the live issues of their business – increasing sales in weeks that had previously been identified as slow periods by an average of 18 per cent. Participants, it seems, had learned formal practices by being taught in an informal way.

Other initiatives have suggested similar potential. The UN cite an intervention in Nigeria which brought together religious leaders to develop a simplified version of Nigeria's 2014 HIV Anti-Discrimination Law. This distilled essential messages from the Act and combined them with examples from religious teachings to make an accessible message that could be spread through pamphlets and posters, as well as training 150 religious leaders to preach messages of tolerance to their followers.[15] The BRAC programme in Bangladesh (El Arifeen et al., 2013) is another good example of how simplified rule-of-thumb messages can bypass problems of literacy. Few in the rural audience could read proficiently, especially women who were a critical audience for many of the health programmes. As El Arifeen et al. describe, 'the perception was that illiterate women could not learn how to use oral rehydration therapy effectively and efficiently'. And yet by 1990, 11 years into the programme, 90 per cent of mothers in the 12.5 million households who had been visited knew how to prepare and give ORT. Van Domelen points to a number of other similar success stories using simple word-of-mouth approaches. She emphasizes the value of 'dissemination through alternate channels of local stakeholders like using community associations and women's groups to complement "official" channels' (2007: vii).

We should also look for where innovation in the global north is already moving towards the concrete and think about how we might employ these new elements in the global south. Whilst the Internet of Things is still a relatively nascent field, many people in the poorest communities may see it as a more logical starting point for access to information than our current dominant method of transmitting digital information via a series of screens. In his description of 'everyware' Greenfield (2006: 32) talks about processing power being 'deployed throughout local physical reality instead of being locked up in a single general-purpose box; and when interacting with it is largely a matter of voice, touch, and gesture, interwoven with the existing rituals of everyday life'. This is much closer to how many people in poor communities approach, learn, and use information.[16]

Last, we should think about how we can make use of the more *concrete habits or 'heuristics'* that the people we are working with use to navigate the world. Jan Chipchase (2008), for instance, investigates some of the ways that non-literate audiences employ physical cues to bypass the written word. He gives the example of bank notes and how non-literate people would use the scent and the texture of the notes to assess whether they were legitimate or not. Another example Chipchase gives is of semi-literate or non-literate people using different-coloured pens in an address book to indicate their different contacts' details. Rather than rely on a written language in which they struggle, people create their own codes. Chipchase argues convincingly that if we can understand these, not always obvious, non-written cues, there may be opportunities to build on them in our own designs in ways that are immediately intuitive to users.

Presentation matters: the role of entertainment and aesthetics

The need to make development solutions more tangible might be overlooked, but it isn't conceptually that surprising. Perhaps less intuitive is the role that aesthetics and entertainment can play in making anti-poverty solutions appealing. It is easy to imagine that poor people have little time to worry about aesthetics and presentational framing, that they care little about how the things we design to reduce poverty look, or feel, or sound. This can be a significant mistake, since aesthetics matter in the lives of the poor just as in the lives of the rich.[17]

Too often, outsiders don't spend enough time thinking about how to make anti-poverty initiatives either culturally engaging or aesthetically pleasing. Yet doing so can have a very significant effect on their adoption and value. Karlan and Appel (2011) cite an example from South Africa of how responses to a microcredit product were transformed by apparently 'superficial' changes, such as removing some of the details from leaflets, or adding pictures of attractive users. They remind us that 'when simple changes to a promotional mailer (like cutting out three rows on the table of sample loans) generate as much new business as drastic price cuts, you can't afford to ignore it' (2011: 47). Braginski describes how Nokia realized that pure functionality and price were not enough to attract low-income audiences to using mobile phones and that the organization needed to take the visual design of their products just as seriously as they would for middle- and high-income people. 'It wasn't just a case of using the simplest visual language, or the one that worked in the west... what the design meant in that market mattered' (personal communication, 2021). This is particularly true with younger and more urban audiences, who are more likely to be exposed to marketing and digital media and who are often becoming more interested in the visuals and iconography of branding. I was struck during a diary project with low-income urban youth in South Asia and West Africa how often their homework came back with the logos of brands – WhatsApp, Facebook – sketched in their margins. It is notable that development organizations who are targeting this audience, such as Girl Effect, are putting significant effort into organizing their development programmes into recognizable and consistent brands.[18]

Development practitioners also often under-estimate how important entertainment is in the lives of the poor. One of the initially most surprising findings from Banerjee and Duflo's work on the poor's finances was how much money those with little money may spend on entertainment. This account from their fieldwork in Morocco (2011: 36–7) brings this reality to life very vividly:

> We asked him why he had bought all these things if he felt the family did not have enough to eat. He laughed, and said, 'Oh, but television is more important than food!' After spending some time in that Moroccan village, it was easy to see why he thought that. Life can be quite boring in a village. There is no movie theater, no concert hall, no place to sit and watch interesting strangers go by. And not a lot of work, either ... it is clear that things that make life less boring are a priority for the poor. This may be a television, or a little bit of something special to eat.

Not only do poor audiences value entertainment more than outsiders often appreciate, entertainment can be the most effective way through which outsiders can promote their new ideas. We saw in Chapter 3 how Paul Polak's IDE has made substantial use of cinema and theatre. Van Domelen (2007) looks at a range of ways in which entertainment media, such as radio shows and live theatre, have been used to seed programmes in poor and remote communities. And a particularly striking example comes from work by GSMA (2016) developing agricultural services for farmers. These services offer tips from agronomic experts that, if followed, should significantly increase farmers' yields and profits. This is information that would surely *seem* to be valuable enough in itself to require no presentational sleight of hand or added spark. But research in Malawi found farmers are much more likely to engage with it if more effort is made to make it entertaining. This led to changes in presentation, such as in creating fictional stories set in farming communities, with elements of drama and music tracks. In a similar example from Bangladesh (GSMA, 2016: 66) researchers describe how at the start of the project 'agriculture was perceived as a very important and serious topic within the target community... Initially, a decision was made to present the content in a monologue style through narration by an agricultural expert'. However, they found that 'when an alternative conversational storytelling style was tested by the product and UX teams, the user feedback was positive and the VAS provider decided to migrate content to this new style'.

I would argue that as poor communities' exposure to media and consumer goods grows, we are likely to have to pay even more attention to entertainment and aesthetics. It's easy to assume that because our messages are more 'important' audiences will give them more attention. But in a world where access to the internet often outpaces access to clean water and sanitation we have to accept that our ideas for reducing poverty may often be competing for attention with a host of other appeals. As Karlan and Appel argue, 'actively marketing development programs does not mean misleading recipients or presuming that they cannot make good decisions on their own. It just means acknowledging that they're like anyone else: susceptible to both reason and to suggestion, subtle and otherwise' (2011: 53).

In conclusion: the power and limits of persuasion

This chapter has explored a range of tactics that can be used to encourage people to embrace new development initiatives and to spend their limited time and money on things they are uncertain about, whether investing their energy in learning new skills, their cash in inputs for their business, or their social capital in supporting their daughters to pursue their career aspirations. These tactics can all be effective, but we have seen that much of their effectiveness rests on context. What works with one initiative or one region may not work in another.

This chapter also shows clearly that the skills needed to create successful development initiatives are expanding. If we want to create programmes and products that are more attractive and useful to the poor themselves we need to learn from industries such as journalism, film, design, marketing, advertising. I hope this book will show how development practice can borrow and learn from these fields and will encourage those working in them to apply their knowledge to the pressing problems of poverty. But there are challenges when disciplines cross in this way. I share the concerns expressed by Schouwenberg (2017) about designers being encouraged to try to solve grand social problems from within the bubble of design. Meanwhile, marketing and advertising are understandably prone to hyperbole and drawn to magical solutions of the kind described just above. For those like me who have come to development work along this path we have to keep our hubris in check, recognize the limits of what we can do, accept that our skills address *some* parts of the problem, and listen to other experts – as well as, of course, to users.

Lastly, whilst I welcome the growing interest in how we can stimulate the 'demand side' of development, this needs to be combined with a clear-eyed assessment of what is being supplied. We may design beautiful or cleverly timed ways to make education more attractive, but if the teachers are often absent and the curriculum archaic and barely relevant, then increasing demand potentially becomes an act of bad faith: a process of tempting and manipulating people to take up services that are fundamentally flawed.

Notes

1. In comparison, it was found that training farmers in financial literacy also increased take-up, but the costs of training were greater than simply offering a discount. J-PAL's paper therefore argues that for insurance to evolve, subsidies may be needed, rather than relying on a commercial market to evolve.
2. They conclude 'this suggests that both a lack of cash and behavioral biases may prevent farmers from purchasing a product they want' (Schickele, 2016).

3. This is the paralysis that the sociologist Ulrich Beck (1992) captured in his notion of 'risk society', where the dynamics that affect us are nearly always distant and 'the unknown and unintended consequences come to be a dominant force in history and society' (1992: 22). Beck sees risks as unequally weighted towards those with least capital: 'like wealth, risks adhere to the class pattern, only inversely: wealth accumulates at the top, risks at the bottom. To that extent, risks seem to strengthen, not abolish, the class society. By contrast, the wealthy (in income, power or education) can purchase safety and freedom from risk' (1992: 45).

4. Survey by the United Nations Economic Commission for Africa (2005), cited by Honwana (2012: 53).

5. Jeffrey (2010: 11) references work in India, Niger, and Zambia that showed a similar tension: 'Educated unemployed men are often unable to marry... They frequently find it hard to leave home and purchase or rent independent living space'.

6. See Albert Bandura's classic work on agency and the differences between personal, social, and proxy agency. For instance, <https://www.uky.edu/~eushe2/Bandura/Bandura1989AP.pdf> [accessed 12 April 2021].

7. The negotiation training programme is available to view here <https://hbsp.harvard.edu/girls-arise/> [accessed 29 July 2020].

8. The inclusion of this third group allowed researchers to monitor the effect of girls simply spending time together with an adult role-model figure versus learning negotiation skills.

9. Duflo et al. (2011) argue that 'this indicates that SAFI's impact came from the features of the program itself, not because people learned about fertilizer through using it. This finding suggests that farmers need incentives to help them overcome procrastination every year'.

10. The World Bank cites that over half of the working population across sub-Saharan Africa work in agriculture. In India the proportion is 42 per cent. <https://data.worldbank.org/indicator/SL.AGR.EMPL.ZS> [accessed 29 June 2020].

11. The World Bank cites literacy rates of 66 per cent across sub-Saharan Africa and 72 per cent in South Asia. <https://data.worldbank.org/indicator/SE.ADT.LITR.ZS?name_desc=true> [accessed 29 June 2020].

12. Chipchase (2008: 80) points out that there are differing definitions of literacy. The UN define a literate person as someone who can 'with understanding, both read and write a short simple statement in his or her everyday life'. The Chinese government's 1993 definition was of the number of Chinese characters that an individual could read, as well as some understanding of basic accounting.

13. See <https://www.technologyreview.com/2012/09/13/18580/emtech-preview-another-way-to-think-about-learning/> for more details [accessed 12 April 2021].

14. <https://haller.org.uk/work/grow/farmer-demo-plot/> [accessed 22 February 2021].

15. Case study at <https://www.undp-capacitydevelopment-health.org/en/legal-and-policy/enabling-legal-environments/stigma-and-discrimination-reduction-programmes/> [accessed 26 February 2021].

16. The designer Ranjit Makkuni who worked for two decades at Xerox's Palo Alto Research Centre is now exploring this premise, building information-processing into everyday objects familiar to people in his native India. Rather than pushing the internet on a computer or tablet, he is incorporating digital information into the objects that people interact with on a daily basis, such as cycle rickshaws, cooking utensils, and jewellery.
17. See Narayan et al. (2000) for the prominence of appearance and aesthetics in their discussions with poor people.
18. See <https://impact.girleffect.org/> [accessed 22 February 2021].

References

Alkire, Sabina (2009) 'Concepts and measures of agency', in Kaushik Basu and Ravi Kanpur (eds), *Arguments for a Better World: Essays in Honor of Amartya Sen*, pp. 455–74, Oxford University Press, Oxford.

Ashraf, Nava, Bau, Natalie, Low, Corinne and McGrinn, Kathleen (2016) 'Teaching girls negotiation skills in Zambia' [online], Evaluation Summary at Poverty Action Lab <https://www.povertyactionlab.org/evaluation/teaching-girls-negotiation-skills-zambia> [accessed 18 June 2019].

Banerjee, Abhijit V. and Duflo, Esther (2011) *Poor Economics: A Radical Rethinking of the Way To Fight Global Poverty*, Public Affairs, New York.

Beck, Ulrich (1992) *Risk Society: Towards a New Modernity*, Sage, London.

Chambers, Robert (2014) *Into the Unknown: Explorations in Development Practice*, Practical Action Publishing, Rugby.

Chipchase, Jan (2008) 'Reducing illiteracy as a barrier to mobile communication', in James Katz (ed.), *The Handbook of Mobile Communication Studies*, MIT, Cambridge Mass.

Crawford, Matthew (2010) *The Case for Working With Your Hands*, Penguin, London.

Cunningham, Gordon (2008) 'Stimulating asset based and community driven development: lessons from five communities in Ethiopia', in Alison Mathie and Gordon Cunningham (eds), *From Clients to Citizens: Communities Changing the Course of their Own Development*, pp. 263–98, Practical Action Publishing, Rugby.

Drexler, Alejandro, Fischer, Greg, and Schoar, Antoinette (2014) 'Keeping it simple: financial literacy and rules of thumb', *American Economic Journal: Applied Economics*, 6: 1–31 <https://doi.org/10.1257/app.6.2.1>.

Drèze, Jean and Sen, Amartya (2013) *An Uncertain Glory: India and Its Contradictions*, Princeton University Press, Princeton.

Duflo, Esther, Kremer, Michael and Robinson, Jonathan (2011) *A Well-Timed Nudge* [online], J-PAL Policy Briefing <https://www.povertyactionlab.org/sites/default/files/publication/2011.9.30-Nudging-Farmers.pdf> [accessed 26 February 2021].

Edström, Jerker and Shahrokh, Thea (2015) 'Poverty, work and employment', in J. Edström, A. Hassink, T. Shahrokh and E. Stern (eds), *Engendering Men: A Collaborative Review of Evidence on Men and Boys in Social Change and Gender Equality*, pp. 24–38, EMERGE Evidence Review, Promundo-US, Sonke Gender Justice and the Institute of Development Studies.

El Arifeen, Shams, Christou, Aliki, Reichenbach, Laura, Osman, Ferdous Arfina, Azad, Kishwar, Islam, Khaled Shamsul, Ahmed, Faruque, Perry, Henry B., Peters, David H. (2013) 'Community-based approaches and partnerships: innovations in health-service delivery in Bangladesh', *The Lancet*, 382: 2012–26 <https://doi.org/10.1016/S0140-6736(13)62149-2>.

Gambhir, Varinder and Kumar, Prerna (2013) *How the People of India Live with Climate Change and what Communication can do*, [online], BBC Media Action, <https://downloads.bbc.co.uk/rmhttp/mediaaction/pdf/climateasia/reports/ClimateAsia_IndiaReport.pdf> [accessed 24 June 2020].

Greenfield, Adam (2006) *Everyware: The Dawning Age of Ubiquitous Computing*, New Riders, Berkeley.

GSMA (2016) *Agricultural Value-Added Services,Toolkit 2.0*, [online], <https://www.gsma.com/mobilefordevelopment/wp-content/uploads/2016/05/mAgri-VAS-Toolkit-2016.pdf> [accessed 29 June 2020].

Heath, Chip and Heath, Dan (2011) *Switch: How to Change Things When Change is Hard*, Thorndike Press, Waterville.

Honwana, Alcinda (2012) *The Time of Youth: Work, Social Change and Politics in Africa*, Kumarian, Virginia.

ISEAL Alliance (2019) 'Evaluation of the early impacts of the Better Cotton Initiative on smallholder cotton producers in Kurnool District, India', [online], <https://www.evidensia.eco/resources/17/evaluation-of-the-early-impacts-of-the-better-cotton-initiative-on-smallholder-cotton-producers-in-kurnool-district-india-final-evaluation-report/> [accessed 22 February 2021].

Jeffrey, Craig (2010) *Timepass: Youth, Class and the Politics of Waiting in India*, Stanford University Press, Stanford.

Karlan, Dean and Appel, Jacob (2011) *More Than Good Intentions, Improving the Ways the World's Poor Borrow, Save, Farm, Learn, and Stay Healthy*, Penguin, New York.

Kottack, Conrad (1985) 'When people don't come first: some sociological lessons from completed projects', in Michael Cernea (ed.), *Putting People First*, pp. 431–64, World Bank, Washington.

Lichand, Guilherme (2010) 'Decomposing the effects of CCTs on entrepreneurship', *Economic Premise*, 41 <https://doi.org/10.1596/1813-9450-5457>.

Mani, Anandi, Mullainathan, Sendhil, Shafir, Eldar and Zhao, Jiaying (2013) 'Poverty impedes cognitive function', *Science*, 341 <https://doi.org/10.1126/science.1238041>.

Mathie, Alison and Cunningham, Gordon (2008) 'Introduction' and 'Conclusions', in Mathie, Alison and Cunningham, Gordon (eds), *From Clients to Citizens: Communities Changing the Course of their Own Development*, pp. 1–10 and pp. 357–69, Practical Action Publishing, Rugby.

Narayan, Deepa, Pritchett, Lant and Kapoor, Soumya (2009) *Moving Out of Poverty Volume 2: Success from the Bottom Up*, a co-publication of the World Bank and Palgrave Macmillan, Washington.

Neumann, Rogerio Arns and Mathie, Alison, assisted by Linzey, Joanne (2008) 'Conjunto Palmeira: four decades of forging community and building a local economy in Brazil', in Alison Mathie and Gordon Cunningham (eds), *From Clients to Citizens: Communities Changing the Course of their Own Development*, pp. 39–62, Practical Action Publishing, Rugby.

Nussbaum, Martha C. (2003) 'Capabilities as fundamental entitlements: Sen and social justice', *Feminist Economics*, 9: 33–59 <https://doi.org/10.1080/1354570022000077926>.
Polak, Paul (2008) *Out of Poverty: What Works When Traditional Approaches Fail*, Berrett-Koehler, San Francisco.
Robb, Caroline M. (2002) *Can the Poor Influence Policy? Participatory Poverty Assessments in the Developing World*, World Bank, Washington.
Schickele, Anna (2016) 'Make it rain', *J-PAL, CEGA, and ATAI Policy Bulletin*, Abdul Latif Jameel Poverty Action Lab, Center for Effective Global Action, and Agricultural Technology Adoption Initiative, Cambridge Mass.
Schouwenberg, Louise (2017) 'Designers can contribute to a better world, but not if we dictate how they do it', [online], Dezeen, <https://www.dezeen.com/2017/10/18/louise-schouwenberg-opinion-designers-save-world-response-marcus-fairs-dutch-design-week-2017/> [accessed 26 February 2021].
Sen, Amartya (1999) *Development as Freedom*, Oxford University Press, Oxford.
Thaler, Richard H. and Sunstein, Cass R. (2008) *Nudge: Improving Decisions About Health, Wealth, and Happiness*, Yale University Press, New Haven.
UNDP (2004) *Unleashing Entrepreneurship: Making Business Work for the Poor*, UN, New York.
Van Domelen, Julie (2007) 'Reaching the poor and vulnerable: targeting strategies for social funds and other community-driven programs', *Social Protection Paper No 711*, World Bank, Washington.
World Bank (2012) *Gender Equality and Development: World Development Report*, World Bank, Washington.

PART III

When Communities Design Aid

Building on what exists: hidden infrastructure and scaled-up solutions

Abstract

One of the big mistakes we make in development is to miss the solutions that the poor create for themselves. Too often, outsiders assume we are innovating in a vacuum and so end up duplicating what already exists, or producing a new solution that is less well-attuned than the ones that people have made for themselves. In so doing we not only waste time and resources, we reduce local people to the passive role of recipients. This chapter examines how to identify, support, and build upon the poor's own solutions to poverty. It discusses the challenges of finding 'hidden infrastructure', the kinds of support that community solutions do and don't need, and the important questions to ask before 'scaling-up' an intervention and the pitfalls involved in exporting a local solution to new regions.

Keywords: asset-based community development; human-centred design; entrepreneurship; Jugaad Innovation; scaling-up

Introduction

Over time I've come to realize that the reason I believe so firmly in community-built solutions is that we know they *work*. Not work in the sense of providing effective return on investment, or delivering optimally when compared to others in a randomized control trial. Indeed, viewed in these terms they may be relatively ineffectual versus other means of, say, raising farm incomes or encouraging participation in schools. What I mean by 'work' is that they have slotted into daily life in our community; they are things that our people can – and do – use. They are accepted, or at least tolerated by our audience. They are alive, in motion, and they address a problem that some at least in the community believe needs to be solved. In this regard they are already one step ahead of whatever I as an outsider have drawn up in my elaborate plans and diagrams. Furthermore, any local solution that has taken hold is likely to be meeting more than one social goal – and almost certainly doing more than meeting its overt objectives. The group that raises farm incomes may also be a place that members swap labour and where frictions between different religious groups are at least partially set aside. Likewise, the informal transport network that helps girls get to school may also be a means of employment for marginalized people and an indirect source of information on markets in the local town. As Wilkinson-Maposa et al. remind us, poor people 'know something about resource mobilization and effective redistribution that serves *multiple purposes* – cohesion, insurance, risk mitigation and survival' (2005: 119, my italics). Most local solutions not only work in practice, they blend multiple benefits.

My central message then is a simple one: that at the start of any project – and well before we begin to design anything ourselves – we should spend considerable time hunting for, identifying, and understanding any local solutions that are already in place. I recognize that this is hard for outsiders to do. First, there is the problem of what exactly you are looking for. What counts as a solution and is your definition flexible enough to capture the things that may have been created on the ground? Next, how do you go about finding activities which may well not be documented in any form, or broadcast anywhere online? Can you rely on remote methods like desk research and expert interviews to establish whether local solutions exist, or do you need to make, or ask other people to make field visits? Then, there is the impossibility of proving a negative. Say you discover, as my colleagues and I recently did, that there is very limited evidence of grassroots female activists in rural Togo; does this mean there *really is* little out there, or (more likely) has your methodology just not allowed you to find it? At the end of the project I did not feel I could answer the question with real certainty.

Some core principles can help us with these difficulties. The first is to be very open about what kinds of groups and resources we are looking for. Imagine we are trying to establish, say, a new adult educational programme. It may be that we can see no evidence of such solutions on the ground, but before we regard this as a blank slate to design from we should recall that community groups tend to have multiple functions. Thus, a local savings group or farming cooperative may have no educational label, but a lot of education may be going on there nonetheless. In addition, it can often be helpful to look for those groups that have the greatest social capital, rather than those that align most neatly with our own project's goals. This is a clear lesson from experiments in Asset-Based Community Development (ABCD): that if you can find a local group that has social cohesion and momentum, then in time it can be the base for many new activities that branch off from its original purpose/s. This quote from a successful organizer in the East Cape, South Africa captures the organic way that diverse initiatives can evolve: 'you know, in small places, if there is a phone and a fax people will all flock there. They don't care if [the office is for] education or health or whatever. So the corner that I was using ended up being a community corner, instead of focusing on schools. Then it went so far that people came from the income-generating activities and business, coming here for faxes and phone and all those things' (Wilkinson-Maposa, 2008: 252).

One of the notable threads in ABCD work is how people in different locations have used different types of community group and activity as their foundation to build on. In Karnakata it was women's savings groups that were the cornerstone (Mathie and Cunningham, 2008). In southern Morocco it was an energy initiative (Iskander and Bentaleb-Maes, 2008). In Oromia in Ethiopia things began with a farming association (Cunningham, 2008). When working in a new community we need to be very open about where the social bonds, skills, and appetite for change may lie and about how our own plans might connect with less obviously related infrastructure.

This touches on two further important things to consider when looking for community infrastructure to build upon. First, that as Mathie and Cunningham (2008) emphasize, this infrastructure can include intangible as well as tangible assets – trust, strong relationships with neighbours, a sense of agency, and knowledge of rights. How can our intervention build upon these – and ensure it does not disrupt them? Second, in some communities, solutions will already be kinetic, alive, and here outsiders can look to support work already under way. But in communities where there is little already in motion, outsiders should not ignore what is latent. The ABCD approach shows the value of encouraging people to reflect on the local strengths and assets that may not have been recognized or considered before. Cunningham, for instance, quotes a member of a community in rural Ethiopia who has taken part in this process: 'We used to think that only the rich had assets, but now we see that we too have assets … our health, our land, our knowledge, and different kinds of natural resources' (2008: 287). This realization was the start of a wide programme of community-led development that included setting up insurance schemes, reforestation efforts, road repairs, and improved farming techniques.

In the rest of the chapter I want to examine what happens when you *do* find local solutions that already exist. Let's say you have found a network of entrepreneurs, or an empowerment programme set up by young women, or a system of informal healthcare that has been created on the ground. How might the well-meaning outsider go about supporting, partnering with, and potentially building on the work of local creators? And what form should this 'building' take? Should they focus on helping people to make the original solution more solid and durable? Should they try to help increase its impact in the local area. Or – and this is where much of our focus will lie – could they try to help expand it to more users and more regions?

At stake here, as ever, are questions of both efficacy and power. I am, of course, interested in what can make insider–outsider partnerships more *effective*: how can outsiders help local solutions reduce poverty more quickly and widely? But I believe power matters too. We need to avoid outsiders, with their bigger budgets, formal roles, and accredited expertise, taking over local solutions. In Chapter 7 we will address the issue of power more fully, examining the value and limitations of outsider expertise and the ways in which people on the ground can lead the work of development. The current chapter starts this process by exploring two fundamental issues. First, where do those on the ground potentially need most help from outsiders? Second, what questions should an outsider ask themselves before deciding whether to develop or scale up a local solution?

(How) can outsiders help?

Increasing reliability and security over time

Informal local networks tend to rest on the commitment of conscientious individuals and on personal ties. And they tend to operate at the level of habit – we meet on Thursday evenings after eating – rather than on regulations. This means a savings club, or nursery run by an informal community group is not like an equivalent one run by an NGO or government programme. If the people who run it fall out with one another or just lose interest, then the infrastructure is likely to disappear. This is one of the central, underlying threats facing millions of poor people who 'depend on the social insurance provided by the strength of their social ties' (Narayan et al., 2000: 9) and for whom a breakdown in these social ties can mean a loss of vital social services.

One possible contribution that outsiders can make can be to help formalize the ad hoc arrangements on which the poor rely, to help local creators to move towards a more regular structure, more formal commitments, roles, and procedures that will endure when the individuals who currently occupy them move on. This is a transition that sociologists Berger and Luckmann (1991) (1966) describe as 'institutionalisation', an idea they capture neatly in the following description:

> As long as the nascent institutions are constructed and maintained only in the interaction of [two individuals] A and B, their objectivity remains tenuous, easily changeable, almost playful... All this changes in the process of transmission to the new generation... The 'There we go again' now becomes 'This is how these things are done'. A world so regarded attains a firmness in consciousness; it becomes real in an ever more massive way and it can no longer be changed so readily (1991) (1966: 76–7).

Formalization of ad hoc services can have real benefits for their users. Collins et al. describe how people who have moved from informal lending to official microfinance services often value the reliability and transparency that the latter brings, a theme clear from this passage:

> Irrespective of how microcredit loans were used, borrowers appreciated the fact that, relative to almost all their other financial partners, microfinance providers were *reliable*. That is, the loan officers came to the weekly meetings on time, in all kinds of weather; they disbursed loans in the amount they promised at the time they promised and at the price they promised; they didn't demand bribes; they tried hard to keep their passbooks accurate and up-to-date; and they showed their clients that they took their transactions seriously (2009: 27).[1]

A good example of a successful shift from ad hoc to more institutional solutions is the *Conjunto Palmeira* project in north-eastern Brazil, documented by Neumann et al. (2008). The original project was highly organic, the result of people in the newly created community of Palmeira coming together to create their own solutions in the absence of any help from local government. In time GTZ, a German NGO, learned about *Conjunto Palmeira*'s transformative work and the two parties, together with representatives of the state government, met to plan a more formal approach to further development. This resulted in a 10-year plan for action, led by the community, but supported by outsiders and which included major projects such as installing a sewage system, paving the streets, and draining local rivers, all of which were achieved in under the planned 10 years. This success was aided by a shift from more improvised activity to something closer to the 'institutions' that Berger and Luckmann described and one critical aspect was the way that the community work was depersonalized. Like many successful organic solutions, *Conjunto Palmeira* had relied on dynamic individuals. But for these solutions to continue and develop they needed to be formalized so that they could be done by multiple, different people, according to a set of agreed rules. Neumann et al. describe how in Palmeira 'while many of the original leaders remain active, forming new leadership among the younger generation is considered so important that the by-laws of the Residents' Association require it' (2008: 57).

But to move from the personal and informal to the institutional is a major challenge. At the simplest level it may require wages to pay for people to attend meetings whatever the season and budgets for administrative staff who keep the necessary bureaucracy in place. It can also require a major change in *attitudes and habits*. Mansuri and Rao describe the transition very clearly when they note how 'organic participation is driven by self-motivated leaders who work tirelessly, with little compensation, often at a high opportunity cost', but that this 'has to be transformed into manageable, bureaucratically defined entities, with budgets, targets, and extrinsically motivated salaried staff as agents of change' (2012: 33). This major change in both culture and practice tends to require training, formal records, and sometimes mediation, all of which outsiders may be able to provide. We may also discover as we attempt to formalize a project, just how much of its initial success was reliant on its founders: typically charismatic individuals, with extraordinary commitment, knowledge, and social skills and very often with experience of life outside the community.[2] It is hard to codify and transfer founders' personality and energy into bureaucratic standards. This is a problem I often missed early in my career: that a project's strength may in fact be hard to separate from its founders and it's a question we need to consider carefully before intervening. In his analysis of successful social innovations in the global north, Manzini (2015) sees this as a recurring theme, noting how many of his signature examples (such as democratic psychiatry and the slow food movement) relied on the personal qualities of their founders. He argues that 'the events that led to these two great social innovations cannot be separated from the personalities, energy and charisma of their promoters... [and] their capacity to create around themselves a group of capable enthusiasts' (2015: 61).

It's important too that if we begin a process of 'institutionalization' we are alert to the potential downsides it may bring. As a solution becomes more formal, it may lose the flexibility that gives life to organic, improvised solutions. Mansuri and Rao (2012) argue that 'participatory projects work well when they are given the freedom to learn by doing, to constantly experiment, and innovate based on feedback from the ground'. They suggest that 'as the project expands, however, experimentation becomes more difficult, and efforts are directed more toward meeting the letter rather than the spirit of project goals' (2012: 33). Outsiders need to be sensitive to this and to carefully judge where increased formalization and standardization will help and hinder the solution as it grows.

Giving community groups more power in their dealings with the outside world

We saw in the previous chapter how poor people can often feel powerless when dealing with outside bodies, such as local government, formal businesses, and, indeed, NGOs. This sense of powerlessness isn't just experienced individually. The groups and networks that poor people build also often lack power and leverage when dealing with these outside actors. After interviews with tens of thousands of poor people across over 20 countries Narayan et al. (2000: 219) conclude that this lack of leverage is one of the major limitations of locally created infrastructure. 'There are innumerable examples of poor people helping each other to overcome survival, safety and social problems. [But] Poor people's informal networks and organizations by and large have not been able to strengthen their bargaining power with states, private enterprises, traders, or NGOs. In the study communities, only a few cases of poor people's networks have transformed into people's movements'.

This is partly a problem of scale. Community groups are typically just too small to bargain effectively on their own. A women's organization or a farmers' group who meet in a single village is more easily bypassed, undercut or simply ignored by local government or by buyers in the nearby city (Bolton, 2019). This may be a matter of pragmatism, rather than deliberate exploitation. Polak (2008) describes, for instance, how 'for a supermarket supplier in Africa, it is much easier to make one stop at a thousand-acre farm to pick up vegetables and to hold one farmer accountable for meeting quality standards than it is to make a thousand stops at one-acre farms'. To address this reality, he argues, small-scale farmers have to build larger networks: 'unless one-acre farmers come up with an effective group collection and quality-control strategy, they lose out to large-farm competitors' (2008: 153).

The challenge is that the things that can give *individual* community groups their strength (long family histories, daily face-to-face interactions, a high degree of public scrutiny) are often missing once people go beyond their own communities and try to build these bigger alliances. Indeed, in many low-income countries trust in strangers can be lower than in the global north. This is where outside organizations, who are used to building broader coalitions, can make a difference. An outsider who takes the time to uncover a local initiative may be able to identify similarities between this project and others in the region and they may have the experience and resources to build links between the fragmented groups. This can not only increase each group's bargaining power with the outside world, it can also improve their effectiveness within their own communities. Narayan et al. describe how 'interventions like Grameen microcredit and the Andhra Pradesh self-help groups have allowed poor people's groups to link up horizontally and vertically so they can gain sufficient scale to access resources *and* gradually gain social and political voice in their communities' (2009: 328, my italics).

To deal more effectively with external bodies, however, you need more than scale. It is also a matter of knowledge and connections; of knowing which bodies to approach, understanding their bureaucracy, and navigating their cultural and social norms. This knowledge is often lacking on the ground. Narayan et al. note how the majority of the informal groups they found in their research 'are not linked to any outside sources of capital and know-how, such as banks, government agencies, or NGOs' (2009: 308). Similarly, Manzini (2015: 80) suggests that there can be a tendency for grassroots initiatives to become insular and 'separated from larger sociotechnical systems'. They are rich in what Wilkinson-Maposa (2008) calls 'bonding capital' – the social ties within a community that bond people together. But they are often much poorer in what she calls 'bridging capital' – the ability to network beyond the community to reach other influential actors.

I saw the difference that 'bridging capital' makes when between 2008 and 2012 I visited over a dozen community projects in poor neighbourhoods in Brazil, some of which were markedly more impactful than others. The most striking success was run by Juan Cabral, who as a teenager had opened a public library, later credited as being the first established in a Brazilian *favela*. Cabral and his neighbours had used the library to cultivate relationships with local officials and to persuade them to give the community better access to technology, education, and infrastructure.[3] This contrasted sharply with many other community groups I visited, where the work was helping people survive in daily life, but the group could point to little long-term progress. The difference to a large degree came down to the ability of the group to identify and negotiate with outsiders in the way Cabral had done.

Outsiders can potentially help here in a number of ways. Some of these are very practical. For instance, a useful first step can be to help local organizations to register as formal entities themselves. This, as researchers like Flodman Becker (2004) have shown, is likely to give them greater legal protection, more chance of bidding for larger projects, and greater access to finance and government grants.[4] Registration is often hard, however. A report by Mama Cash/ FRIDA (2018) on grassroots gender projects notes that 'registration processes are often complicated, expensive, and require organizations to establish legal representation, to have financial systems in place and to have hired full-time staff' (2018: 16). This is an area where outsiders potentially can help, both helping with the logistics of formalizing informal groups and in lobbying to make the process less burdensome.[5]

Outsiders are also often more aware of grants and programmes provided by governments, NGOs, or commercial partners from which local organizers can benefit. Even where development is, or becomes highly community-led, this can be a role that outsiders may usefully play. Cunningham gives the example of how Ethiopian NGO REST continued to connect community groups 'to government-sponsored initiatives in soil and water conservation, agroforestry, and pasture improvement' even as its input to daily development work declined (2008: 294). Similarly, outsiders may be able to help identify and build productive collaborations between formal and informal actors and structures. Myers et al. describe how the charity Practical Action helped informal sanitation initiatives in South Asia to reach formal service agreements with the local municipality. Joining up with government infrastructure transformed how the local solution could operate, allowing them to 'lease pumping equipment from the municipality... operate freely during the daytime, charge more predictable rates to customers, and dispose of the waste safely' (2018: 92).

Lobbying is another area where outsiders can often bring greater resources. Whilst social media is helping local actors reach larger audiences, they may still lack the tools and connections for forcing effective political action from the authorities. Jamal Khadar (2020) emphasizes the role that professional NGOs can play here for youth groups, arguing that 'social media may have given activists the tools to voice issues, but lobbying to turn this into political action and effective legal safeguards is harder without the resources and expertise of a specialised NGO'.

As well as these specific areas of intervention, outsiders can help more broadly with bridging the *cultural* divides between local actors and formal bodies. Working independently, local groups often develop norms and habits very different from those of government bodies, corporations, and formal NGOs. They are unfamiliar with the latter's bureaucracies, habitual use of technology, formal application processes, and more literal and insistent application of time-frames. The two worlds may also be divided by power dynamics bound up with issues of education and class. To start and run a project in a very poor community requires substantial social skills, but slightly different ones to those that get you ahead in a formal company, NGO, or government office.[6] Some organizers like Cabral find it easy to speak to local government officials and businesses in a language the latter understand. In Cabral's case, he explained to me, it was both literally in the sense of speaking 'good Portuguese' and more subtly knowing how to fill in forms, work around bureaucracy, stand up to, and bargain with councillors or business people. Many communities are less able to interact with outsiders so confidently, during their early dealings especially. Staff in the latter may unconsciously or consciously patronize and under-estimate local innovators.[7] Offering support at this stage can be another useful 'bridging' role that outsiders can play.

Across these examples, I would stress that outsiders should avoid becoming unnecessary intermediaries in the relationship between community groups and formal infrastructure. Outsiders like me may be able to spot, set up, and facilitate connections with local government, banks, or large-scale NGOs, but we should seek to remain in the background. The goal should be to build direct relationships, where insiders engage with these bodies themselves, rather than relying on a third party. See, for instance, Mathie (2008: 221) for how successful savings groups in southern India benefited from 'a clear strategy... to ensure [they] could link directly with institutions such as banks and government agencies so as to be able to function independently'.

There is also a risk that by connecting community groups to formal actors, especially local government, we make the former too reliant on the latter and take some of the energy out of local solutions. There is a balance, as John Kretzmann (2008: vii–viii) describes, of helping 'local communities recognize and grow the capacities of local residents to define and accomplish development goals themselves, while still recognizing that support from governments, larger NGOs and funders is essential, and in fact an obligation'. This tension, as Kretzmann acknowledges, often disappears in practice, since very often communities find ways for their organic solutions to combine with, and benefit from, the formal services supplied by the state. In the best outcomes, the state may even learn from and adapt to what they see being done on the ground (something we will explore in more detail in the next chapter). But we should not ignore the potential for tension here between the power that communities get by acting independently and the power they have in demanding their rights as citizens.

As ever, much depends on context. Myers et al. illustrate this with the example of community-led sanitation. In rural areas it can work as a relatively self-contained activity, which communities can, at least in time, manage for themselves. But in urban contexts safe sanitation is much more likely to require lobbying of, and collaborations with, local government. This is because, as Myers et al. (2018) show, the nature of the physical sanitation problem is more complex in many cities. Open defecation is less common than in rural areas, but waste contamination is widespread. Fixing problems like open drains, leaking pits, and water contamination is a major infrastructural undertaking, one that Myers et al. say requires 'collectively advocating for access to safe services from service providers and government' (2018: 6). This example shows that whilst self-empowerment is critical, it is also locally grounded and the degree to which communities can act autonomously is heavily context specific.

Opening up new income opportunities

The last area I want to explore is how outsiders can help local groups expand their income-generating activities by connecting them with more formal economic networks. One of the most common blind spots among poor-owned businesses and cooperatives is an awareness of marketplaces outside their locality. Polak (2008) gives the example of how 'many of the small-acreage farmers in the hill areas of Nepal have perfect weather and soil conditions to grow off-season vegetables, but they... lacked information about prices and demand in the markets in Pokhara and the Kathmandu valley, where they could sell their crops' (2008: 201). Even when insiders have formed local cooperatives and business groups it is often outsiders who are more likely to be able to link them to external buyers. Manzini (2015) gives the example of *Ainonghui*, a project established in China's Guangxi province, where the urban citizens of Liuzhou arranged to source organic produce from farmers a few hours drive away. This has led to increases in farmers' incomes and the conservation of traditional farming knowledge and practices. In Ghana, a US NGO called TechnoServe has formed a connection between a major fruit exporter and 322 small-scale farmers. The deal increased their incomes by an average of over $1,000 in a county where per capita income was $290 at the time. The NGO Farm International, meanwhile, works with a Commercial Villages Model to help small-scale farmers across many parts of Africa to work collectively to meet the demands of commercial buyers and achieve new and higher prices for their produce.[8]

There has been a lot of positive discussion of these kinds of interventions and in particular how they can be enhanced by digital technology. The e-Choupal initiative, for instance, has been widely celebrated for giving rural Indians the chance to sell to new, more distant market places (Wharton School, 2009; UNDP, 2004). The UNDP describe how 'in India small-scale soybean farmers use a village internet kiosk to check spot prices for their products on the Chicago Board of Trade's website, bypassing local intermediaries and getting better prices' (2004). There are, though, important caveats that outsiders need to keep in mind. First, there is the risk that the poorest and most vulnerable are less able to take advantage of these opportunities that outsiders can bring. For instance, five years after the launch of e-Choupal, only 10 per cent of the farmers using the digital service were classified as poor, and studies of the service found that poorer farmers were less able to understand and confidently use the technology or to travel to the towns where the hubs were based (Garrette and Karnani, 2010; Mukerji, 2020). Second, as outsiders we are prone to see these opportunities in quite abstract terms – they are cases of 'market failure' and 'asymmetric information' that can be fixed by following sound economic principles and increasingly by introducing disruptive technology. The reality is that the reasons why poor people struggle to sell their goods outside their local area can have very grounded and local root causes. These require us to pay as much attention to insider knowledge as we do to our panoramic 'expert' point of view and to think about knotty political struggles as well as clean technical solutions. Narayan et al. give an example from a fishing community in Cambodia that captures this reality very clearly and I'll quote directly here from some of these fishers to whom they listened:

> Rich middlemen who buy crabmeat and sell it at the Kampot market are also people who have the ability to control economic opportunity in this village. As of now, there are three middlemen in Somrampi village, and

all of them are classified rich and have multiple business activities. The price of crab depends on these middlemen. If they give us 10,000 riels per kilogram of crab meat, it's okay, and if they give us only 8,000 riels for the same weight it's also okay. They can help us, and they can also cause us problems by reducing the price. We are so poor, and we don't have enough productive assets such as fishing tools, agriculture tools, and so forth; hence we have to borrow money from them to buy all these instruments. Because we borrow money from them, when we get something from the sea such as marine fish, crabs, and shrimp, we have to sell to them at locally set prices. There is no choice for us to select our buyers according to what we want (2009: 190).

As an outsider it would be easy to focus on technical solutions to the community problems. We could create a virtual marketplace, which we would train fishers to use in order to sell directly to people who shop at the Kampot market and beyond. I have seen and been involved in a number of ideas of this kind. But the critical question would be how would the middlemen respond to our attempt to fix the 'market inefficiency'? Would they accept the change? Or try to prevent their captive audience from using the service? Would they find new uses for it themselves? We have quickly moved here from the clean principles of supply and demand to the messiness of neighbourhood politics. And it is among the weeds of the latter that many development initiatives stand or fall. For outsiders to be useful we need to recognize that our broader perspective is only half of the story, a reality that we will pick up in the next section and explore in much more detail in the next chapter.

Appreciating and assessing local solutions: critical questions to ask before 'scaling up'

So far, we have looked at the ways that outsiders can help local solutions. This has included ways to support and reinforce what already exists. But much of our emphasis has been on how outsiders can increase the *scale* of local solutions – whether by adding to its local impact, building links with similar work in other areas, or by replicating the local work in new locations. Scaling up is an inviting idea and one that is integral to the way the professional development industry thinks and acts. As Polak (2008) writes approvingly, the Gates Foundation has a central tenet that they will only fund projects that can deliver on a mass scale. Polak set himself the demanding (and initially counter-intuitive) goal of working at a very local level *and* reaching mass audiences. His solutions were typically low-tech and very attuned to local geography, but they also had to be replicable nationally or internationally.

This, I'd agree, is an ideal ambition for development work. And when we identify local projects we should be hoping to find those that are both highly locally attuned *and* able to expand and replicate. In this section, though, I want to encourage outsiders to pause and reflect on the challenges expansion involves. What can hold expansion back? What kinds of benefits might be lost when a solution grows? What value might small and 'inefficient' solutions have for those on the ground. To scale up successfully, we need to acknowledge its difficulty, be sensitive and selective about where we seek to add scale, and accept that sometimes remaining small is the best option. Below I sketch a number of questions that I believe outsiders should ask themselves before seeking to 'scale up'.

How much appetite is there to expand?

The first question one should ask is a very simple one. Do the people who created the solution want to expand it, or even formalize it, in any way? Many community solutions are created by people who are already working full-time, often on several jobs, or combining study, work, and family commitments. They created the local infrastructure you have excitedly discovered *because they saw it was needed*, not with any great plan to grow it, see it replicated elsewhere, or get recognition as a formal enterprise. I remember asking one youth organizer in northern Brazil what his dream was for the future. I imagined maybe branches across the city and hundreds more participants, but no, his dream was the government would increase funding for the area and he would not be needed any more. Even when projects are less reliant on individuals, some groups won't want to scale up, or become more involved in the formal sector. This is despite the benefits that we outsiders can see in doing so. In a study researching girl-led activist groups, the NGOs Mama Cash and FRIDA (2018) emphasize this point, noting that some girls don't register formally, even though it cuts them off from some sources of funding and help: 'some do not feel ready to take on the legal and financial responsibility of registration while others believe registration would restrict their work'. Sunil Babu Pant, a community organizer from Nepal, meanwhile describes the frustrations that grassroots leaders can experience when making formal agreements with official NGOs. In a critical article, Pant (2017) argues that 'you end up spending more time on paper work, and your actual work of promoting human rights, slowly falls down your list of priorities. To become professional and efficient you are encouraged, over time, to get rid of the "emotional" side of your personality, which not only makes you less of an activist but also makes you less human'.

Are we scaling up the things that matter to users?

When outsiders identify local solutions our instinct is to view them through the lens of our own projects. Say we are trying to build an agricultural service and we find a group of farmers meeting in the area; well, we naturally frame it as a farming group. In so doing, though, we may miss the very *varied* roles that local infrastructure plays on the ground. We have seen above that in communities where resources are stretched, activities may have rich and multiple purposes that are not immediately obvious to the outsider. Muradian

(2013) describes, for instance, how many farming cooperatives, especially among the poorest communities, are geared as much towards social support (e.g. literacy, HIV prevention) as they are to helping grow and market crops. There is a risk that an outsider bringing in money and resources to 'develop' these local solutions ends up ignoring or even undermining these less obvious but vital benefits. As outsiders we need to take the time to ensure that what we are scaling up is what matters to the people on the ground.

How organic is the solution?

It is also useful to ask how far the local solution we have identified may already have benefited from, or been stimulated by, outside help. We have seen above examples of how community initiatives may be encouraged or supported even at an early stage by national and international NGOs. Whilst this may only occur in a small minority of cases, it is more common among the *obvious* cases, the ones that outsiders are most likely to discover through desk research. This doesn't make the solution any less authentic or potentially powerful, but it does mean that it may not expand, either within its region, or out to other regions, without similar help from outsiders. Khadar (2020) makes this argument in his analysis of female youth groups, where, he suggests 'the role of formal organisations in stimulating activism is often left out'. He argues that 'by over-emphasising how "spontaneous" activism is, we risk underplaying the barriers and dangers girls and young people face in becoming activists without the support or encouragement of others. It may be unrealistic to expect some – with limited freedom and exposure to others – to do it alone'.

Is the solution a stopgap?

We should also remember that some informal solutions only exist to help people to *endure* their current poverty, rather than to *escape* it. As eager outsiders, we need to be cautious about trying to expand projects that were only meant to be interim and which are created as a last resort, rather than a vehicle for change. Narayan et al. argue that often 'informal associations and networks may help poor people to survive. They serve a defensive function and usually not a transformative function. That is, they do little to move poor people out of poverty' (2000: 8). Outsiders can miss this reality. A notable example is recent attempts to expand the entrepreneurial activities of poor-owned businesses – a trend that has been encouraged in recent years by stories of the poor as 'natural entrepreneurs' (Khanna and Palepu, 2010; Khanna, 2011; Yunus, 2007). This is a powerful narrative and, to be fair, not without evidence. On almost every field visit I've made to poor communities, I've met resourceful business people: families turning living rooms into video-game parlours, or DVD rental stores; young men parsing the city's streets for valuable plastic to recycle; groups reviving traditional artisan skills to sell craft products to middle-class homes. Polak (2008) cites a survey of the Dharavi slum in

Mumbai, which found 1,044 manufacturing operations and 85 organizations who were making products for export. India's Honeybee network documents thousands of small-scale innovators and entrepreneurs.[9]

The problem is that outsiders often over-estimate the potential to scale up what are in reality projects of last resort. Banerjee and Duflo (2011) remind us that 'many of the businesses are run because someone in the family has (or is believed to have) some time on hand and every little bit helps. This person is often a woman, and she typically does it in addition to her housework; indeed, it is not clear that she always has much of a choice when the opportunity to start a business comes up' (2011: 226). Ayadi and Ben Aissa agree that 'where paid employment opportunities are limited and social protection is non-existent or weak, people are driven mainly by survival needs. It is their inability to be hired as employees that pushes them into running their own business rather than a proactive identification of a new market opportunity' (2015: 105).[10] Hence, whilst *some* poor-owned businesses provide a compelling route out of poverty, the potential is far from universal. In fact, studies often find a negative association between self-employment and escaping poverty. Strode et al. compared African workers above and below the $2 line and found that the former were more likely to have moved into wage employment, with regular pay.[11] This doesn't mean there is no role for outsiders to support defensive, or interim solutions – stepping stones that will help poor people before a longer-term solution arrives. But we do need to distinguish clearly between stopgaps and solutions that have potential to scale. If one risk lies in ignoring informal structures, another risk lies in pushing them to be more than they are.

How much does the solution rely on human relationships?

Work like Polak's *Out of Poverty* (2008) and Radjou et al.'s *Jugaad Innovation* (2012) suggest the rich potential for identifying locally created engineering solutions that can be developed, mass-produced, and distributed across whole regions. But many of the local projects that function in poor communities rely heavily on social capital and personal relationships more than on technical innovations. We should remember that the risks of trying to expand are higher when the basis is human relations, rather than physical engineering; a cooperative group is more likely to buckle than a treadle pump. Mansuri and Rao (2012) give the example of a participatory farming project in rural India, where 'a huge burden was placed on a complex and shaky system: the project had to create a new organizational structure, to quadruple the size of its operations' (2012: 107).

Is the solution reliant on its local context?

There is an understandable impulse in development to try to transplant local success stories to as many new places as possible. The problem is that local successes are often reliant on local *context*. We saw this in Chapter 1, where

I and many others over-estimated the potential to replicate the impact of mobile phones that Robert Jensen (2007) identified among Keralan fishers. Some of the problems were in hindsight obvious. First, the rules on the sea don't necessarily hold on land. As journalist Michael Hobbes (2016) points out 'these fishermen sell a perishable good. They have to sell it to someone, they have to sell it today and it's the same distance back to the shore regardless of which port they pick. But the typical African or Indian farmer does not live perfectly equidistant from several produce markets'. Some of the other ways that local context mattered were harder than this to spot and only emerged in later analysis. Srinivasan and Burrell (2013) argue that further south in Kerala the steep slope of the ocean floor results in heavy surf, meaning small, fibreglass, and plywood boats are more common than large vessels and a single, sheltered harbour did the majority of business. With smaller catches and fewer competing markets, it was much less useful for fishers to be able to call around different ports. Hence, Srinivasan and Burrell claim fishers in the southern study rarely mentioned checking prices or making decisions about where to sell based on price when they described their use of the mobile phone. Like Hobbes, Srinivasan and Burrell also question the premise that intermediaries are necessarily parasitic and that interventions should seek to bypass them. On the coastline that Srinivasan and Burrell studied they found that in fact 'society auctioneers were *introduced* between buyer and seller in order to reduce the exploitation of fishers' and that 'the presence of middlemen cannot automatically be assumed to introduce exploitation in a market' (2013: 7). An intervention that cuts out the intermediary in one context may be much less useful to poor people in a different one. In another, more polemical, paper Steyn and Van Greunen (2014) also claim that the insights from Jensen's paper were not automatically transferable to other locations and point to other such context-specific factors as the price and distribution of fuel. They claim that in the south of the state fishers are heavily incentivized to return and sell at their home port, in order to qualify for subsidized fuel, making it less inviting to shop around between different markets. Meanwhile, Chambers (2014) gives an older and similarly sobering example of the challenges of transplanting local success stories. He describes how in the early 1980s irrigation experts in India saw the *warabandi* irrigation system that had been pioneered in north-west India as a solution that could transform water supplies across the whole country. However, the system relied on conditions that rarely existed in other parts of India and hence attempts to expand it soon foundered. Chambers writes despairingly that 'the outcome was major investment in metal *warabandi* boards giving fantasy timings erected to rust and decay all over India as monuments to top-down ignorance and folly' (2014: 57).

It is understandable that we can get swept along by stories of breakthrough solutions. Poverty is so intractable and good news so rare that when we find a successful local intervention it's hard not to suppress the hope that it will work equally well elsewhere. This is particularly tempting when the intervention involves a new technology, like, in its day, a mobile phone. The same is true when the intervention is counter-intuitive, as with a famous Kenyan RCT which found that supplying deworming tablets to students had a bigger effect on educational behaviour than more obvious ploys like free textbooks or incentives for teachers. Findings like this naturally generate a lot of discussion and hope, but they should also evoke caution. As a World Bank report (2004) says of the Kenyan RCT, 'these results from a hundred schools in an isolated area of Kenya have been getting enormous academic attention because there are so few rigorous, randomized evaluations of schooling interventions'. Reviewing over 500 empirical (mainly econometric) studies of participative development, Mansuri and Rao (2012) invite us to be wary of the potential for transporting interventions. 'Outcomes from interventions are highly variable across communities', they write. 'History; geography; and the nature of social interactions, networks, and political systems all have a strong influence. As a result, a successful project designed for one context may fail miserably in another' (2012: 286–7).

Thus, before we try to export locally created solutions we need to stop and consider carefully the different ways in which their success may rely on their locale. And if we attempt to export a solution we need to look afresh at each new context, rather than assuming that the model will work in similar ways and similarly well. A good example of how this can work *in practice* is the hugely successful programme of rural electrification carried out in Morocco during the early years of the 21st century (Iskander and Bentaleb-Maes, 2008). It was heavily influenced by an initial community-led initiative in the Souss valley, which set something of a blueprint for expansion across the country. But, as Iskander and Bentaleb-Maes make clear in their account of the programme, people recognized very clearly the need to adapt approaches in each new community and to spend time at the outset carefully understanding local differences. As Iskander and Bentaleb-Maes describe, the government recognized that 'in order to build a network that addressed village-specific energy usages patterns, a thorough needs assessment needed to be conducted *in each community*' (2008: 174, my italics).

How will expansion change the solution?

It's not just that local solutions might not transplant easily to new locations, they may also not be able to function at an increased level of scale. Something that reduces poverty among a small group of people won't necessarily work among a bigger population. First, it may lose the human scale which first made it intuitive and practical to its users. One reason why microfinance programmes *were* able to expand beyond the original experiments in Bangladesh was that Grameen and later followers retained the small-scale nature of transactions. Even as the customer-base expanded enormously, users were able to make very small, frequent payments in sync with their daily finances. Collins et al. argue that 'much of their success in showing that the poor are bankable has depended on this feature, which acknowledges and respects the small cash flows of poor households' (2009: 57).[12]

Second, we need to think carefully about the mechanics of each local solution to consider how large an audience can actually benefit from it. Sometimes an initiative that works well for a few people will have diminishing returns as it reaches a larger audience. Microfinance itself has been criticized very much along these lines, as a solution which got less efficient and useful as it grew to mass levels and attracted borrowers who used the money for consumption, rather than investment (Karlan and Appel, 2011). In the worst instances, bringing in a wider audience may even undermine the benefits of the original solution. Deaton (2013) presents this as a significant risk for the kinds of initiatives aimed at farmers or small businesses, such as improved market information or advice on inputs, which we discussed above. He argues that the competitive advantage given by such activities may be lost once the knowledge is spread throughout the whole market. He gives the example that 'one farmer can increase his productivity, but if all do so, the prices of the crops will fall, and what is profitable for one may not be profitable for all... So once again, a project may be successful on its own terms, but scaling up to the national level may be a failure' (2013: 293).

There could be further twists in the story that Deaton tells. The rise in production levels might, for instance, make it worthwhile for local entrepreneurs to supply better transport for farmers to get their crops to market. A foreign buyer might enter the market now that the increased output levels make it worth their while. One of these new actors might then provide RFID chipped bags, thereby reducing the losses to theft and corruption. With these denouements, the farmers' income might still rise and the market might function more efficiently, even as the price fell. But it would be folly to count on such outcomes and once again this shows the myriad variables we need to consider when planning to scale up a successful programme. The kinds of critical and focused questions we can ask include:

- Who makes most use of the original solution and where can you find similar groups elsewhere?
- What differences are there between the original and future audiences and how will you have to adapt the service as it grows?
- As you expand, are you reaching the intended audiences and how are they using the solution?
- What competitive advantages could be gained or lost as more people get to use your solution?

Moving forward: caution and context

I have argued that as outsiders we need to do more to acknowledge and search for local solutions to poverty that already exist. Rather than starting from scratch, our starting point should be what is working already. Often, I have suggested, there are opportunities for outsiders to use their skills and resources to support and develop local projects. We can help formalize ad hoc practices and relationships to make local infrastructure more reliable and likely to last in the long term. We can build up coalitions between individual groups to give them more information and bargaining power. We can help local actors to negotiate and benefit from formal organizations and resources (government grants, contracts, NGO support), and we can introduce local groups to new marketplaces and income-generation possibilities. But the message, as throughout the book, is one of caution and context, as well as ambition and scale. As outsiders we should be very respectful of the local knowledge that underpins local infrastructure and of the individuals who have built it. We should differentiate between expandable and stopgap solutions *and* we should recognize the valuable role the latter can play in poor people's lives. We should recognize the risks of scaling up, especially the impact on social relations and not romanticize away the flaws within 'organic' solutions. We should remember the importance of context and avoid assuming that a highly impactful local solution can transfer neatly to a new geographical location. Furthermore, whilst I am clearly an advocate of taking small-scale solutions seriously, I believe we also need realism about what small-scale initiatives can achieve compared with broader government-led changes in public policy. In communities with major structural and infrastructural problems (terrible roads, erratic digital connections, low education, high corruption, mass unemployment, limited consumer markets) even the best planned local intervention may make only limited impact.[13] We should do more to seek out and build up individual micro interventions, but we cannot ignore the importance of the macro in politics, economics, and social policy. Without improvements in governance and public policy, scaling up may only take us so far.

Notes

1. Narayan et al. (2009) report a strong association between informal banking and higher levels of poverty: 'communities that rated their economies as strong or very strong at the time of the survey were also more likely to rely on government banks as a source of credit. Almost 40 percent of the economically strong communities, but only about a quarter of the economically weak communities, said that government banks were among the top two sources of credit in their area. Households in local economies rated weak or very weak were more likely to rely on friends, relatives, and moneylenders than on banks for their financial needs' (2009: 209).
2. Reflecting on the consistent role of migrants in community-led development, Mathie and Cunningham (2008) note that migrants into the community often bring new ideas, energy, and resilience, whilst those who have left can offer new knowledge and links to the outside world. They argue that 'migration is a common thread running through all the cases, whether the energy and determination of new migrants, or the reliance on the skills and resources of people who have moved away, or the legacy of cooperation during earlier periods of migrant settlement reflected in a community-wide volunteer spirit' (2008: 5).

3. His story of how he managed to do this can be seen in a short film I made with Carla Rollo and Jamie Singh Robertson available at <https://vimeo.com/105213889> [accessed 9 May 2021]. Many of the tactics that Cabral and others I met in Brazil have used are captured in Neumann et al.'s account of one of the country's most effective community organizations, Conjunto Palmeira (Neumann et al., 2008).

4. Evidence suggests a strong association between businesses that have formal licences and economic success. Narayan et al. claim 'the ease with which local governments make business licenses available was an important factor distinguishing high-performing communities from those where the local economy was considered weak' (2009: 217). Of course the correlation may work both ways (richer areas and businesses are more likely to register themselves) but there are clear advantages to being formally registered, as noted.

5. In the early part of the century, for instance, the Tanzanian government dramatically cut the time it takes to register a business from three months to three days (UNDP, 2004).

6. Pierre Bourdieu's idea of 'habitus' can be helpful here (1990) (1998) (1977). It refers to the dispositions we have unconsciously learned through our upbringing and cultural and social experiences, ranging from the ways we have learned to carry ourselves physically to the styles of speaking we have internalized to the values we hold and categories we use to order the world. Whilst these are not determining (and an important part of the idea is the scope that it allows for individual improvisation), Bourdieu sees them as heavily influencing both the way we react to the world and how the world reacts to us. He describes habitus as 'durable, transposable dispositions, structured structures predisposed to function as structuring structures, that is, as principles which generate and organize practices and representations that can be objectively adapted to their outcomes without presupposing a conscious aiming at ends or an express mastery of the operations necessary in order to attain them' (1990: 53).

7. Jeffrey (2010) captures a very similar dynamic in his account of how poor and marginalized young people are unfairly rejected when applying for jobs in the formal economy. 'We lack the demeanour for the new jobs, and our accents give us away' one young farmer explained to Jeffrey, after seeing members of the *Jat* caste consistently fail to be hired at recently opened factories and offices (2010: 85).

8. See their latest case studies at <https://www.farmconcern.org/commercial-villages#case-studies> [accessed 14 February 2021].

9. See <http://honeybee.org/index.php> [accessed 14 November 2019].

10. Similarly, in her study of unemployed and marginalized African youth, Alcinda Honwana (2012) found that despite the rhetoric around emerging market entrepreneurs, most of the people she spoke to didn't have the skills, networks or support to start profitable businesses. 'Entrepreneurship is often presented as an alternative to getting a job, particularly in view of the contraction in the labor market. However, young people are not being adequately prepared to become successful entrepreneurs and very few policies and programs promote and support those who attempt to start their own businesses' (2012: 39–40).

11. This reveals an association rather than a pattern of cause and effect. And the correlation may work in reverse: i.e. people with higher incomes find it easier to take time to look for and find salaried jobs, or are able to dress and present themselves more effectively when called for interview. But there is a plausible story that the stability of a salaried job allows people to manage their finances better, withstand economic shocks, and plan for and invest in their future through education. This is the narrative put forward by Strode et al. (2015: 82). 'Casual workers lack job security; their hours are unpredictable, and their benefits are few. Salaried employees, on the other hand, enjoy steady and predictable working hours and pay, which enable them to better plan for the future'.
12. As such, the research on microcredit gives quite a rich picture of the problems of scaling up. It would seem from these studies that microcredit has been undermined by one problem (of over-estimating audience size) whilst avoiding another (increasing the scale of interactions for its users).
13. For example, analysing economic self-empowerment projects, Hickel argues that 'this kind of self-help is impossible on a large scale without market regulations and state subsidies that favour small enterprises, and without welfare arrangements to support people when they fail' (2014: 1366).

References

Ayadi, Mohamed and Ben Aïssa, Mohamed Safouana (2015) 'Entrepreneurship', in Mthuli Ncube and Charles Leyeka Lufumpa (eds), *The Emerging Middle Class in Africa*, pp. 102–30, Routledge, London.

Banerjee, Abhijit V. and Duflo, Esther (2011) *Poor Economics: A Radical Rethinking of the Way To Fight Global Poverty*, Public Affairs, New York.

Becker, Kristina Flodman (2004) *The Informal Economy: Fact Finding Study*, Sida, Swedish National Press.

Berger, Peter L. and Luckmann, Thomas (1991) (1966) *The Social Construction of Reality: A Treatise in the Sociology of Knowledge*, Penguin, London.

Bolton, Laura (2019) *Economic Impact of Farming Cooperatives in East Africa*, Institute of Development Studies, Brighton.

Bourdieu, Pierre (1990) *The Logic of Practice* (trans. Richard Nice), Stanford University Press, Stanford.

Bourdieu, Pierre (1998) (1977) *Outline of a Theory of Practice* (trans. Richard Nice), Cambridge University Press, Cambridge.

Chambers, Robert (2014) *Into the Unknown: Explorations in Development Practice*, Practical Action Publishing, Rugby.

Collins, Daryl, Morduch, Jonathan, Rutherford, Stuart and Ruthven, Orlanda (2009) *Portfolios of the Poor: How the World's Poor Live on $2 a Day*, Princeton University Press, Princeton.

Cunningham, Gordon (2008) 'Stimulating asset based and community driven development: lessons from five communities in Ethiopia', in Alison Mathie and Gordon Cunningham (eds), *From Clients to Citizens: Communities Changing the Course of their Own Development*, pp. 263–98, Practical Action Publishing, Rugby.

Deaton, Angus (2013) *The Great Escape: Health, Wealth, and the Origins of Inequality*, Princeton University Press, Princeton.

Garrette, Bernard and Karnani, Aneel (2010) 'Challenges in marketing socially useful goods to the poor', [online], *California Management Review*, Summer, <http://www.societyandorganizations.org/wp-content/uploads/2010/06/Garette-CMR-su10.pdf> [accessed 23 June 2020].

Hickel, Jason (2014) 'The "girl effect": liberalism, empowerment and the contradictions of development', *Third World Quarterly*, 35: 1355–73 <https://doi.org/10.1080/01436597.2014.946250>.

Hobbes, Michael (2016) 'How Mark Zuckerberg should give away $45 billion: it's complicated', [online], *Huffington Post*, <https://highline.huffingtonpost.com/articles/en/how-to-give-away-45-billion/> [accessed 26 February 2021].

Honwana, Alcinda (2012) *The Time of Youth: Work, Social Change and Politics in Africa*, Kumarian, Virginia.

Iskander, Natasha and Bentaleb-Maes, Nadia (2008) 'The hardware and software of community development: migrant infrastructure projects in rural Morocco', in Alison Mathie and Gordon Cunningham (eds), *From Clients to Citizens: Communities Changing the Course of their Own Development*, pp. 161–80, Practical Action Publishing, Rugby.

Jeffrey, Craig (2010) *Timepass: Youth, Class and the Politics of Waiting in India*, Stanford University Press, Stanford.

Jensen, Robert (2007) 'The digital provide: information (technology), market performance, and welfare in the South Indian fisheries sector', *The Quarterly Journal of Economics*, 122: 879–924 <https://doi.org/10.1162/qjec.122.3.879>.

Karlan, Dean and Appel, Jacob (2011) *More Than Good Intentions, Improving the Ways the World's Poor Borrow, Save, Farm, Learn, and Stay Healthy*, Penguin, New York.

Khadar, Jamal (2020) '*Are NGOs Fetishising Youth Activism?*', [online], Medium, <https://jamalkhadar.medium.com/are-ngos-fetishising-youth-activism-13b0755246d2> [accessed 12 February 2021].

Khanna, Tarun and Palepu, Krishna (2010) *Winning in Emerging Markets*, Harvard Business School Press, Cambridge.

Khanna, Tarun (2011) *Billions of Entrepreneurs: How China and India Are Reshaping Their Futures and Yours*, Harvard Business Review Press, Cambridge.

Kretzmann, John P. (2008) 'Foreword', in Alison Mathie and Gordon Cunningham (eds), *From Clients to Citizens: Communities Changing the Course of their Own Development*, pp. vii–ix, Practical Action Publishing, Rugby.

Mama Cash and FRIDA|The Young Feminist Fund (2018) *Girls to the Front: A Snapshot of Girl-Led Organising*, [online], <https://www.mamacash.org/media/publications/girlstothefront_report_web.pdf> [accessed 21 February 2021].

Mansuri, Ghazala and Rao, Vijayendra (2012) *Localising Development: Does Participation Work?* World Bank Policy Research Report, World Bank, Washington.

Manzini, Ezio (2015) *Design, When Everyone Designs*, MIT, Cambridge Mass.

Mathie, Alison (2008) 'People's institutions as a vehicle for community development: a case study from southern India', in Alison Mathie and Gordon Cunningham (eds), *From Clients to Citizens: Communities Changing the Course of their Own Development*, pp. 207–35, Practical Action Publishing, Rugby.

Mathie, Alison and Cunningham, Gordon (2008) 'Introduction' and 'Conclusions', in Alison Mathie and Gordon Cunningham (eds), *From Clients to Citizens: Communities Changing the Course of their Own Development*, pp. 1–11 and pp. 357–69, Practical Action Publishing, Rugby.

Mukerji, Maitrayee (2020) 'Re-examining strategic and developmental implications of e-Choupal, India', Practitioner Paper, *Electronic Journal of Information Systems in Developing Countries*, 86 <https://doi.org/10.1002/isd2.12132>.

Muradian, Roldan (2013) 'The potential and limits of farmers' marketing groups as catalysts of rural development', Paper Presented to UNRISD Conference, 6–8 May 2013, Geneva.

Myers, J., Cavill, S., Musyoki, S., Pasteur, K. and Stevens, L. (2018) *Innovations for Urban Sanitation: Adapting Community-led Approaches*, Practical Action Publishing, Rugby.

Narayan, Deepa, Chambers, Robert, Shah, Meera K. and Petesch, Patti (2000) *Voices of the Poor: Crying Out for Change*, Oxford University Press for the World Bank, New York.

Narayan, Deepa, Pritchett, Lant and Kapoor, Soumya (2009) *Moving Out of Poverty Volume 2: Success from the Bottom Up*, a co-publication of the World Bank and Palgrave Macmillan, Washington.

Neumann, Rogerio Arns and Mathie, Alison, assisted by Linzey, Joanne (2008) 'Conjunto Palmeira: four decades of forging community and building a local economy in Brazil', in Alison Mathie and Gordon Cunningham (eds), *From Clients to Citizens: Communities Changing the Course of their Own Development*, pp. 39–62, Practical Action Publishing, Rugby.

Pant, Sunil Babu (2017) 'Why grassroots activists should resist being pressurised into an NGO', [online], *Guardian*, <https://www.theguardian.com/global-development-professionals-network/2017/jul/07/why-grassroots-activists-should-resist-being-professionalised-into-an-ngo> [accessed 22 February 2021].

Polak, Paul (2008) *Out of Poverty: What Works When Traditional Approaches Fail*, Berrett-Koehler, San Francisco.

Radjou, Navi, Prabhu, Jaideep and Ahuja, Simone (2012) *Jugaad Innovation: Think Frugal, Be Flexible, Generate Breakthrough Growth*, Wiley, London.

Srinivasan, Janaki and Burrell, Jenna (2013) *Revisiting the Fishers of Kerala, India*, [online], Paper presented at the International Conference on Information and Communication Technologies and Development 2013 in Cape Town, South Africa, <https://markets.ischool.berkeley.edu/files/2013/07/revisiting_fishers_kerala_wp.pdf> [accessed 8 April 2021].

Steyn, J. and Van Greunen, D. (eds) (2014) 'ICTs for inclusive communities in developing societies'. Proceedings of the 8th International Development Informatics Association Conference held in Port Elizabeth, South Africa.

Strode, Mary, Crawfurd, Lee, Dettling, Simone and Schmieding, Felix (2015) 'Jobs and the labor market', in Mthuli Ncube and Charles Leyeka Lufumpa (eds), *The Emerging Middle Class in Africa*, Routledge, London.

UNDP (2004) *Unleashing Entrepreneurship: Making Business Work for the Poor,* UN, New York.

Wharton School (2009) 'Why companies see bright prospects in rural India', [online], Knowledge at Wharton, University of Pennsylvania, <https://knowledge.wharton.upenn.edu/article/why-companies-see-bright-prospects-in-rural-india/> [accessed 30 June 2020].

Wilkinson-Maposa, Susan, Fowler, Alan, Oliver-Evans, Ceri and Mulenga, Chao F.N. (2005) *The Poor Philanthropist: How and Why the Poor Help Each Other,* Centre for Leadership and Public Values, University of Cape Town, Cape Town.

Wilkinson-Maposa, Susan (2008) 'Jansenville Development Forum: linking community and government in the rural landscape of the Eastern Cape Province, South Africa', in Alison Mathie and Gordon Cunningham (eds), *From Clients to Citizens: Communities Changing the Course of their Own Development,* pp. 237–60. Practical Action Publishing, Rugby.

World Bank (2004) *Making Services Work for the Poor,* World Bank, Washington.

Yunus, Muhammad (2007) *Creating a World Without Poverty: Social Business and the Future of Capitalism,* Public Affairs, New York.

CHAPTER 7

Who decides? Who acts? Shifting the power in participative development

Abstract

Despite the growing influence of participative development and human-centred design, power in development still largely rests in the hands of outside 'experts'. This chapter explores what a truly community-led approach to development could entail. It shows first the limits of outside expertise. Outsiders' social models like Utilitarianism and agreed lists of priorities like the SDGs provide only partial and imperfect guides. Outsiders' attempts to identify 'poverty traps' and 'adaptive preferences' can be fraught with difficulty. It then explores how communities can be given the lead role in decision-making and the steps needed to make these decisions more informed and equitable. This includes practical ways to make participation more democratic, to diffuse information from experts to users, and to help the latter make trade-offs and navigate dilemmas. In the final section it explores how communities can play a leading role in every stage of the development process, from inception to implementation and evaluation. We see the considerable challenges involved, but also the ample scope to redesign development so that it maximizes the knowledge and resources already present on the ground.

Keywords: participative development; human-centred design; Sustainable Development Goals; capabilities approach; adaptive preferences

In the last of my main chapters I want to address two issues of power and control that have been bubbling below the surface in the book so far. The first issue is who gets to choose between different competing development options. Participative development is all very well, but we have seen continually that listening to the poor isn't an easy or neutral exercise that yields clear answers. Do it properly and the different people we listen to want different things – sometimes directly opposed to one another. The second issue is that the aspirations and concerns of the poor don't always match the goals of development organizations, or the evidence amassed by expert research studies. What should the well-meaning outsider do when the people they consult have 'the wrong' priorities?

We have seen these two clashes regularly in the pages above and how they leave us with difficult dilemmas, not obvious answers. Young women tell you that pleasing their family is more important than completing their education; should you try to persuade them to change their mind? Your new farming approach will increase the incomes of a disadvantaged group, but will also undermine social cohesion; should you continue? We consistently find ourselves having to weigh up one development goal against another, or to decide between competing interests within the same community, or to balance our expertise with the expertise of our end users. Who, then, gets to choose in these situations and on what basis? We will see there are no easy ways of resolving this tension, but in this chapter I set out some ways we can tackle it more confidently, honestly, and sympathetically.

This will bring into relief one of the book's other recurring questions: how far can people on the ground take control of the practice of development? I have argued throughout (and especially in the previous chapter) that we need to place more value on the knowledge, skills, and networks that exist within communities, and we need to acknowledge the capacity of the poor to create and manage their own solutions to poverty. In this chapter I want to look at this capacity more critically and comprehensively, including:

- Which parts of the development process do people on the ground tend to have more and less capacity to manage and lead?
- How can this capacity be better identified and developed?
- How do we create more productive exchanges between insider and outsider knowledge that ultimately let the former take more control?
- How can we create solutions that limit the need for outsiders' 'technical' expertise?

The chapter has three parts, starting more with the question of 'who decides' and moving gradually into the question of 'who leads'. The first part is a critical examination of what the outside development 'expert' brings to debates over development choices. It shows the strengths, but more often the limits of an outsider's perspective and the lack of a rationale for privileging outsider over insider knowledge. I look at what, if any, objective principles or criteria the outside expert can turn to for help when trying to decide between competing courses of action, or competing voices in a community. I explore how established theories of social choice such as Utilitarianism, Libertarian, and Rights-based approaches give us models with which to weigh development outcomes against one another, but few categorical answers. Similarly, outsiders can use the concrete priorities for development, such as the United Nations' Sustainable Development Goals or Martha Nussbaum's list of universal 'capabilities',[1] but I argue that these provide only frameworks for making choices and invariably rely on consulting with people on the ground. This leads into a stronger critique of the tendency to privilege outside expertise and a clear argument for giving end users a greater say in development.

Having made this case, the second part of the chapter starts to explore what happens when those on the ground do lead decision-making. I begin by addressing openly the major challenges this raises. I highlight the kinds of information that insiders lack when making decisions and the ways in which more dominant groups can unconsciously (or very consciously) gain greater sway over discussions. From here, I explore the tactics that we can use to mitigate, if not overcome, these problems and to make community decision-making more equitable and effective.

The final part of the chapter takes to a logical conclusion the argument that has been building throughout the book. It asks how we might move beyond mere consultation with communities to an entirely community-led approach to development. This involves examining each stage of a typical development project in some detail for how it could be managed and run by local people and for how outside input can be scaled back. I will try to show how even in areas typically reserved for outsider 'technical' expertise, there is scope for communities to have far greater input and control. I will introduce examples of development practitioners who have pushed far down this path and I will examine what practical steps might allow outsiders to cede control more quickly and effectively in the near future. This clears the way for some short and concrete recommendations that I will set out in the eighth and concluding chapter.

Who decides? Development dilemmas and the (limited) value of outside expertise

What happens when we are working in the field and find ourselves faced by a clash between two imperatives? (Should we, say, continue to focus on our new farming intervention with its ability to raise incomes, even if it will undermine important cultural traditions?) As we struggle with such decisions, should the outside 'expert' leave it to those on the ground to choose – or to argue it out among themselves? Or can they reach for any objective principles or standards that would help them assess the competing options and make a better, more objective choice? This is the tension with which I want to begin, as we start to examine critically the value of the outsider's expertise.

Using models of social choice to resolve real world dilemmas

In his book *Development as Freedom*, Sen (1999) provides a guide to some of the conceptions of justice we might use when trying to evaluate different development priorities against one another. In particular, he examines three standpoints: Utilitarianism, the Libertarian philosophical traditions, and the concept of Human Capabilities that Sen himself has developed in parallel with Martha Nussbaum. The first, Utilitarianism, is an immediately appealing model for the development professional, since it offers an apparently simple gauge for weighing one choice against another. When faced with competing priorities, Utilitarianism demands that we choose the one that brings most satisfaction to the total population. So if maintaining a traditional mode of farming makes the majority of the community more satisfied than using new practices to increase revenue from the land, we should support tradition, even if, say, this prevented some younger and more marginalized members of the community from getting land and getting ahead.

For Sen (1999), Utilitarianism has the advantage that it demands ongoing, empirical analysis. It obliges us to keep evaluating the reality in front of us – whether our efforts are maximizing people's satisfaction or not. But Utilitarianism has several shortcomings too, as Sen explores in detail. First, it can be very hard in practice to measure satisfaction – or other proxies for satisfaction. Second, Utilitarianism is, classically at least, concerned with maximizing satisfaction for *the society as a whole*, rather than examining how satisfaction is distributed across different people. So we may find that a community *in total* is more satisfied by maintaining the traditional farming system, but some groups within the community will see quality of life decline harshly. Are we happy with this result? A third, connected problem Sen raises is that marginalized people may adapt their expectations and preferences, so they 'come to terms with their deprivation because of the sheer necessity of survival ... and may even adjust their desires and expectations to what they unambitiously see as feasible' (1999: 63). If this happens, and it seems particularly likely to do so among the poorest, then our measure of satisfaction becomes problematic. We will look further at this idea of 'adaptive preferences' below.

If Utilitarianism is an imperfect guide, an alternative way of thinking about social choice is Libertarianism. Utilitarianism starts from the basis that no one goal is intrinsically superior to any other and that we can only judge them against the broader empirical goal of maximizing total satisfaction. In contrast, Libertarian philosophy does privilege one goal over everything else: people's individual freedom. This is perhaps an even more inviting way to resolve dilemmas, since our yardstick now seems even clearer: which of our two development options gives people more freedom? If this means, say, breaking up the traditional farmholdings and giving each individual their own plot of land we should choose this option, even if it means, say, creating tension within families and across generations. Our aim should be to increase people's *freedom,* in order that they themselves may choose.

As my rather blunt example reflects, Libertarianism is unlikely to be a wholly satisfactory approach to development either, at least when applied in a purist way. As Sen outlines very clearly, Libertarianism rests on a basic misconception: that if people have liberty then all else will follow. The reality, Sen argues convincingly, is that there is no guarantee that liberty will lead to other social goods such as equality, security, or rising incomes. Instead, Sen argues, 'the operation of these entitlements can, quite possibly, include rather terrible results ... as is shown in my *Poverty and Famines* even gigantic famines can result without anyone's libertarian rights being violated' (1999: 66).

Hence Sen concludes that neither Utilitarianism nor Libertarianism provides a practical basis for setting or judging development goals. In their place he turns to his own conception of development as the practice of increasing people's 'capabilities' – the things that poor people are able to *do*. Here Sen is not focused on freedom as an abstract principle, to be supported for its own sake, but on supporting people's freedom *to do the specific things that they regard as valuable*, whether this is to go to school, maintain a farming tradition, work outside the home, or maintain close and stable family relationships.[2] There is, though, an intrinsic tension within the Capabilities approach too, which is how do we decide what capabilities are valuable to people? Do we ask our audience to define this for themselves, or do we as outsiders have a list of capabilities that we believe everyone should enjoy in any society? This is a question to which the two architects of the approach have responded differently.[3] Sen (1999) is wary of looking for universal capabilities (Robeyns, 2005). Nussbaum (1997) has created – and updated – a detailed list of the 'capabilities' that she believes development should work towards. It is the strengths and limitations of such lists that I will now move on to explore.

Development goals as criteria for making development choices

Nussbaum is not the only prominent development figure or organization to have sought to distil the aims of development practice into a set of priorities or goals. In this subsection I will briefly examine a number of different lists, exploring what they contain and specifically how they might help us in the field when we are trying to decide between competing development priorities. I have summarized four prominent examples below.

1. The *Capabilities List:* As noted, Nussbaum has put forward a list of specific and essential capabilities that she believes human development should work towards. These capabilities are wide-ranging and include being able to live a human life of normal length, enjoying physical health and security, being free from assault of any kind, having freedom of speech, freedom from discrimination, the right of political participation, and being able to hold property. Notably, Nussbaum also includes less obvious and more joyful – one might say more human – capabilities. These include the ability to play, laugh, love and be loved, and to use our imaginations. Her list has been detailed and explored extensively and my short summary only hints at its richness, but I introduce it to give an indication of the kind of criteria that we might apply. Nussbaum emphasizes that this list is not meant to be conclusive or universal, but rather 'open-ended and humble; it can always be contested and remade' (1997: 286).

2. *Multidimensional Poverty Index*: Another useful place we may look is the Oxford Poverty and Human Development Initiative.[4] This research group produces a global index of multidimensional poverty that captures financial and non-financial measures, including assets owned, nutritional levels, school attendance, access to clean water, and sanitation. Their focus on measurement over time gives their work a specific emphasis, but they are concerned with the same fundamental

questions of what aspects of poverty are critical (and in their case should therefore be measured). Like Nussbaum's lists, the OPHI is also a work of continual development, one which can be followed at the OPHI website and in the many research papers collected there. The initiative encourages countries to adopt and measure national multidimensional indices, which are notably based on the country's *own choices*. At the time of writing Sierra Leone had become the latest of over 20 countries to provide a national index.

3. The *SDGs:* Probably best known of all the criteria in play are the Sustainable Development Goals, or SDGs, set by the UN in 2015. These are 17 very broad global goals that again focus on non-financial as well as financial aspects of poverty and include achieving gender equality, providing quality education, and achieving good health and wellbeing. Each of the 17 SDGs comes with more specific targets to be met by 2030. The 'Quality Education' goal, for instance, has 10 subtargets, including ensuring 'that all youth and a substantial proportion of adults, both men and women, achieve literacy and numeracy'.[5]

4. *Grameen Goals*: Other specific lists of development priorities and goals are provided by individual organizations, such as the one developed by Muhammad Yunus, founder of Grameen (Yunus, 2007). This influential organization uses a set of 10 criteria when determining whether they have helped one of their customers to move out of poverty. These include whether you live in a tin-roofed house, drink pure water, have a hygienic and sanitary latrine, and if your children are able to finish primary school (Yunus, 2007). The list is framed more in terms of resources and outcomes than capabilities.

A lot has been written elsewhere about the problems of constructing lists of development goals (Crocker, 2007; Nussbaum, 1997; Nussbaum, 2003; Robeyns, 2005; Sen, 1999). What I am interested in here is the *practical application* of such lists to resolving development dilemmas. How might lists of the kinds above help us to choose between competing priorities in the community, or between the priorities of outside 'experts' and those of insiders on the ground? The answer again, I'd suggest, is that they can provide useful frameworks, but rarely conclusive answers.

First, having a list of our ideal *eventual* goals doesn't free us from having to make choices in our *immediate* everyday practice. Our ultimate aim may be a situation where all the SDGs are met, or where all the capabilities Nussbaum describes are in place, but the immediate reality of project work will often force us to choose *between* different criteria on the list. If we want to increase freedom of assembly we may lose some security in the community. If we push for greater female access to education perhaps we risk reducing social affiliation. The SDGs or the Capabilities list are effective beacons for where development as a whole is heading, but the designer of an individual project may still be forced to make choices.

Second, we will often find in practice that insiders may want to 'go off-list' and have other things they regard as more important than the Capabilities we regard as primary, or the SDG we wish to pursue. Nussbaum herself is very open about this reality, emphasizing that her list 'is continually being revised and adjusted, in accordance with my methodological commitment to cross-cultural deliberation and criticism' (1997: 277). OPHI and Grameen (Yunus, 2007: 110–11) similarly allow for differences across countries and regions, and the former encourages new users of the index to add their own criteria.[6] This returns us once more to consulting insiders. Once the capability approach is used for policy work it is 'the people who will be affected by the policies who should decide on what will count as valuable capabilities in this policy question' (Robeyns, 2005).

Third, the goals on these lists often rely on qualitative value judgements. What constitutes 'free speech', or an 'adequate education'? Or at what level of violent crime do we say someone can live 'free from fear of violent assault'? Nussbaum is very aware that any list of priorities involves value judgements and notes that hers has a tendency towards emphasizing freedom versus authority. The OPHI guide is similarly frank, emphasizing that their indexes of non-monetary poverty involve 'implicit or explicit assumptions about what people do value or should value'.[7] This means again that if we are going to use these lists in practice, we need to work with those on the ground to flesh out what these broad concepts *mean in the specific context we are working*. Lastly, even if we could arrive at a universal list, our audience might not feel it was legitimate unless they had been consulted in developing it. As Robeyns (2005: 199) writes, 'it is thus not sufficient that people can agree about the different items on the list of capabilities; instead, the process by which the list has been created itself needs to be legitimate. If the people to whom the list will apply reasonably feel that it is imposed on them, then the list will lack the necessary legitimacy that is needed for the list to have any political effect'.

None of these concerns is meant to question the value of identifying and applying priorities for development. Personally, I use all of the lists above as reference points when thinking about the range of different impacts a project might have. I find that consulting these lists can also help flush out our personal values and preferences, forcing us to be open about the positions we are taking. (For instance, I would instinctively give Nussbaum's 'security from assault and domestic violence' precedence over other concerns, no matter the context, or what insiders told me they believed.) These lists can also encourage us to think productively about the *relationship* between the different goals that are in play and where one goal might be very efficient at solving multiple other aspects of poverty. We saw a clear example of this earlier in how improving female literacy can have dramatic effects on infant mortality and as Sen writes 'these interlinkages are particularly important to seize in considering development policies' (1999: 40).

But, however much we might desire a universal model which tells us which elements of poverty to address first, second, and third, the reality is that context matters. Sen (1999) reminds us that incomes may be a 'prime mover' in some contexts, but not in others.[8] Narayan et al. (2009) highlight how education may be transformative in some instances, but a lower priority in others.[9] Once again, then, we are led away from objective criteria and back to context and consultation. Once more, we return to listening to insiders, to deciding together through conversation and exchange, rather than through any predetermined principles. I will move on shortly to examine how we can make these conversations more productive. Before that I want to double down on the importance of listening to insiders, by highlighting how difficult it is for outsiders to make objective assessments, and drawing further into question the nature of outside 'expertise'.

The strengths and weaknesses of the outsider's perspective

Let me start with an example from a project I was involved in a decade ago.

> I am talking to a company who are looking to create digital services to help poor owned businesses in South Asia. We have just finished ethnographic research and I am describing the daily life of one of the respondents I met, when one of the clients stops me with what should be a simple question: 'What does he do?' I pause for a second: 'He runs a road-side kiosk'. 'Right'. 'But, it's closed at the moment whilst he's working on the family land, near the town'. 'OK'. 'And he helps his cousin with his repair shop in the evenings, but actually most of his money comes from paintings he sells as an artist to tourists in Udaipur'. The meeting lapses into silence briefly and the client looks understandably uncertain. 'How can I help this man with his business?'

The 'correct' answer to my client's question would be to help him get a single job. Academic analysis suggests that many of the poorest people on the planet are held back by their 'portfolio' approach to work, their tendency to switch between many different economic activities – farming, a small business, seasonal work in the city and so forth – instead of focusing on one source of income. Analysis by Strode et al. (2015) of the job market in four African countries shows that households which have at least one 'portfolio' worker are more likely to be living below the poverty line of $1 a day than households where people work in a single sector.[10] Banerjee and Duflo (2011) similarly find across multiple studies that portfolio work tends to be economically inefficient.[11] Meanwhile, Narayan et al.'s (2000) global survey concluded that finding dependable, salaried work was an effective pathway out of income poverty.[12] Look at the evidence from robust social science approaches and you will see that the portfolio approach is a bad choice.

However, when you spend time with poor portfolio workers you realize that this way of living and working has its own logic and rewards. Not *all* are happy to work this way, but many see real benefits. I have heard workers say they feel they are mitigating risk by keeping multiple options open. I have seen how people use the flexibility of their working patterns to coordinate their time with other members of the family, developing habits and bonds that might be lost if they worked full-time. And many people I have met obviously enjoy the freedom that having several sources of income gives them – the chance to vary their tasks according to their mood, for example, rather than follow the routine of a regular job in the formal economy.

This illustrates both the strengths and the weaknesses of the outsider's perspective. On the one hand outsiders can identify where poor people's choices are suboptimal or even self-destructive. On the other hand insiders may have their own logic for making these choices, which the outsider can easily miss. Collins et al. (2009) give the example of poor people taking out loans in order to be able to invest. To an outsider this might seem a poor choice: why would someone with only a few dollars a day pay higher rates for loans than they will get as a return on their savings? But there is often an underlying social logic; for instance, a young South Asian woman may take a loan in order to invest in gold, because gold is one of the only assets that she knows *she can own personally*, whatever happens through her life. It is, Collins et al. argue, 'a substantial life-long asset offering security against the disruptions in family life so common and so painful for women like her – divorce, desertion, or death of her husband' (2009: 23). A similar example is given by Caroline Robb (2002) who found people in Mali with very low incomes were spending surprisingly large sums on clothing. This apparently 'irrational' use of money had the very functional explanation; that clothing kept its value better than other goods and was a sound investment for people with few secure financial assets to buy. Another example is cited by Rao in Karnataka where poor villagers spent on average 15 per cent of their annual income on contributing to, and participating in, local festivals – a surprising sum given the difficulty of meeting many basic needs. But Rao (2002) also found that this money brought concrete economic rewards for those who had participated, such as paying lower prices for food. These examples are a sharp reminder of the pitfalls of ethnocentrism in development and just one example of how the solutions to poverty that people come up with themselves can be very effective and entirely at odds with outside experts' expectations.

There are also instances of 'irrationality' where insiders are very aware of the self-defeating nature of their behaviour. When the poor adopt short-term expedient solutions which damage their long-term interests they are often more acutely aware of this damage than any eagle-eyed development expert. As Narayan et al. argue, 'poor people want to be able to take the long view, but they cannot. Having to live "hand to mouth" is not a choice, but an immensely frustrating necessity' (2000: 37). As outsiders we are often quick to congratulate ourselves for identifying 'poverty traps' and 'sub-optimal behaviour' among poor communities, but very often the poor are a step ahead of us – aware that their choice is not ideal and aware of why they nonetheless have to make it.[13]

It can be especially hard for outsiders to judge whether a choice is leading to greater suffering or not. Alkire illustrates this very clearly via a number of hypothetical but convincing examples. These include 'a hard-packed dirt floor in a leading indigenous household that has an eco-lodge... low body mass, for fashion reasons... water from an unprotected spring [that] may in fact be safe although the conventions would code it differently' (2018: 9). In each, outsiders might identify a deprivation that isn't experienced as such by those (literally) on the ground. Nussbaum points to a similar potential for misunderstanding between outsider and insider, with examples including, 'a deeply religious person [who] may prefer not to be well-nourished, but instead prefer to engage in strenuous fasting' (1997: 288), Mohanty's critique of western commentary on the veil shows how the meaning of a covering relies on understanding the specific cultural logic of actors in each context. For instance, she argues that 'Iranian middle-class women veiled themselves during the 1979 revolution to indicate solidarity with their veiled working-class sisters' (1988). This, she argues, was 'both an oppositional and revolutionary gesture on the part of Iranian middle-class women' (1988), and a complex and multi-layered act that extends far beyond most outsiders' interpretation of veiling. This illustrates how outsiders can have particular difficulty in analysing the subtleties of power relations and the degrees to which particular groups are, or aren't, being oppressed.

Outsider clarity and 'adaptive preferences'

Some of the most difficult calculations come around the idea of 'adaptive preferences' alluded to earlier. Adaptive preferences (or AP) has been used to describe moments when marginalized members of a community learn to expect less from life than their more privileged neighbours. The problem can be illustrated with a jarring example from Nussbaum and Sen's work (Nussbaum, 1997). Looking at data from post-independence India they found that at that time 48.5 per cent of widowers described themselves as suffering from ill or indifferent health, but that the equivalent for widows was a tiny 2.5 per cent. Taken at face value, this would suggest a huge investment was required in health and care services for older men – and much, much less for older women. Nussbaum's explanation for this enormous difference, however, is more compelling. She suggests that women – and especially widowed women – had assimilated such low expectations for themselves that even when their health conditions were materially worse, they had learned to downplay their problems. She argues that 'people who have regularly been malnourished, who have, in addition, been told that they are weak and made for suffering, and who, as widows, are told that they are virtually dead and have no rights, will be unlikely to recognize their fatigue and low energy as a sign of bodily disease'. She suggests this is 'not so for males, who are brought up to have high expectations for their own physical functioning' (1987: 282).

This example is stark, but the underlying dynamic is common. Marginalized groups are more likely to undervalue their priorities and underplay the extent of their need. So when an outsider asks what they would want from a new initiative they may ask for less and they may ask less forcefully. When asked what goals we should prioritize, they may downplay the importance of their own.

To some extent the outsider's perspective may be valuable here. The development professional can potentially help marginalized people to see disconnects between their perceived needs and actual needs, and to expand their ideas of what they might be able to gain from development. But the idea of 'adaptive preferences' needs to be used with care. First, I would agree with Serene Khader (2009) who argues that outsiders are rather prone to employ the label 'adaptive preferences' when insiders' priorities disagree with their own. If I believe in education as a development priority and am working on a project to improve access among young women, then when a young woman tells me that following family traditions is more important than staying in school I may quickly assume that she is not expressing her 'true' desires, but rather a learned, 'adaptive' preference. And by jumping in with my label, I may not spend enough time listening to her rationale for doing so.

This brings us to a second point that Khader (2009) raises, which is that 'adaptive preferences' can be formed in more reflective and conscious ways than outsiders often acknowledge. Poor people often find themselves in social conditions where pursuing their ideal goals is simply unrealistic and hence they adapt their preferences not in a naive or unthinking way, but as a pragmatic calculation of what they can currently achieve. When a young woman in northern India tells me she is going to help her husband with his business rather than start her own, or a man from a minority ethnic group in Kenya tells me he is going to vote for 'someone who can win', rather than stand for local election himself, they may be very aware of what is going on and are making an active calculation. This doesn't mean they are expressing their ideal choice, but neither are they acting naively. Their choices are, as Khader describes, 'formed in response to unjust social arrangements' (2012: 303). If an outsider wants to be useful, they shouldn't just be trying to encourage greater reflection or expand people's horizons, they should be looking to address these underlying social arrangements.

Khader's conception of 'adaptive preferences' also emphasizes the tensions and layers within any adaptive behaviour. Drawing on fieldwork by Uma Narayan (one of the critics of AP), she gives the example of the varied and sometimes conflicting layers that come with religious veiling and seclusion for the Pirzada women of Delhi. I will quote from her description at length to reflect the complexities involved and how they go far beyond a simple label of 'adaptive preference':

> These women a) are sometimes right when they describe their options as limited; b) experience internal conflict about the acceptability of the norms that oppress them (they disapprove of women whom they

perceive as immodest, yet simultaneously envy those who have married into less restrictive families; they also criticise purdah for making them 'look like water buffalo' and limiting their educational access); c) gain objective benefits from their compliance with oppressive norms (such as class status and the ability to move anonymously in public); and d) would thus possibly have their lives worsened by coercive policies aimed at changing their behaviour (2012: 304).

Such tensions almost inevitably surface once you get into the field. People hold contradictory views that don't neatly correlate with a simple notion of either free choice or oppression. Their views play out quite differently depending on the context they find themselves in – more resistant in one moment, more accepting in another. The choices that people make are also the result of active trade-offs and calculations, which take into account norms and strictures over which they have limited personal control. An outsider needs to take time to observe, discuss, and absorb these tensions and contradictions before trying to assess what someone's true preference is.

What I hope this section has shown is both the value and the deficiencies of the outsider's perspective. We have seen how the 'irrational' behaviour we try to eradicate may have a compelling logic that the poor see much better than us. The 'poverty traps' and 'adaptive preferences' that we identify may already be very familiar to the poor, who also know more than us about how the trap or preference comes about. The suffering or oppression we identify may not be experienced as such by the 'sufferers'. All this means outsiders cannot easily step back and evaluate one option over another from the comfortable position of expertise. We can use our distance from the situation, our knowledge of multiple contexts, our ability to draw on and model data of outcomes across locations. But we should be extremely cautious about deciding what is the right option, highly attentive to context, and more patient in understanding the options from the insiders' point of view. It is to the challenges of doing the latter that I'll turn now.

Who decides? How can communities lead decisions?

In the pages above we have continually come back to the impossibility of outsiders deciding between development priorities on their own and the importance of consulting with those on the ground. And yet when it comes to choosing between development options, communities are no more infallible than outside experts:

- They are often divided in their priorities.
- Dominant groups are prone to take over the process and push their vested interests.
- Whilst insiders have knowledge that outsiders lack, the reverse is also true.
- And the goals the community prioritize and the solutions they prefer may not be the most effective at meeting their actual wishes.

In the next section I want to draw out these problems in more detail and look at what (often very practical) steps can be taken to address them. How do we ensure decisions have input from marginal as well as dominant voices? How do we help people gain and use more information in making their choice? How can we help people with limited experience of social and economic change to think more concretely about alternative possible futures?

Including all voices

When we ask a community to guide a development project two slightly different but related things can happen. First, the people we hear from are the most powerful groups; second, we end up designing something that benefits the most powerful. There are numerous references in development research to the first dynamic. Oosterlaken (2009) argues that participative design methods too often fail to canvass the views of the marginalized. The World Bank's *Sleeping on Our Own Mats* report describes how 'members of community development committees tend to be predominantly community elites, and male' (2002: 3). Mansuri and Rao conclude that 'absent some kind of affirmative action program, groups that form under the aegis of interventions tend to systematically exclude disadvantaged and minority groups and women' (2012: 9).

It doesn't automatically follow that a group dominated by the powerful will pursue their interests over those of weaker groups. The 'elite' may take on leading roles not out of self-interest, but because they have more free time to devote to helping the community. Sometimes, they may use their education and connections to make sounder choices that will benefit the community as a whole. This rosy interpretation is not impossible. For instance, Mansuri and Rao (2012) cite a study by Dasgupta and Beard that found that 'community development boards that were dominated by elite groups delivered more benefits to the poor, who fared much worse under apparently more egalitarian community development boards' (2002: 130). But in my experience this is not the norm. And in their wide-reaching review of participative development work, Mansuri and Rao conclude that overall 'the poor often benefit less from participatory processes than do the better off, because resource allocation processes typically reflect the preferences of elite groups' (2012: 5). Fung and Wright (2001) note how this may happen even in celebrated cases of participative development, such as the Brazilian city Porto Alegre's participative government experiment. They conclude that 'even if both strong and weak are well represented, the strong may nevertheless use tools at their disposal – material resources, information asymmetries, rhetorical capacities – to advance collective decisions that unreasonably favor their interests' (2001: 34).

Elite takeover is a widespread problem, and one that is hard to combat. But there are several practical steps we can take to minimize it. The first is to not take the easy option of focusing on the community's *current* representatives – local government, community leaders, and elders. As Robb notes, 'in many communities, it is easier and quicker to interact with the local elite, thereby missing the poorest (who are often less articulate, overworked, and unable to attend meetings) and women (who do not often leave their homes and are used to being excluded)' (2002: 59). Similarly, we should be wary of asking the community to choose the people who will represent them in our new development initiative. If there is little democratic tradition and no quotas, the new group we convene is likely to be elite-dominated and liable to design interventions that play to their agendas.

Hence a lot of effort is often needed at the outset to identify, approach, and encourage less powerful members of a community to be part of the representative group. Many participative projects have tried to tackle this directly by applying quotas for gender, ethnicity, caste, neighbourhood, land ownership, or religion.[14] Wong and Guggenheim (2018: 18) suggest that this mandatory route has had some success, noting that when gender quotas are mandated, women's participation in community development becomes 'exponentially higher than it is in traditional councils or in sectoral community-wide programs'. Persistence is also required. Iskander and Bentaleb-Maes's account of community electrification in Morocco emphasizes the time it took for both the privileged and marginalized to feel comfortable with a more democratic group being in charge. The former saw it as an attack on their powers, whilst the latter were unsure their contributions were really wanted. It was only through persistent invitations and encouragement – and the 'proof of concept' that came with persuading outside technical professionals to give their help – that the group started to function as planned.

We should also consider the mundane but vital factors that will make it easy for all groups to take part. Marginal groups often work longer hours and live further from likely meeting points. Women's ability to participate in community work is often constrained by the time they are expected to give to parenting and domestic work (Hamaus et al., 2015), and they may not be able to travel far from their homes. The poorest may be unable to give up hours to attend, when they could be earning. Hence it really matters where we hold these events, at what time, and what incentives and support we provide to get people there. There may also be softer signals we can use too, to help draw in representatives of the whole community. When you choose a community hall to hold the meetings, is it in a higher-class or higher-caste area, or somewhere everyone feels comfortable? Who owns the hall and who normally meets there? Are the media you are using to invite people (local radio, word of mouth, written documents, town criers) clearly aimed at everyone?[15]

Getting people to attend is only half of the story. Even if we overcome the many challenges and bring together a truly representative group, the dominant members are liable to take control of the discussions that get under way.[16] As Fung and Wright remind us, 'participants in these processes usually face each other from unequal positions of power. Citizens who are advantaged in terms of their wealth, education, income, or membership in dominant racial and ethnic groups participate more frequently and effectively than those who are less well off'. However solemnly we may state that 'all opinions are equally valid and valued here', normal power relations will never be fully suspended in any group – and especially not when the participants will meet again the next day when our idealistic democracy has dissolved. As Abraham and Platteau ask: 'how can a youngster talk on an equal footing with an elder in a meeting of a participation-minded village association while he simultaneously has to address himself to the leader respectfully and humbly as soon as he steps out of the meeting?' (2004: 222). If, as is not uncommon, you are working in a region used to authoritarianism and oppression, people may reasonably suspect there will be repercussions if they speak as openly as we naive outsiders suggest. Mansuri and Rao (2012: 34) point out that our participants may have good reasons to doubt 'that the increase in local power brought about by a project will result in lasting change ... making them more fearful of eventual retaliation by local elites'.

There are varying ways to respond to these problems, some more direct or even confrontational than others. At the more indirect end of the spectrum, we can try to *work around* elite domination by conducting smaller and less formal consultations and by talking to people in distinct groups: men and women only; particular age bands; similar classes, castes, and ethnic groups. This is an approach I have often used and one with which I feel more naturally comfortable. In field, it can require a lot of preparation and sometimes subterfuge. On many occasions I have settled down to listen to a father holding court, whilst my colleagues have peeled off to interview his wife and children, or I have waited for a formal meeting of farmers to end before arranging to talk to the quieter and poorer members separately. The growth of digital technology is potentially transformative here. Already, online networks are making it easier for traditionally less powerful groups to gather and discuss ideas away from 'dominant' voices. The NGO Plan, for instance, run a programme called Girls Out Loud designed to allow more natural, organic conversations among girls and young women online (Westerberg, 2020).

We can also address the power imbalances during the analysis phase, by making power relations an explicit and central part of the way we review and interpret the views we have heard. What goals, priorities, assumptions were put forward by more and less powerful groups? What was said and not said by those with less power? Making power an explicit part of the analysis of consultations is an important step.

A more direct approach is to run public, open consultations and include very clear mechanisms that encourage marginal or minority voices. Van Domelen (2007), for instance, suggests formal, secret voting is one way that outsiders can both highlight the idea that *all* members of the community should be listened to equally and provide a method for collecting opinions equally. However, care needs to be taken when choosing our methods – the idea of a secret vote may be seen suspiciously in a very communal culture with no tradition of this method (Dowden, 2008). Another approach is to design incentives that encourage more equal participation and representation.

For instance, Van Domelen (2007) outlines how some projects have scaled their funding, so that the amount of funding increases when projects can demonstrate they have benefited all groups in a community, or specific marginal groups in particular.

The most striking approach, though, is not to *work around* inequalities but to try to bring them into the open, to *make manifest* how poorer and weaker members of a community are being held back or exploited and to challenge the community to address this inequality. I have not had the opportunity, or courage, to do this myself; however, there are case studies of interventions that have done so very directly, and successfully. I want to look briefly now at one exemplary case and consider what we might learn from it. The project was run by Banerjee et al. (2015) in Bihar, North India, a state with high levels of poverty and discrimination, and it sought to address the way that dominant groups were monopolizing ownership of land. The method was to work with villagers to record maps (first on cloth and paper and then eventually on a PC) that showed who owned and controlled each square metre of land in the area. Equally importantly, the *reasons* why certain people exercised control over certain pieces of land were recorded. The map that the researchers and community members created made manifest the abuses of power that were occurring within the community. The map showed, for instance, that 'many landless families from *dalit* and tribal communities have been unable to make use of land that was allotted to them by the state government because of an inability to establish control over holdings' (Banerjee et al., 2015). It was also found – and very clearly shown on paper and then on screens – that less than 2 per cent of land was owned by women.

What is particularly striking about this project is the way that the methodology was designed first to work around, but then eventually *against*, established power groups. The maps were constructed initially by the poorest members of the community and then put on general display, where they were authenticated by a broader range of people. The first voices to be heard in the project were those of the poorest groups, and, notably, the powerful groups had little chance to influence the process until the former had spoken. But rather than merely talking to marginalized groups solely in private, the project deliberately and very publicly found a way to broadcast their voices to the community as a whole and to lay down a challenge to the elites. This project had rapid and tangible effects. Banerjee et al. cite a number of villagers who 'successfully secured land rights in their favour following a land-mapping process and with use of land maps' (2015). The authors give the example of one man who 'was able to wrest control over 6 acres and 62 decimals of land (around 6.6 acres) belonging to his ancestors. The land had been misappropriated by a village landlord, but the land-mapping process brought clarity regarding the particulars of encroachment of land in the village' (2015).

One final, important way that less powerful members of a community may be encouraged centre stage is by shifting the emphasis of work from discussion to action. Less affluent and influential members of the community may be less confident participating in debates about abstract plans, but they may have similar, or greater, levels of knowledge of more practical questions. Cunningham (2008) describes how 'ownership' of the development process can shift from elites to poorer people if or when we focus on more tangible steps for development. Giving an example from rural Ethiopia, he describes how the development programme was 'initially dominated by educated, affluent community members who pushed the agenda of electrification' (2008: 292–3). But 'once it became clear that this was too ambitious, these members became less active, while those less accustomed to leadership spearheaded groups concerned with poultry, beekeeping, and embroidery initiatives' (2008: 293).

Beyond listening to the poor: sharing knowledge from the outside

So far, we have been looking at how to increase representation across a community so that decisions are taken by, and on behalf of, all. I now want to turn to a second challenge, which is how to increase the knowledge base on which these decisions are taken. This is because insiders, like outsiders, have only a partial perspective and incomplete information with which to make choices. Thus, I would argue, the role of outsiders is not just to listen to the poor, but to help poor people to think about a wider range of potential futures and to consider critically the trade-offs that these will involve. This section examines three ways we can do this in practice.

Introducing new information. We have seen throughout the book that poor communities are increasingly affected by changes in fields beyond their traditional knowledge. Globalized supply chains, changing weather patterns, evolutions in media, breakthroughs in agricultural technology all affect the daily lives of people in remote and very traditional communities. They often do so in ways it is hard for people to trace. Over 15 years ago Alkire argued that development workers should do more to help poor people to think about the transformations that these external forces are liable to bring. Her advice, from which I quote below, has become even more pressing today.

> Every field worker knows the difference between the city and the countryside; most have heard stories of how villages or neighborhoods have been transformed within one generation. Many even write up and publicize their case studies in glossy print for fund-raising purposes. Some call themselves 'change makers'. And yet the communities are not themselves dignified with so much as a forthright discussion of what is coming so that they can address the changes reflectively and protect what is most treasured (2004: 196).

This is a justifiable critique. To respond, I have often found it useful to bring into the field information on emerging trends, future projections, and plans that may affect the communities where I'm working. This information can be gathered in desk research and distilled in various ways, and includes:

- *Simple statistics:* For instance, sharing with members of the community data that shows the growing number of young women in higher education in the country, or the returns by farmers who are or aren't members of cooperatives.
- *Possible futures:* Speculative design projects that show possible future scenarios. For instance, exhibitions and websites such as Design for the Other 90% and Open IDEO's social challenges[17] give examples that can be condensed, developed, and critiqued.
- *Proof/disproof of concept:* Evidence from past projects is also rarely shared with communities, but I believe it is vital when working on a new programme to tell people what has and hasn't worked in similar past initiatives. There is a growing number of resources we can use here, such as J-PAL's publicly available catalogue of past research, which distils lessons from individual trials into short summaries.
- *Concrete comparisons:* Showing people examples of local initiatives from other parts of the region can also help people think about what changes they would, and would not, like to see. For instance, Sristi's Honeybee Network[18] or DESIS's clusters of social innovation projects (Manzini, 2015) provide catalogues of community and development projects to share.

Some of these resources are largely designed for, and accessed by, outsider audiences, but much of the material can be fairly easily adapted to share with people on the ground. A project from the global north that illustrates this potential is the City Eco Lab Scenarios created in St Etienne, France (Manzini, 2015). Here, designers worked with six families from the city, giving them examples of 50 existing but often embryonic environmental projects from the region and asked them to imagine how they might use and interact with these projects in the course of their everyday lives. The families were encouraged to create stories of their future lives, captured in photographs, collage, and text. These were then shared with other residents in displays and local media, allowing them to talk about how potentially abstract urban planning ideas would play out in their everyday lives.

There is, of course, a delicate balance here about how and when one introduces such stimulus. We need to be careful we aren't only selecting material that supports our own hypotheses and priorities. Typically too, I believe, it works best to understand the issues spontaneously from insiders' perspectives before introducing future possibilities that might shift the conversation away from people's instinctive priorities. Ideally also, we design consultations so that they allow repeated back and forth between outsiders' and insiders' knowledge and priorities. Outsiders introduce ideas that may not have been considered before. Insiders can react to these, rejecting, reworking, and adding to them. The outsider can respond in turn with updated versions.

With persistence, empathy, and good fortune neither outsider nor insider imposes their priorities on the other, but rather both revisit and reset their goals. Crocker (2007) gives further illustrations of fluid facilitation of this kind.

Grounding choices in tangible examples, places, and practices. When we ask insiders to choose between development outcomes we are often asking them to weigh up things they haven't experienced before. How can someone anticipate whether, for instance, a digital land map or an RFID tagged bag for transporting cashew nuts will bring more benefits than problems if they – like most people – have never seen such a thing before? One way we can help is to create stimulus and prototypes that bring out future scenarios to life in vivid and locally grounded ways. Over time I've learned the value of working with graphic and digital designers to create such future scenarios and to depict them in simple and grounded ways (see Figures 7.1 to 7.3 below). The scenes you show and the benefits you imagine are often as useful for what you get wrong as what people actively want.

I have also come to appreciate how we can use the physical environment of the community as stimulus for imagining the future. A simple approach I have often used is a guided walk around the community, where you stop at important spaces in people's everyday lives and discuss the potential for new innovations *in situ*. Standing where the cooperative meet, or where children gather to walk to school, you have all the physical and social cues right there in front of you. How would these RFID tagged bags actually be used

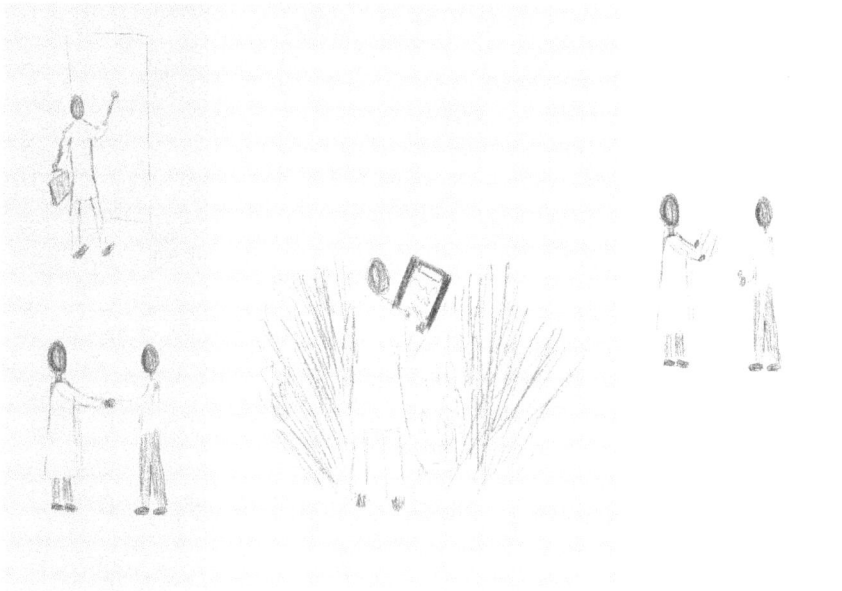

Figure 7.1 Drawing for early concept for farming service, used in field, 2018.

Figure 7.2 Drawing for early concept for farming service, used in field, 2018.

Figure 7.3 Drawing for early concept for citizens' rights service, used in field.

in the reality of the cooperative's sorting office, for instance? How would a safe transport-to-school solution actually work along these streets? Manzini (2015) describes how this approach was developed further in the global north during the 2012 Human Cities project. Designers captured on cards examples of new environmental initiatives from cities around Europe. Residents were then asked to walk around their own neighbourhood with these cards and to think about where and how these outsider projects could be applied to their own community – as well as where they would fail to connect. To make the possibilities more nuanced and real they were asked to photograph the card held up against the location in which they imagined it being used – creating a visual map of how outside ideas could work in their community.

The aim of all these activities and tools is twofold. First, they encourage people to critically assess their current reality and its potential for change in the way that Praxis achieved with who owns the land. Second, they ask people to imagine, evaluate, criticize, and develop possible concrete, alternative futures. Or as Manzini writes rather more poetically, 'by putting different promising cases together and showing them as they could appear in people's daily lives ... they generate a metavision of a possible but as yet unrealised life' (2015: 132).

Obliging people to make choices. Lastly, consultations should oblige insiders to make choices. As Robb (2002) argues, it is easy to turn a consultation process into a wish list of all the things that participants would want. The real job of the outsider, I would argue, is to ask people on the ground to consider and make *trade-offs* for themselves. This means being open about how well previous initiatives have worked and being frank about what the potential downsides of our initiative might be. To move from wish lists to choices, outsiders can also encourage the community to debate and consider the risks and benefits from *a variety of different angles*: individual and communal; economic and social; shorter-term and longer-term perspective.

The trade-off between long and short term is particularly critical, since in many places the poor face a growing tension between the long-term desire to preserve communal resources and the short-term necessity of making a living. The latter, understandably, frequently wins, but people will often feel regret, as this passage from Narayan et al. (2000: 51) clearly describes:

> In all regions communities are experiencing the effects of deforestation, and poor people see the loss of forest areas and its impacts as threatening their livelihoods and food security. In most places where the problem is identified, the poor attribute deforestation to human pressures and lack of alternative livelihoods, fuel and food. In Adaboya, Ghana the researchers indicate that economic hardships and the lack of jobs push many into charcoal burning and cutting wood to sell. Similarly poor people rely heavily on firewood and rattan collecting, charcoal burning, and hunting to generate income in the highland forest communities of

Ha Tinh, Vietnam. Women and men acknowledge the pressures that their activities place on the local environment, but they see few alternatives.

We need to ensure that longer-term communal, natural resources are in play when priorities are compared and choices are made. And if we are to take sustainability seriously we need to ensure that non-human needs – the requirements of the land, water, plant life, and non-human organisms – are part of the nexus of choices. This means more collaboration with environmental specialists and making room for less anthropocentric perspectives. Or as Despret (2016) provocatively puts it, 'what would animals say if we asked the right questions?' It also means taking the time to draw out knowledge of the environment that exists within the community, and which may sometimes be taken for granted – the multiple ways that particular trees or plants are used, the sources of water throughout the year, the *de facto* ownership, and usage of different plots of land. The environmental resources within a community, and the habits that sustain or deplete them are unlikely to be captured in a neat audit, or even always consciously in people's minds. We have to take care that they are included as factors within community decision-making.

Who leads? Accelerating the transfer of power across the development cycle

The steps that I've described so far represent only a very partial transfer of power from outsiders to communities. Let's say we do all the things I've advocated above. We foster informed, subtle, and democratic debate within the community. We enrich it with outside data and imaginatively designed future scenarios. We find ways to draw out and appreciate important assumed knowledge. And then we go back to our offices in Nairobi or north London and design the new programme on our own. In this process has the community really decided?

Preece et al. (2015) criticize a lot of the research that is conducted with poor communities for exactly this kind of 'extractive' approach. The problem is, they argue, that outsiders extract a lot of knowledge from the community in the name of 'participation' but then give very little in return. This process may briefly give poor people a voice, but it is outsiders who retain control of the important choices. They decide what services to make and how these services are delivered. Preece et al. argue that the poor cannot really be said to have chosen if they are merely consulted at the outset, rather than co-creating and implementing the programmes and products they go on to use. I will quote their critique at some length.

> In the context of large-scale aided development, project information systems have predominantly served as mechanisms to facilitate the 'upward' transfer of knowledge about communities to project management. Whilst this may suit agencies interested in planning and managing programmes, the effect has often been to consolidate a system

of externally driven intervention, wherein beneficiaries do not influence the programme beyond a contribution to the planning stage (2015: 41).

When I think about the work I have done during the last 15 years and particularly earlier in my career I must recognize a good measure of truth to this criticism. In many cases the transfer of knowledge *has* been largely one way. Lots of research may have been done with people on the ground. But, most of the time, major decisions have been made outside the community. We may have listened, but we have also tried to guard our roles as outside experts, crediting ourselves with an objectivity that allows us to go into the field, find the truth, and then come back and analyse and explain what it all 'really means'.[19] In such moments, the transfer of power from outsider to insider is far from complete.

In this final section I want to explore how the entire arc of development work could be reworked to give much more power and control to those on the ground. I look at five broad areas or stages in the development process (inception, research, analysis, implementation, and evaluation) and examine where we can help insiders to do more and outsiders do less. Our ultimate goal should be a fully community-run process, but we need to be honest that some parts of the process are more difficult for communities to run. It would be folly to pretend that it's straightforward to ask people to run regression analysis on quantitative data, write an algorithm in a farming app, or maintain a complex regional plumbing network.[20]

On the other hand, those of us who are paid for our 'technical' expertise should take more care about how we judge what requires 'technical support'. Are there ways to reframe our initiatives so that they make more use of the strengths of local knowledge versus outside expertise? Users may not be able to program the app themselves yet, but what kinds of new software would let them do so? Can we design a pipe system that is easier for local people to repair, or which mirrors the technical understanding of plumbing that already exists in the region? The evidence we have seen – and will continue to see below – suggests we should be asking such questions much more often.

Inception: sourcing ideas from communities

Firstly, I'd suggest outside agencies need to think much more carefully and creatively about the source of development ideas. Even as the number of participative and community-driven projects has increased, the planning and design of these projects has often remained in the global north. The projects may seek to let communities lead, but the original idea for the work still tends to arise far outside the community. This means agencies are missing out on the countless ideas that originate on the ground. It matters, because as Iskander and Bentaleb-Maes (2008: 177) argue, successful development 'does not proceed by "invitations to tender", according to agendas elaborated in the North, but by responding to proposals put forward by local populations and migrants'.

If we are to take this notion seriously then actors in the global north need to shift their role fundamentally, from project instigators to project supporters. NGOs and funding bodies need to find ways to be usefully reactive. Rather than taking ideas out to communities, they should become much more accessible to community actors finding them. Community leaders can then bring development agencies their own new ideas, to which the outside experts can supply guidance, as well as technical and financial assistance. The growth in access to digital technology makes such an approach increasingly viable. There appears rich potential here for agencies in the global north to work together to create platforms that would allow communities on the ground to pitch and instigate new ideas, rather than waiting for outsiders to arrive.

Community-led research and consultation

This is an area I would suggest is gathering momentum. On several occasions I have helped to train people in low-income communities to conduct their own qualitative and quantitative research. These are fairly abstruse skills to transfer, compared to teaching a man or woman to fish. But they can benefit both individuals and community. For the former, there can be immediate employment and improved future career possibilities. My colleague Jamal Khadar, for instance, ran a long-term training programme in Rwanda that both created a local research team and increased employment amongst young women.[21] More importantly, the community as a whole acquires valuable skills and becomes less reliant on outsiders. Research by community members also has certain inherent advantages. Banerjee et al. (2015) found that respondents interviewed by researchers from their community 'generally related much better to the community representatives than the way they might have been expected to relate to non-community evaluators'. The charity Girl Effect similarly claim that teenage girls can be more willing to talk about sensitive subjects when interviewed by their peers from the same or similar communities.[22] There are growing examples of community members taking on a larger proportion and a greater range of research skills, including more complex ones. Mathie (2008) gives the example of the NGO Myrada training people in a remote and poor area of Karnataka, southern India, to conduct techniques such as wealth ranking, mapping, and transect walk: the same techniques which I often recommend to my graduate students.

As communities take on more active research roles, the question of bias is often raised. Whilst anyone conducting research will bring their own subjective expectations and prejudices, community members may have more skin in the game. This can allow them a richer, more vivid understanding of what is being discussed, but it may also make it harder for them to blot out their own agenda. When the researcher (or their friends or family) may stand to gain from certain outcomes of the consultation more than others, it can take heroic efforts not to steer discussions. Thus, any community-run research effort does need to identify, consider, and account for potential bias within the methodology and analysis.

Community analysis and planning

We have seen above that often the process of consultation happens in communities, but the analysis and planning that follows is done elsewhere. Preece et al. (2015) describe how in the Avahan study they realized that this was occurring: 'the monitoring itself was creating rich fields of understanding that, though shared with communities, was ultimately analysed outside the domain of community'. Training people to analyse and interpret the material generated in consultations is in my experience more difficult than training people to conduct primary research. Qualitative data from interviews and discussions can strike new practitioners as a barrage of individual stories and competing anecdotes. (Personally, it was only after many months and numerous studies that I could see themes and patterns easily emerging from my notes and recordings.) Quantitative data from surveys requires some formal education in mathematics at least and often far more sophisticated statistical understanding. Many of the judgement calls needed in analysis also tend to come from experience – what sources of data to trust, what mechanisms may lie behind the correlations we see. Furthermore, some programmes (most obviously medical ones) have technical elements which require extensive training to judge. As a World Bank report (2004: 65) argues, 'Patients – as individuals or health boards – are good judges of courtesy and attendance. But they are much less able to judge clinical quality or the appropriate mix of curative and preventive services'. All of this is harder still if members of the team struggle with literacy.

We shouldn't, though, regard these challenges as an excuse to maintain the wall between insiders and outsiders. Instead, we should look for ways to work around them, to think about how we change our methods of analysis to bring in insiders to analysis and planning. Preece et al. (2015) describe, for example, how they built an analysis toolkit using colour-coding to group results into clear themes. They then worked with community groups to develop how these codes were used in analysis. Over time, groups became more confident about taking control of the analysis and to move from following the rules to improvising in order to ground discussions in the material that was emerging. Another study run by Praxis (Banerjee et al., 2015) asked community members to devise the categories on which a programme would be evaluated. This not only ensured that they were analysing the programme on criteria that mattered to the community, it acted as a first step in training people to do their own analysis. Outside facilitators then helped local participants to distil the 77 initial different criteria into a smaller number of directive themes.

This study challenged the assumption that analysis requires formal education and social science training. It started instead with the premise that local knowledge and life experience could be equally if not more valuable and it then built the analysis tools from this principle. The authors describe how 'in the design and the running of the evaluation, credit was given to held knowledge, popular knowledge, and primary knowledge as opposed to bookish, academic, and secondary knowledge'. Researchers can also address problems of literacy by conducting analysis using more visual methods. These include drawings and images and recording people's thoughts on video. The affordability and accessibility of digital technology makes this approach increasingly viable.

Even when later elements of analysis and planning do take place outside of the community, outsiders can do more to share preliminary findings and plans with insiders, and thereby ensure their voice returns to the fore. This is one area where I feel I and most other development practitioners fall down. As Crocker (2007: 440) notes, 'outside investigators, even participatory ones, often neglect to return to the community to share with their informants the investigators' assessments and the donor's funding decisions'. There are, of course, practical barriers to doing so. How do we send reports to remote communities and ensure everyone gets to see them? How do we include non-literate audiences? There is also the cost and time of translating the written material and the challenge of writing in a style that talks to both participants and technical audiences. There is the underlying question too of when the process of consultation stops; should I send my responses to their responses?

Community design and implementation

So far, we have looked at how the poor can be more involved in the research and planning of products, services, and programmes. I now want to explore how they can be involved in their fuller implementation. Community implementation is far from mainstream, but the evidence of projects under way is often very encouraging. One example is Community Led Total Sanitation (CLTS) discussed above. Whilst many aspects of CLTS are standardized and the process has been practised in dozens of countries, it gives each new community some control over the design and production of the toilets that are made and used in their area. The first latrines in each location are based on ideas from members of the community. Bongartz et al. describe how they are typically 'low-cost, made from locally available materials and constitute the first step on the sanitation ladder' (2010: 31). Then, over time, the latrines are developed, with guidance from outside experts to address any shortfalls in the original design (Bongartz et al., 2010; Myers et al., 2018). Rather than being designed by experts, experts are a *backup resource, who help* local people to create their own designs. Notably, this process is considerably cheaper; the cost is typically $15 per household, compared with up to $600 per household for latrines designed and produced by outsiders.

I would argue that outsiders should be less quick to assume that technical assistance is needed with the implementation work of development, and instead should challenge themselves about where outside and 'technical' help really is needed. First, the growth of technologies such as 3D printing that allow manufacture to occur on a local and small scale are likely to offer increasing opportunities for poor communities to create physical solutions for themselves in their own neighbourhoods (Manzini, 2015). Second, the evidence suggests that if outsiders devote time to drawing out and clearly mapping the skills and assets that already exist in a community the requirements for 'technical assistance' may be much smaller than is assumed. Writers like Cunningham (2008) and Neumann et al. (2008) illustrate this clearly with examples, from Ethiopia and Brazil respectively, of communities leading the implementation of irrigation, land management, and building work. Cunningham describes how through using the 'appreciative enquiry' approach described above, the community realized that they 'had the labour along with most of the tools and skills, as well as the natural resources needed to carry out these activities'. He continues, 'all they needed from outside the community was some legal advice to demarcate areas for tree planting, technical assistance with irrigation from the woreda, and some help from a Hundee-supported community nursery to access large numbers of tree seedlings' (2008: 271). Neumann et al. (2008) meanwhile show how community members in Fortaleza, Brazil were able to take on responsibility for the delivery of complex infrastructural projects such as the building of a canal. This was a long-term project with major social, economic, and technical challenges to delivery, but it was planned, supervised, and constructed almost entirely by people from the community. Control over the project remained with the community and whilst outsiders were brought in to help with some technical aspects of construction, management remained with the community. Neumann et al. describe how 'at the time, the usual practice was for government to manage the construction of infrastructure projects. But on GTZ's insistence, the community had to be in charge of construction, through the Residents' Association. "The Canal", as it is known locally, became a landmark not only because it improved the living conditions in the community, but also because of the experience people gained in administering such a large project' (2008: 49).

Community delivery brings numerous benefits. It can boost the skills and confidence of individual residents. It can add to the sense of agency within the community. It can keep local residents on board during difficult moments of evolution. (Neumann et al. relate how when homes in Fortaleza had to be moved or demolished, residents trusted that they would be given new homes because they were hearing this from their neighbours.) Community implementation can also lead to more innovative solutions, through the effective and surprising combination of local and outsider knowledge. The rural electrification programme in Morocco is a prime example of this latter benefit. By establishing forums where local people could talk directly with volunteer engineers from Electricite de France, two different types of expertise were combined: insider and outsider. And through this exchange, novel, practical solutions were discovered. Iskander and Bentaleb-Maes describe how:

> This sort of ongoing and collaborative improvisation ultimately produced a network that differed significantly both from the blueprints that the electricians had brought with them and from the standards

set by Moroccan government, but that was, as a result, well-suited to the local needs and local environment. Local materials, including recycled hardware, were used; the network capacity was scaled down to local usage requirements; and maintenance needs were simplified so that the villagers could manage the network on their own (Iskander and Bentaleb-Maes, 2008: 169).[23]

This last point is an important one to note, since we saw above that it is the *maintenance* of solutions, rather than the creation of solutions that can often be hard for communities to manage on their own. If we are to create initiatives that are truly community owned, we should look to adapt the materials and processes used, so that management and repair can be undertaken by local people.

Community implementation can bring one further essential benefit: cost savings. In their recent review of community-driven development (or CDD) projects, Wong and Guggenheim (2018) found that CDD have often delivered equivalent services at a lower price, due to the cheaper cost of local labour and by cutting out intermediaries. They write that 'studies from the Philippines, Indonesia, Nepal, Burkina Faso, and Malawi, for example, have demonstrated 15 percent to 40 percent lower costs, depending on the type of investments' (2018: 16). Mansuri and Rao (2012: 8) find that in the few cases where CDD have been directly compared with 'top down' programmes, 'community engagement seems to improve both the quality of construction and the management of local infrastructure – implying lower levels of corruption relative to government provision. When the Moroccan government reviewed community-led electricity services, they reached a similar conclusion, that 'electricity networks could be built using materials that were adapted to the topography of rural Morocco, that were locally sourced and less expensive, without compromising service or safety' (Iskander and Bentaleb-Maes, 2008: 174).

It is encouraging to see that in recent years community implementation is happening at a larger scale, with agencies handing control of budgets and planning for whole programmes to communities. Notable examples include the Kecamatan Development Program in Indonesia, which has reached over half the villages in the country and which grew to $7.3 billion in funding by 2017. It is cited in several of Narayan et al.'s (2009) research locations as a major contributor to people escaping poverty. Other examples include the Social Action Fund in Tanzania and the participatory budgeting initiative in Porto Alegre (Bhatnagar et al., 2003). The Moroccan rural electrification roll-out, meanwhile, is an example of how a small-scale community implementation can lead to transformation on a nationwide level (Iskander and Bentaleb-Maes, 2008). The Moroccan government borrowed heavily from the original community-led project and applied the same principles to its national programme, helping bring a huge increase in government-backed electricity in that country – from 21 per cent of rural homes in 1996 to 81 per cent in 2005.

There are, though, serious potential challenges with community design and implementation that need to be considered and mitigated. As with consultation, the implementation of projects can be taken over by the more powerful people in the area. Narayan et al. (2009) found cases where CDDs had been hijacked by elites who were using the extra money and power they had gained not just to bypass but actually to exploit the weaker members of the community. These results from a project in rural Tanzania were troubling and far from unique: 'most decision making about projects is concentrated in the hands of these elites, and poor people see demands to participate and contribute as infringing on their freedom. One poor man in Bugokela said, "Freedom is when you can sleep and nobody comes to disturb you at night, telling you to go and fetch water for building a school"' (2009: 317).

We also have to be realistic and honest about the extent of local knowledge. The examples above suggest that communities may possess much more 'technical' expertise than the development industry often allows. But there will frequently be significant gaps in this knowledge, which we should not underplay. For instance, Khwaja (2004) looked at 132 infrastructure projects in rural Pakistan and found that community input into the non-technical aspects had a significant positive effect on their standard of maintenance. However, community participation in *technical matters* had a negative effect. This is also an issue in Mansuri and Rao's review of water projects, which found that 'community members were unable to make informed choices about the type of project to build, monitor the work of contractors, or maintain projects after they were constructed without adequate training' (2012: 187). Hence it is standard practice in many CDDs to appoint an outside facilitator who works with the community group giving them advice to help them decide how to spend the funds. Wong and Guggenheim (2018: 11) note that 'in most CDD projects, facilitators not only explain the government's fiduciary rules for the program, but they also serve to help communities access technical expertise, to monitor performance, and to help handle complaints'. Whilst I would argue strongly that we should try to minimize the amount of technical input needed on each project, we should recognize that this minimum will vary by type of project, scale, and local area, and that we need to take seriously the risks, as well as the benefits of outsiders stepping back.

Community monitoring and evaluation

The final phase of a typical programme, monitoring and evaluation (or M&E), can be a particularly challenging one for communities to take on. The problem of bias naturally creeps in here once more. And to track a project over time, long-term, bureaucratic procedures also need to be put in place, procedures that are likely to be unfamiliar in many poor communities. In addition, most evaluation requires quantitative data-analysis skills, which again are rare on the ground.

It's perhaps not surprising then that studies in this area have found that community members have found it easier to contribute to the design of development plans than to carry out ongoing monitoring and evaluation. The authors of a World Bank study in this area, entitled *Sleeping On Our Own Mats* (2002: 3–4), report that whilst community members were more at home designing and implementing programmes, they 'were not nearly as at-ease in supporting re-evaluating their plan'. As a result, there was no feedback loop: communities did not make new development choices based upon measured, consistent assessments of the past development activities (2002: 3–4). The authors conclude that outside help was needed in these later monitoring stages.

The same researchers also suggest, though, that there may be more potential to transfer power even during this more technical phase in development. Their report draws an interesting line between traditional M&E conducted by outside professionals and the kind of evaluating work they did achieve with communities at the forefront. The latter, they emphasize 'is not formal monitoring and evaluation. It does not aim to make a statement about the impact of a community development project'. It is, instead, they write, 'a tool for building communities' capacity to direct their development' (2002: i). This is a useful distinction, I'd suggest. The team were not asking the community to assess the project's impact using quantitative measures, but rather to reflect more richly on development as a whole – how it is progressing, what they want from development, and how to reshape future programmes.

In conclusion

This chapter has explored a number of connected questions: first, how do we choose between competing or conflicting development priorities? Second, how do we value and use local knowledge versus the expertise of outside professionals? Third, how do we empower local people to take control of the majority, if not all, of the development process? I have sought to illustrate the potential for, as well as the challenges involved in, making development a community-run endeavour. We are still some way from the point that Preece et al. (2015) hope to reach, where 'the role of the NGO gradually diminishes as the CBO [community based organization] equips itself with skills in the kind of monitoring, interpretation, planning, and analysis that is traditionally the domain of the NGO'. But we have seen already the range of initiatives under way to help communities collect and analyse data, to design programmes, to contribute to their implementation, and to monitor their results. Banerjee et al. (2015: 129) argue that this transfer of power is not just the logical development of participative approaches to development, but also a practical way of ensuring that more money ends up in the hands of the poorest:

> Conventional evaluations subvert the aims of development projects insofar as they drain resources (time, money and knowledge) away from the poor and towards development professionals. A community-led evaluation process such as the one discussed here is much more consistent

with the thrust and priorities of the project as a whole, since resources are directed towards the intended beneficiaries.

I would agree with these writers that the goal of external development workers should be to make our jobs redundant. We should fight the urge to hold on to our privileged position as experts and think continually and creatively about how our knowledge and power can be transferred to the people we aim to help. The imperative to shift power, money, skills, and knowledge is becoming much more urgent with the climate emergency. We have to move away from a model which involves flying in 'technical expertise' from the global north to communities which are already suffering from the effects of climate change. But we cannot assume this transfer can be easy or fast. This chapter has tried to show the current value of outside knowledge, the benefits of conversations between insiders and outsiders, and the very significant challenges of transferring power to those on the ground. I believe it is an area of development where we have to pursue radical change. But ambition and circumspection are needed in equal measures. In the next, concluding, chapter I will start to unpack what this might look like.

Notes

1. These projects, as we will explore, of course vary widely in scope and agenda. Nussbaum is more concerned with first principles, OPHI's multidimensional poverty work with what and how we should measure progress (or lack of), and the SDGs with coordinating development work over a set period.
2. The Capabilities approach has a number of broader strengths that help us in daily development work. First it encourages us to look not just at development outcomes but at the routes people took to get to these outcomes. Imagine, for instance, two communities with low female employment. The data on outcomes (i.e. the percentage of women working) may look very similar. But imagine in one community most women are *choosing* not to exercise the right to work outside the home, and in the second many men are preventing women from doing so. The outcomes are the same, but the two groups' capabilities are very different. A second strength is that Nussbaum and Sen both encourage us to see capabilities as multiple and interlocking. The capability to choose to work needs to be reinforced by other capabilities – for example – critical reasoning, free speech, and political participation. This approach discourages us from pursuing one narrow goal in our work (say nutrition levels, or employment) without considering the other things people are or aren't capable of doing.
3. For a detailed comparison of their approaches, see Robeyns (2005).
4. For more information see <https://ophi.org.uk/research/multidimensional-poverty/alkire-foster-method/> [accessed 19 June 2019], and for discussion see Alkire (2018).
5. See <https://www.un.org/sustainabledevelopment/sustainable-development-goals/> [accessed 14 April 2021].

6. Similarly, the countries that have constructed measures of multidimensional poverty have chosen to focus on different criteria. For instance, whilst education and health criteria are ever-present, Chile includes a measure of social cohesion, and Panama, sanitation. See OPHI's National MPI Reports.
7. They go on to highlight the necessary fuzziness this can involve in daily practice. 'At times these assumptions are the informed guesses of the researcher, in other situations they are drawn from convention, social or psychological theory, or philosophy'. <https://ophi.org.uk/research/multidimensional-poverty/how-to-apply-alkire-foster/> [accessed May 16 2019].
8. As he describes 'the instrumental relation between low income and low capability is variable between different communities and even between different families and different individuals' (1999: 40).
9. Narayan et al. quote one respondent who summarizes this starkly. 'For people who cannot afford even two square meals a day, education means nothing at all. Electricity is of no use to them. The first important thing for them is to perform work from which they can earn and get food' (2009: 206).
10. Note the difference is more pronounced in urban areas than rural areas.
11. They point out that 'women who run three different businesses and men who cannot commit to a fixed job in the city because they want to keep the option of returning to the village every few weeks, give up the opportunity to acquire skills and experience in their main occupations ... [and] the gains from specializing in what they are really good at' (2011: 143).
12. They write 'especially for those without access to land or the ability to grow their own food on other people's land, access to dependable wage labor emerged as a major factor defining poverty. Whether in the countryside or in the city, poor people can rarely find permanent, salaried employment. Instead, poor people without land engage in informal, casual, and daily wage labor with no security and low earnings' (2000: 30).
13. Polak (2008: 65) gives the example of an early IDE project in Somalia, where he sold repair tools to donkey cart owners and was surprised to find that poor-quality $6 wrenches were much more popular than the $12 version: 'I realised a donkey cart operator could generate enough income in one month to buy ten British-made lug wrenches, but if he didn't have the money to buy a lug wrench to fix today's flat tire, he would earn nothing and might end up losing his donkey cart. So he bought the wrench he could afford in order to stay in business today and earn more money for tomorrow. Hundreds of poor people I talked to told me the same kind of story. For the 2.7 billion people in the world who earn less than $2 a day, affordability rules'.
14. Van Domelen describes examples including 'in the Brazil Northeast Poverty Alleviation Projects, 80 percent of the members of the project-formed Municipal Councils are comprised of representatives from rural communities and local civil society, and 20 percent from the public sector ... The Zambia Social Investment Fund requires that a minimum number of women be represented on the local project management committees ... In India, the Tamil Nadu Empowerment and Poverty Reduction Project ...

has representation from the scheduled castes and scheduled tribes and the disabled. At least 50 percent of the representatives must be women' (2007: 44).

15. See Myers et al. (2018: 25) for a valuable list of ways in which people might be excluded from a consultation process.

16. Crocker (2007) makes a useful distinction here between layers of participation. He distinguishes 'nominal participation', where people are named part of a decision-making group, but don't choose or aren't allowed to attend; through passive participation, where people are told of plans that have already been made; through to deliberative participation, where local people make all major decisions themselves.

17. See <https://www.designother90.org/> and <https://www.openideo.com/challenges> [accessed 5 May 2021].

18. <http://honeybee.org/index.php> [accessed 22 June 2020].

19. Bruno Latour employs an analogy of Plato's cave here, where 'only the expert can come in and out of the cave and pass from the social world to the world of external realities'. Cited by Carpousis (2019).

20. The difficulty of the last is illustrated by a review of community-run piped water projects in Malawi, which found that only half of the schemes were still running well (a minimum of three years into the project). As Mansuri and Rao (2012: 188) describe, 'community groups were capable of making small repairs necessary to keep water flowing, but they were unable to undertake more substantive preventative maintenance and repairs'.

21. See <https://global.girleffect.org/stories/girl-research-unit-trainer-handbook/> [accessed 22 February 2021]. In another example, Preece et al. (2015) recount how the NGO Avahan in India trained local community-based organizations with the research skills to develop their own programmes to combat HIV.

22. See <https://www.girleffect.org/what-we-do/mobile-platforms/tega/> [accessed 30 June 2020].

23. One example they give is of how 'finding it impossible, for example, to haul the ten-metre high concrete columns, mandated by French and Moroccan safety standards, up to the isolated village on rough dirt roads, the villagers and electricians decided instead to make the poles for their network out of stripped eucalyptus trunks, which were available locally and were easier to transport' (2008: 169).

References

Abraham, Anita and Platteau, Jean-Philippe (2004) 'Participatory development: where culture creeps in', in Vijayendra Rao and Michael Walton (eds), *Culture and Public Action: An Introduction*, pp. 210–33, World Bank, Washington.

Alasuutari, Pertti (1995) *Researching Culture: Qualitative Method and Cultural Studies*, Sage, Thousand Oaks.

Alkire, Sabina (2004) 'Culture, poverty, and external intervention', in Vijayendra Rao and Michael Walton (eds), *Culture and Public Action: An Introduction*, pp. 185–210, World Bank, Washington.

Alkire, Sabina (2018) 'The research agenda on multidimensional poverty measurement: important and as-yet unanswered questions', *OPHI Working Paper: 119*, University of Oxford, Oxford.

Banerjee, Abhijit V. and Duflo, Esther (2011) *Poor Economics: A Radical Rethinking of the Way To Fight Global Poverty*, Public Affairs, New York.

Banerjee, Anindo, Preece, Rohan and Chandrasekharan, Anusha (2015) 'Breaking the barriers to information: community-led land mapping in Bihar', in T. Thomas and P. Narayan (eds), *Participation Pays: Pathways for post-2015*, pp. 5–23, Practical Action Publishing, Rugby.

Bhatnagar, Deepti, Rathore, Animesh, Torres, Magui Moreno, and Kanungo, Parameeta (2003) 'Participatory budgeting in Brazil', [online], Empowerment case studies, World Bank, <http://documents1.worldbank.org/curated/en/600841468017069677/pdf/514180WP0BR0Bu10Box342027B01PUBLIC1.pdf> [accessed 30 June 2020].

Bongartz, Petra, Musyoki, Samuel Musembi, Milligan, Angela and Ashley, Holly (2010) 'Tales of shit: community-led total sanitation in Africa', *Participatory Learning and Action*, 61: 27–49.

Carpousis, Alicia (2019) 'Being a humanistic designer in a technocratic world', Unpublished MA Dissertation, Royal College of Art, London.

Chambers, Robert (2014) *Into the Unknown: Explorations in Development Practice*, Practical Action Publishing, Rugby.

Crocker, David A. (2007) 'Deliberative participation in local development', *Journal of Human Development*, 8: 431–55 <https://doi.org/10.1080/14649880701462379>.

Cunningham, Gordon (2008) 'Stimulating asset based and community driven development:lessons from five communities in Ethiopia', in Alison Mathie and Gordon Cunningham (eds), *From Clients to Citizens: Communities Changing the Course of their Own Development*, pp. 263–98, Practical Action Publishing, Rugby.

Denzin, Norman K. and Lincoln, Yvonna S. (1994) *Handbook of Qualitative Research Methods*, Sage, Thousand Oaks.

Despret, Vinciane (2016) *What Would Animals Say if We Asked the Right Questions?* University of Minnesota Press, Minneapolis.

Dowden, Richard (2008) *Africa: Altered States, Ordinary Miracles*, Portobello, London.

Fung, Archon and Wright, Erik Olin (2001) 'Deepening democracy: innovations in empowered participatory governance', *Politics and Society*, 29: 5–41 <https://doi.org/10.1177/0032329201029001002>.

Hamaus, Julia and Edström, Jerker with Shahrokh, Thea (2015) 'Public and political participation', in J. Edström, A. Hassink, T. Shahrokh and E. Stern (eds), *Engendering Men: A Collaborative Review of Evidence on Men and Boys in Social Change and Gender Equality*, pp. 151–65, EMERGE Evidence Review, Promundo-US, Sonke Gender Justice and the Institute of Development Studies.

Iskander, Natasha and Bentaleb-Maes, Nadia (2008) 'The hardware and software of community development: migrant infrastructure projects in rural Morocco', in Alison Mathie and Gordon Cunningham (eds), *From Clients to Citizens: Communities Changing the Course of their Own Development*, pp. 161–80, Practical Action Publishing, Rugby.

Khader, Serene J. (2009) 'Adaptive preferences and procedural autonomy', *Journal of Human Development and Capabilities*, 10: 169–87 <https://doi.org/10.1080/19452820902940851>.

Khader, Serene J. (2012) 'Must theorising about adaptive preferences deny women's agency?', *Journal of Applied Philosophy*, 29 <https://doi.org/10.1111/j.1468-5930.2012.00575.x>.

Khwaja, Asim Ijaz (2004) 'Is increasing community participation always a good thing?', *Journal of the European Economic Association*, 2: 427–36 <https://doi.org/10.1162/154247604323068113>.

Mansuri, Ghazala and Rao, Vijayendra (2012) *Localising Development: Does Participation Work?* World Bank Policy Research Report, World Bank, Washington.

Manzini, Ezio (2015) *Design, When Everyone Designs*, MIT, Cambridge Mass.

Mathie, Alison (2008) 'People's institutions as a vehicle for community development: a case study from southern India', in Alison Mathie and Gordon Cunningham (eds), *From Clients to Citizens: Communities Changing the Course of their Own Development*, pp. 207–35, Practical Action Publishing, Rugby.

McCracken, Grant (1998) *The Long Interview*, Sage, Thousand Oaks.

Mohanty, Chandra Talpade (1988) 'Under Western eyes: feminist scholarship and colonial discourses', *Feminist Review*, 30: 61–88 <https://doi.org/10.1057/fr.1988.42>.

Myers, J., Cavill, S., Musyoki, S., Pasteur, K. and Stevens, L. (2018) *Innovations for Urban Sanitation: Adapting Community-led Approaches*, Practical Action Publishing, Rugby.

Narayan, Deepa, Pritchett, Lant and Kapoor, Soumya (2009) *Moving Out of Poverty Volume 2: Success from the Bottom Up*, a co-publication of the World Bank and Palgrave Macmillan, Washington.

Neumann, Rogerio Arns and Mathie, Alison, assisted by Linzey, Joanne (2008) 'Conjunto Palmeira: four decades of forging community and building a local economy in Brazil', in Alison Mathie and Gordon Cunningham (eds), *From Clients to Citizens: Communities Changing the Course of their Own Development*, pp. 39–62, Practical Action Publishing, Rugby.

Nussbaum, Martha C. (1997) 'Capabilities and human rights', *Fordham Law Review*, 66: 273–300.

Nussbaum, Martha C. (2003) 'Capabilities as fundamental entitlements: Sen and social justice', *Feminist Economics*, 9: 33–59 <https://doi.org/10.1080/1354570022000077926>.

Oosterlaken, Ilse (2009) 'Design for development: a capability approach', *Design Issues*, 25: 91–102.

Ostrom, Elinor (2017) (1990) *Governing the Commons: The Evolution of Institutions for Collective Action*, Cambridge University Press, Cambridge.

Oxford Poverty & Human Development Initiative (OPHI) (no date) *National MPI Reports*, University of Oxford <https://ophi.org.uk/publications/national-mpi-reports/> [accessed 23 May 2021].

Polak, Paul (2008) *Out of Poverty: What Works When Traditional Approaches Fail*, Berrett-Koehler, San Francisco.

Preece, Rohan, Joseph, Stanley, Sarangan, Gayathr and Bharadwaj, Sowmyaa (2015) 'Knowledge base: towards a community-owned monitoring system', in T. Thomas and P. Narayan (eds), *Participation Pays: Pathways for post-2015*, pp. 41–61, Practical Action Publishing, Rugby.

Rao, Vijayendra (2002) 'Experiments in participatory econometrics: improving the connection between economic analysis and the real world', *Economic and Political Weekly*, 22: 1887–91.

Robb, Caroline M. (2002) *Can the Poor Influence Policy? Participatory Poverty Assessments in the Developing World*, World Bank, Washington.

Robeyns, Ingrid (2005) 'Selecting capabilities for quality of life', *Social Indicators Research*, 74: 191–215 <https://doi.org/10.1007/s11205-005-6524-1>.

Sen, Amartya (1999) *Development as Freedom*, Oxford University Press, Oxford.

Strode, Mary, Crawfurd, Lee, Dettling, Simone and Schmieding, Felix (2015) 'Jobs and the labor market', in Mthuli Ncube and Charles Leyeka Lufumpa (eds), *The Emerging Middle Class in Africa*, pp. 82–101, Routledge, London.

Thomas, Tom, Kader, Moulasha and Preece, Rohan (2015) 'Lost policies: locating access to infrastructure and services in rural India', in T. Thomas and P. Narayan (eds), *Participation Pays: Pathways for post-2015*, pp. 63–84, Practical Action Publishing, Rugby.

Van Domelen, Julie (2007) 'Reaching the poor and vulnerable: targeting strategies for social funds and other community-driven programs', *Social Protection Paper No 711*, World Bank, Washington.

Westerberg, Anneli (2020) 'Girls out loud: amplifying the voices of girls' [online], <https://medium.com/innovationhub-planinternational/girls-out-loud-amplifying-the-voices-of-girls-c4adfae11ead> [accessed 11 February 2021].

Wong, Susan and Guggenheim, Scott (2018) 'Community driven development: myths and realities', *Policy Research Working Paper*, World Bank, Washington <https://doi.org/10.1596/1813-9450-8435>.

World Bank (2002) *Sleeping on our Own Mats: An Introductory Guide To Community-Based Monitoring and Evaluation*, World Bank, Washington.

World Bank (2004) *Making Services Work for the Poor*, World Bank, Washington.

Yunus, Muhammad (2007) *Creating a World Without Poverty: Social Business and the Future of Capitalism*, Public Affairs, New York.

CHAPTER 8
Setting participative development goals

Abstract

How do we make development something that is led and enacted by communities themselves? To get there we need to set clear and time-specific goals. These goals need to accelerate the transfer of power, knowledge, and skills from development professionals to participants and from the global north to the global south. This chapter makes an initial proposal for what these goals might be. Based on insights from the book as a whole, it sets out a list of 12 participative development goals. These are intended as a starting point for discussions, and further refinement and development.

Keywords: participative development; community design; Sustainable Development Goals; asset-based community development

Poor people sometimes don't want the things that are designed to lift them out of poverty. This was the counter-intuitive idea with which we began the book. Through the pages that followed I have tried to explain some of the reasons why this problem occurs more often than we might imagine, and what we can do to prevent it.

I have sought, first of all, to show a number of principles that we can adopt to make anti-poverty initiatives more likely to succeed. These are summarized below as six **core design principles**.

1. Poor communities tend to be more communal than those found in the global north. This creates opportunities for word of mouth, collective action, and shared ownership, as well as creating barriers to new ideas, which stems from a fear of breaking social conventions.
2. Power in poor communities is very unevenly distributed, sometimes in ways that are hard for outsiders to spot. We continually need to find ways to ensure weaker and marginal members of communities can use the interventions we design. This requires a combination of indirect and direct means of addressing inequality.
3. The poor often have their own solutions to poverty that have traction and power. But these are often hard for outsiders to identify and only some have the potential to expand. We need to devote more time to finding these solutions and to think critically about how we can add support and scale.

4. Poor people have many reasons to be sceptical about change. We need to do more to consider and mitigate the risks that even our most benign interventions offer and to increase people's sense of individual and collective agency.

5. The cultural details of how aid interventions are presented and communicated matter. We need to think more carefully about the role of aesthetics, experience, and entertainment as we increasingly battle to capture our audience's attention.

6. Poor people have more assets and resources than outsiders typically recognize. There are significant opportunities to transfer leadership of the development process to communities themselves and to design initiatives that can be implemented and maintained using local skills.

Experience and evidence from the field suggests that if we apply these principles our anti-poverty initiatives have a better chance of working. But we have seen that in the messy reality of daily development work, broad guidelines such as these can only take you so far.

First, the principles I have described aren't boxes to tick on a straight path to success; rather, they are sometimes competing considerations that have to be assessed and weighed against one another. So, for instance, focusing on the weaker and marginal and recognizing the communal nature of resources are both useful principles when designing for the poorest, but we just need to look back to Chapter 1 and Simon Harragin's account of famine relief in South Sudan to see how one can undermine the other.

Furthermore, the principles may be useful as initial guides, but we have seen on countless occasions that success relies primarily on adapting to local context. We've seen how an innovation that is transformative in one region adds limited value in another; an inclusive community with strong social capital lies only a few kilometres from another where prejudice and discrimination saps the scope for change. Development theory – and development practice – tends to valorize people working at a conceptual level with 'models' and 'strategies' and with stories of globally transformative solutions. Such models and stories are understandably alluring, because they promise efficiency and scale – the two things we desperately need to solve poverty. But out on the ground, development programmes stand or fall on getting very specific local details right.

To take a recent example, my colleagues Jamal Khadar, Matthew Strickland, and I spent several months at the end of 2018 attempting to design a service for low-income dairy farmers in Tanzania. The service allowed farmers to digitally log their milk collections at their local depot, which in turn aimed to let dairies identify underperforming farmers and target them with information and inputs to help them produce more milk and earn more money. We spent time carefully designing a logical way to collect and manage the flow of this information, considering myriad factors such as the range of different possible reasons for milk rejection, the location of scales at a collection agent, the quality of mobile phone signal in different rural districts. PowerPoint charts were created and honed. A prototype was built, based on our neatly organized model. The model then met the reality of dairy collection in rural Tanzania. Within two days we had half a dozen clear lessons in how we needed to adjust it.

This is how I've found development works: through constant and often mundane improvisation and flexibility, rather than the dogged pursuit of plans or the execution of precise pre-prepared models. As Neumann et al. (2008: 57) write, 'building a community is like a game of chess, demanding patience, flexible strategies, and an awareness of risk'. Richard Sennett (2008) provides a useful, if rather grand, historical parallel when he argues that in the Roman Empire the 'menial' craftsmen didn't simply put into practice the vision of planners and architects, but rather, 'a great deal of improvisation occurred on the ground. Many formal "errors" had to be committed to get the houses, roads, and sewers to function. The thinking of menial workmen involved correction and adaption' (2008: 134).

This book has touched repeatedly on the difficulties of development. Often, development enthusiasts – and critics – talk about ending poverty in impatient terms: on the one hand, that we just need to embrace these policies and we can *end poverty now*; on the other hand, that no progress is being made and that aid *just isn't working*. I have tried to tell a more cautious story. It is a story where improvement is often slow and halting; a story where progress in one area of development may be offset by negative changes elsewhere; a story where we recognize – and publicize – failures, so that we can learn from them· It is a story where we accept, as Papanek argues, that 'design as a problem-solving activity can never, by definition, yield the one right answer: it will always produce an infinite number of answers, some "righter" and some "wronger"' (1972: 5–6).

The vision of making the development industry redundant is sadly a long-term one. In the short-term there will be roles for outsiders, but not, I hope, as principal actors. Instead, outsiders should be facilitators and guides, who are actively engaged in transferring power, knowledge, skills, money, and responsibility for development to those on the ground.

To accelerate this transfer, I believe we should be setting ourselves goals as ambitious as the MDGs or SDGs. These should make clear the nature of transformation we expect and a time-frame for achieving it. So to conclude the book, I would like to sketch an initial draft of what these goals and principles should be. These are, of course, highly provisional and inevitably very subjective and partial. But I hope that these **participative development goals** provide a useful starting point for a wider conversation, one that is geared towards sustained and urgent action.

1. Every project will transfer the skills used in the project to members of the beneficiary community.
2. Every major decision point in every project journey will have input from community members.

3. Outside agencies commit to sourcing ideas for new projects from the communities in which they are working. To aid this, we build a platform that allows communities to send their ideas for interventions, which NGOs commit to consulting before planning an intervention of their own.
4. A commitment to apply the ABCD principles on every project: to start with the assets and strengths of a community, rather than an immediate focus on its problems.
5. An assumption that the community will lead delivery of projects. And a principle that all outside technical expertise needs to be justified, rather than assuming it is required.
6. Ongoing targets to monitor *and reduce* the share of development spending that goes outside of communities, including five-yearly targets and review of progress.
7. An industry-wide initiative to develop, share, and use concrete, visual tools that make participation in development decisions easy and compelling for people with lower formal literacy.
8. The building of a catalogue of peer-reviewed community-led development success stories, which are made easily accessible to people within poor communities globally.
9. A commitment to ensure the top-rated university departments for development studies are all located in the global south within 10 years.
10. A new argument for development funds aimed at the public in high-income countries. One that acknowledges the uncertainty that comes with community-led development, but which shows a vision of development that is ultimately less reliant on aid from high-income countries.
11. Recognition of potential tensions and problems within the goals: for instance, the risk of trying to meet community spending targets before ensuring communities have the capacity for spending these funds.
12. Open discussion of setbacks and failures, and a shared commitment to testing, challenging, and revising the goals themselves.

References

Neumann, Rogerio Arns and Mathie, Alison, assisted by Linzey, Joanne (2008) 'Conjunto Palmeira: four decades of forging community and building a local economy in Brazil', in Alison Mathie and Gordon Cunningham (eds), *From Clients to Citizens: Communities Changing the Course of their Own Development*, pp. 39–62, Practical Action Publishing, Rugby.

Papanek, Victor (1972) *Design for the Real World*, Thames and Hudson, London.

Sennett, Richard (2008) *The Craftsman*, Allen Lane, London.

APPENDIX
A note on methodology

This book draws extensively on primary research conducted by myself and by my colleagues first at 2cv Research and then at Copa Research. Whilst the studies vary widely in scope and topic (from improving agricultural extension advice to creating inspirational role models for poor teenage girls), the majority have employed relatively similar ethnographic methods: face-to-face interviews, informal observation, focus groups, diary exercises, and local expert interviews. The majority of these trips have been what Mansuri and Rao (2012) call 'touch the water buffalo': one- or two-week field visits. Whilst typically short, there have been many of them, including several dozen I've conducted personally.

Some of these fieldwork projects are available in the public domain and I have referenced published data throughout where this is the case. Many other studies, though, particularly those conducted for commercial clients, are not, and they can only be referenced briefly. In these cases I regret that readers can't scrutinize the methodology or how the data was analysed and interpreted, and so I try to mitigate this in a number of ways: by supporting my findings where possible with references to academic research that is in the public domain and that covers similar themes and findings; by providing quotes and descriptions of projects where permissible; and by encouraging readers to question and critique my findings.

I make reference to numerous field studies by other researchers, including many randomized control trials. They are by their nature trials, benefitting from outside technical expertise, funding, and the commitment and focus that come with a time-limited project. A business training or agricultural inputs trial that works under these conditions may not work so well when it is expanded to be run by local government and members of the community over a longer stretch of time. (Or indeed it may work much better, due to the superiority of local knowledge and the intensity of personal commitment. The point is that we cannot be sure.) In addition, I recognize we need to be careful about transposing results to other regions or countries. A project that works well in, say, Mtwara region, Tanzania won't necessarily replicate well across the border in Mozambique, or in fact in the Tanga region of Tanzania, where the social, economic, cultural, and geographical context is different. It is possible, even, that its effects will be harmful when re-created outside its original environment. Deaton (2010) makes the comparison with the (genuine) example of an arthritis drug passing an RCT with 18–65 year olds, but leading to fatalities when given to older patients. Furthermore, as Deaton argues, RCTs sometimes have little to say about how the impact is distributed across the population: the net result may be positive, but results often don't tell us much about winners and losers within the community. There's a risk that when we export it we will export the inequalities that go with it.[1] These are serious criticisms and as development practitioners we should be more cautious than is sometimes the case about generalizing from single studies. But neither would I be quick to dismiss evaluations of any kind. First, many of the practitioners of RCT are themselves very aware of the limitations of the method and try to address them in their reporting. We have seen above a number of examples of researchers highlighting the uneven distribution of impacts across different populations. Second, we can only build a picture of what works by comparing and combining evidence assembled through multiple approaches in multiple locations. Whilst RCT have their limitations and a single RCT may tell us very little about what might work elsewhere, we can combine findings from multiple evaluations and other sources of data, such as qualitative research and diagnostic quantitative studies. Our conclusions may remain tentative, but if multiple sources point at the success or failure of a particular approach, we should take this seriously. In the course of this book I have tried wherever possible to find more than one example of any finding or argument I explore. Where this isn't possible – and indeed even when it is – I'd encourage readers to approach them critically and to return to my prevailing theme: the importance of context.

Note

1. The seriousness of this question will, of course, vary on the initiative you are exporting – with a new way of advertising a loan to farmers, huge differences behind the mean may not worry us as much as if we were bringing a new form of medical service.

References

Deaton, Angus (2010) 'Instruments, randomization, and learning about development', *Journal of Economic Literature*, 48: 448–9 <https://doi.org/10.1257/jel.48.2.424>.

Mansuri, Ghazala and Rao, Vijayendra (2012) *Localising Development: Does Participation Work?* World Bank Policy Research Report, World Bank, Washington.

Index

Abraham, A. and Platteau, J.-P. 7, 75, 151
abstract information vs concrete skills 100–4
adaptive preferences (AP) 146–8
aesthetics: presentation of
    information 104–6
Africa
    poverty reduction 34
    unemployed young people 94–5
    see also sub-Saharan Africa; specific
        countries
agency-building 92–6, 99
AIDS/HIV prevention 59, 103
Alkire, S. 21, 94, 146, 153
Asset-Based Community Development
    (ABCD) 10, 95–6, 114–15

Banerjee, A.V.
    and Duflo, E. 7, 8, 15, 17, 23, 39, 58, 96,
        97, 102, 105, 126
    et al. 152, 160, 161, 166–7
Bangladesh 48, 79, 128
    agency-building 93
    local vs outsider knowledge 19, 21
    presentation of information 105
    rule-of-thumb messages 103
    word of mouth approaches 56, 57
BBC Media Action 71–2, 94
behaviour change 97–9
Berger, P.L. and Luckmann, T. 116, 117
'bonding capital' and 'bridging capital' 119
Bongartz, P. et al. 53, 162
Bourdieu, P. 14
Braginski, P. 56, 57, 104
Brazil 38–9, 49–50, 58–9
    agency-building 92–3, 96
    community infrastructure design and
        implementation 163
    Conjuncto Palmeira and GTZ NGO 116–17
    digital technology 100
    favela library project 119
    visual voting system 102

Cabral, J. 119, 120
campaigns see word of mouth approaches
capabilities approach 139, 140–1
Capabilities List 141, 142–3
Chambers, R. 9, 10, 13, 36, 40, 53, 102, 127
change vs tradition 13–15
change strategies 89–90
    agency-building 92–6, 99
    power and limits of persuasion 106

presentation: entertainment and
    aesthetics 104–6
risk mitigation 90–2
tactical nudges 96–9
tangible design 100–4
children
    mortality 70
    nutrition 98–9
    oral rehydration therapy (ORT) 103
    see also education
Chipchase, J. 103–4
citizen status 96
collective agency-building 95–6
collectivism and individualism 6–8, 53–5, 82
Collins, D. et al. 9, 38, 116, 128, 145
communal cultures 47–9, 60–1
    shared designing 49–51
    shared resources, protecting existing 51–3
    total community vs individual
        adoption 53–5
    word of mouth approaches, potential and
        problems of 55–60
community analysis and planning 161–2
community design and implementation
    162–5
community monitoring and evaluation
    (M&E) 165–6
community research and
    consultation 160–1
community-driven development
    (CDD) 164, 165
community-led total sanitation (CLTS) 53–4,
    120, 121
    latrine design 162
concrete skills vs abstract information
    100–4
Conditional Cash Transfer programmes 92
context see local/context-reliant solutions
core design principles and goals 173–6
Cornwall, A. 36, 75
COVID-19 pandemic 33, 34
Cunningham, R. 9, 95–6, 101, 115, 120,
    153, 163
    Mathie, A. and 10, 95, 115

Deaton, A., 129, 177–8
deforestation 157–8
development goals and development
    choices 141–4
digital technology
    3D printing 162–3

digital technology (*contd.*)
  abstract information vs concrete
    skills 100–4
  and broadcast media access 39–40, 50,
    58–60
  new income opportunities 122–3
  visual methods 152, 155–7, 162
  voice of less powerful groups 151
discrimination 67–8
  direct tackling of 74–80
  indirect tackling of 72–4
  see also gender inequality/discrimination;
    intersectional thinking
Dowden, R. 59, 151
Drèze, J. and Sen, A. 34, 39, 57, 70, 96
Duflo, E.
  et al. 98
  see also Banerjee, A.V.

e-Choupal 122
Edström, J.
  and Shahrokh, T. 75, 76–7, 78–9
  see also Hamaus, J.
education
  gender inequality 70–1, 72–3, 74, 80, 95,
    97–8
  randomized control trials (RCTs) 12,
    127–8
  school fees 98
El Arifeen, S. et al. 56, 57, 103
electrification, Morocco 51, 128, 150, 163–4
elite groups and inclusive strategies 149–53
employment 22–3, 38, 144–5
  unemployment/underemployment 22,
    94–5
  women 79–80, 97–8
entertainment: presentation of
    information 105
entrepreneurship 125–6
  Conditional Cash Transfer programmes 92
  women 22, 75
Ethiopia 96, 101, 102, 120, 153, 163
  poverty reduction 34
ethnicity and intersectionality 77
ethnocentrism 3, 13, 145
ethnographic methods 10, 177
excluded groups *see* discrimination;
    inclusivity; intersectional thinking
experts *see* outsiders
exploitation 40, 58

face-to-face approaches *see* word of mouth
Fairs, M. 41
farmers/smallhold farmers 3–4, 9, 12, 14, 17,
    19, 38, 40
  agency-building 93
  cooperatives 61, 124–5
  dairy 174–5
  'demonstration plots' 102
  inequalities 69, 74–5, 118

new income opportunities 121–2
  participatory project 126
  presentation of information 105
  risk mitigation 90–2
  risk of scaling up 129
  sharing resources 51
  tactical nudges 98, 99
  word of mouth programme 60
finance
  informal arrangements 9
  see also microfinance
financial vs non-financial concerns 20–1
fishers
  Cambodia 122–3
  Congo 75
  Kerala, India 11–12, 17–18, 20, 52, 126–7
Fung, A. and Wright, E.O. 149, 150–1

Gambhir, V. and Kumar, P. 71–2, 94
Gates Foundation 123
gender inequality/discrimination 17–18, 23,
    34–5, 39, 40, 48, 61
  pay gap 69, 77
  resister's perspective 78–80
  see also intersectional thinking; women/
    girls
Girl Effect NGO 49, 73–4, 79, 104, 160
global north–global south comparisons
    13–14, 16–17, 22–3
global poverty line 33, 35, 36
global poverty reduction 33–4
good and services, shared design of 49–51
Grameen Bank 55, 56, 128
Grameen Goals 142, 143
Greenfield, A. 103
GSMA 41, 69, 105
  and Frog Design 59
guided walks 155–7
guidelines, short and practical 102–3

Haller Foundation 102
Hamaus, J.
  and Edström, J. 78
  et al. 150
hands-on experience 101–2
Harragin, S. S. 5, 6, 10, 19, 174
health and healthcare 39, 56, 57, 59–60
  accessible messages 103
  adaptive preferences 146
  behavioural interventions 98–9
  citizen status 96
  COVID-19 pandemic 33, 34
  see also children
heuristics/concrete habits 103–4
Hickel, J. 71, 82
Hobbes, M. 127
Honwana, A. 94–5
horizontal support networks vs vertical
    aid 8
human-centred design (HCD) 6, 19

ILO 38, 61, 73
inclusivity
  importance of 68–71
  strategies and tactics 71–2, 149–53
  see also discrimination
income-generating activities 121–3
India 7–8, 9
  adaptive preferences 146, 147
  agency-building 94, 96
  community-led research and
    consultation 160
  existing infrastructure and scaled-up
    solutions 121, 122, 126, 127
  films 13–14, 78
  fishers, Kerala 11–12, 17–18, 20, 52, 126–7
  land ownership mapping 152
  poverty 34, 39–40
  promoting inclusivity 71–2
  sharing resources 51, 52
  tackling discrimination 72–3, 74, 75,
    77–8, 80
  word of mouth approaches 56, 57, 58, 59
individual level poverty 34
individualism and collectivism 6–8, 53–5, 82
Indonesia 34, 39, 77, 164
inequalities within poor communities 16–19
information
  introducing new 153–5
  presentation of 104–6
infrastructure *see* local infrastructure and
  scaled-up solutions
insiders *see entries beginning* local
'institutionalisation' and participation
  116–18
insurance, weather 91–2
International Development Enterprises
  (IDE) 3, 12–13, 56, 57, 105
intersectional thinking 76–8
  and navigating dilemmas 80–3
'irrationality' of the poor 145, 148
ISEAL Alliance 102
Iskander, N. and Bentelab-Maes, N. 51, 115,
  128, 150, 159, 163–4

J-PAL 12, 91, 154
Jensen, R. 11–12, 20, 72–3, 127
  and Oster, E. 58
Jugaad Innovation 15, 126

Karlan, D. and Appel, J. 4, 54, 56, 104,
  105–6, 129
Kenya 74, 75, 92, 98, 127–8, 147
Khadar, J. 49, 77, 120, 125, 160, 174–5
Khader, S. 147–8
Khanna, T. and Palepu, K. 58, 125
knowledge *see* outsiders; power shifting in
  participative development
knowledge transfer 158–9
Kottack, C. 6, 101
Kretzmann, J. 121

La Ferrara, E. et al. 58–9
land ownership 52
  and asset ownership 38–9
  gender inequality 69, 76–7, 152
  mapping, India 152
Libertarianism 139, 140–1
Lichand, G. 92
life expectancy and life stages 39
literacy/illiteracy 70–1, 101, 102, 103–4
lobbying 120
local infrastructure and scale-up solutions
  113–15
  assessment for scaling-up 123–9
  caution and context 129–30
  outsider help 116–23
local/context-reliant solutions 114–15,
  126–7, 129–30
  disregarding differences and needs 10–13
  vs outsider solutions 8–10
local/insider vs outsider knowledge 8–10,
  19–21, 165
  see also power shifting in participative
    development
Lofchie, M. 14, 49

Malawi 40, 60, 82, 105
Mama Cash/FRIDA 119, 124
Mann, L. and Nzayisenga, E. 58
Mansuri, G. and Rao, V., 16, 51–2, 69, 74–5,
  117, 118, 126, 128, 149, 151, 177
Manzini, E. 61, 117, 119, 122, 154, 157,
  162–3
marginalized groups *see* discrimination;
  inclusivity; intersectional thinking
marketing *see* word of mouth approaches
Mathie, A. 52, 121, 160
  and Cunningham, G. 10, 95, 115
Mbaye, A.A. and Golub, S. 22
microfinance 48, 54–5, 116, 128, 129
  and gender 75, 82–3
  presentation of information 104
  see also Grameen Bank; Grameen Goals
mistakes/misunderstandings 6–23
mobile phones 41, 48, 49
  Airtel 60
  fishers, India 11–12, 17–18, 20, 126–7
  intermediaries 58
  money transfer (M-Pesa) 12, 57, 58
  Nokia 4, 56, 104
  Vodaphone Ghana 38
Morocco
  electrification 51, 128, 150, 163–4
  entertainment 105
Moving Out of Poverty *see* Narayan, D. et
  al. (2009)
multi-country studies 36–7
Multidimensional Poverty Index (OPHI)
  141–2, 143
Muradian, R. 61, 124–5
mutual self-reliance 8

Myers, J. et al. 7, 54, 55, 120, 121
Myrada NGO 160

Nair, C. 50
Narayan, D. et al.
    (2000) 10, 16, 17, 18, 20, 36–7, 38–9, 40,
        67, 68, 69, 116, 118, 125, 144, 145,
        157–8
    (2009) 9, 22, 34, 35, 48, 49, 73, 82, 93–4,
        96, 119, 122–3, 144, 164, 165
National Rural Employment Guarantee 69
natural resources
    sharing 51–2
    trade-offs 157–8
NCube, M. 34
Neumann, R.A. et al. 102, 116–17, 163, 175
NGOs 120, 124, 125, 166
    see also specific NGOs
Nigeria 9, 39, 55, 79, 103
Nokia 4, 56, 104
nudge tactics 96–9
Nussbaum, M.C. 68, 82, 94, 139, 141,
        143, 146

Open Defecation Free (ODF) communities
        53–4
Oral Rehydration Therapy (ORT) 4, 103
Orientalism 19
outsiders
    contribution of 116–23, 146–8, 153–8
    strengths and weaknesses of 144–6
    vs local/insider knowledge 8–10,
        19–21, 165
    see also power shifting in participative
        development
Oxford Poverty and Human Development
        Initiative (OPHI) 141–2, 143

Palmer, T. and Darabian, N. 38, 60
Pant, S.B. 124
Papanek, V. 59–60, 175
participative development 19, 21
    goal setting 173–6
    see also power shifting in participative
        development
Plan NGO 74, 77, 151
Polak, P. 3, 12, 14, 19, 21, 49, 56, 93, 105,
        118, 121–2, 123, 125–6
'the poor'
    definitions and measures 33–5
    diversity in individuals, countries and
        cultures 36–7
    life on the poverty line 37–41
    terminology 41
'poverty traps' 21, 145, 148
power relations
    community groups and formal
        organizations/local government
        118–21
    intersectionality 76–8

power shifting in participative development
        137–9, 166–7
    across development cycle 158–66
    local communities as decision
        makers 148–58
    outsider experts as decision
        makers 139–48
Praxis NGO 53, 157, 161
Preece, R. et al. 158–9, 161, 166
presentation of information 104–6
public scrutiny 7–8

Radjou, N. et al. 15, 126
randomized control trials (RCTs), 12, 127-8,
        177–8
Rao, V. 61, 145
    and Walton, M. 5, 15, 18
    see also Mansuri, G.
registration of local organizations 119, 124
rejection of aid 3–6
    mistakes/misunderstandings 6–23
reliability and security, increasing 116–18
research
    community-led 160–1
    methodology 177–8
resistance 13–15, 74–5, 78–80
Retamal, M. and Dominish, E. 50–1, 60
RFID tagged bags 155–7
risks
    of interventions 15–16
    mitigation of 90–2
    of scaling up 129
Robb, C.M. 97–8, 145, 149–50, 157
Robeyns, I. 141, 143
role models 76
rule of thumb approaches 102–3
Rwanda 51, 58, 160

Said, E. 19
sanitation *see* community-led total
        sanitation (CLTS)
Saudi Arabia 79–80
scaling-up *see* local infrastructure and
        scale-up solutions
Schickele, A. 91–2
self-help groups 9
Sen, A. 21, 35, 70, 94, 139–41, 143–4
    Drèze, J. and 34, 39, 57, 70, 96
Sennett, R. 175
shared designing 49–51
shared resources 6–7, 49–50
    protecting existing 51–3
sharing economy 49
shopping collectives 61
Sinha, D. 13–14
smallhold farmers *see* farmers/smallhold
        farmers
social capital
    'bonding capital' and 'bridging capital' 119
    and personal relationships 126

social choice models in real world
dilemmas 139–41
social media 50, 120
social ties 48–9, 54–5, 61, 116, 119
sourcing ideas from communities 159–60
Sreekumar, T.T. 17–18, 20, 52
Srinivasan, J. and Burrell, J. 20, 127
Stern, E. and Clarfelt, A. 74, 80
stopgap solutions 125–6
Strickland, M. 174–5
sub-Saharan Africa 7, 8, 14
    communal cultures 51, 59–60, 61
    marginal/excluded groups 69, 74–5, 79, 82
    poverty 34–5, 38, 39, 41
    see also specific countries
Sudan famine relief 5, 6, 174
Sustainable Development Goals (SDGs) 142–3

tactical nudges 96–9
tangible design 100–4
Tanzania 100, 164, 165, 174–5
technology *see* digital technology
terminology
    generalizations 37
    users, recipients, consumers, people 41
Thompson, J.B. 13
time
    cyclical vs linear 14
    increasing reliability and security
        over 116–18
    of poor vs rich 22–3
timing of interventions 92, 98
toilet facilities *see* community-led total
    sanitation (CLTS)
total community approaches 53–5
trade-offs in decision making 157–8
tradition vs change 13–15
transport
    sharing 50, 51
    Tata Motors mini-truck 58
travel restrictions, women/girls 73–4, 97–8

Udry, C. 9, 17
urban and rural communities
    links 7

toilet facilities 54
word of mouth 58
Utilitarianism 139–41

Van Domelen, J. 73, 77, 103, 105,
    151, 152
visual methods 152, 155–7, 162
visual vs written material 102
Vodaphone Ghana 38
Voices of the Poor *see* Narayan, D. et al.
    (2000)
voting 77, 102, 151

water
    chlorine dispensers 97
    irrigation system 127
    Oral Rehydration Therapy (ORT) 4, 103
    shortages 71–2
weather and risk mitigation 91–2
Wilkinson-Maposa, S. 6, 114, 119
    et al. 7, 8, 35, 50, 114
women/girls
    adaptive preferences 146, 147–8
    education 70–1, 72–3, 74, 80,
        95, 97–8
    employment 79–80, 97–8
    entrepreneurship 22, 75
    land ownership 69, 76–7, 152
    microfinance 75, 82–3
    reputation 7–8
    role models 76
    rule-of-thumb messages 103
    travel restrictions 73–4, 97–8
    see also gender inequality/discrimination
Wong, S. and Guggenheim, S. 150,
    164, 165
word of mouth approaches 103
    potential and problems 55–60
working hours, global north–global south
    comparison 22–3
World Bank 9–10, 35, 40, 70, 77, 97,
    128, 161
    Sleeping on Our Own Mats report 149, 166

Yunus, M. 55, 56, 142, 143

www.ingramcontent.com/pod-product-compliance
Lightning Source LLC
Chambersburg PA
CBHW070929030426
42336CB00014BA/2598